CHOOSING SUSTAINABILITY
Your Guide to the What, Why and How

Mindy Mutterperl

Bankhouse Publishing

Printed in the USA
ISBN 978-0-692-06322-4

Library of Congress Control Number: 2018909289

Subjects: Sustainability. Sustainable living. Green living.
Localism. Community resiliency. Sharing.

Book design and cover design by CranCentral Graphics, LLC

Editorial review by Amanda McBride

Bankhouse Publishing
New Hope, PA
sustainablechoices.net

This publication is intended to provide accurate and timely information.
All content is provided for information purposes only to help readers explore
sustainable lifestyle choices. The author and publisher accept no liability for
actions inspired by any part of this book. Where applicable, readers may wish
to obtain professional advice and guidance. Mention of specific companies,
organizations or authorities does not imply endorsement of those entities by
the author or publisher, nor does it imply that those entities have endorsed
this book, the author or publisher.

Bankhouse Publishing is committed to supporting a strong local economy
by keeping design, editorial and other related publishing and marketing
services within the local community.

To my family and friends, the generations that follow and all those already involved in taking a leap— large or small—toward a better way of life

Acknowledgements

As I developed the copy that would become *Choosing Sustainability*, my husband, teenage son and close friends all offered their unconditional support and patience along with a healthy dose of insight and perspective. Their encouragement came early, spurring me on to the task, and it was sustained through the many years that it took me to transform my initial idea into tangible form. As my beta reader, my dear friend Audrey Bleich, a language instructor, translator and editor, assured me that the book was worthwhile, helpful and readable. My long-time business partner, designer and natural problem solver Eileen Vincent Smith, was always available to point me toward answers to the next set of challenges…and to remind me that "I get to do this one my way." My subject-matter experts, Mitch, Pia, Silvia and John, played a critical role in reviewing the text for accuracy. The expertise and wisdom of my editor, Amanda McBride, was invaluable. And my design team, Max and Anita Crandall of CranCentral Graphics LLC, offered their talent, flexibility and generosity of spirit throughout page and cover design, layout and print production. Thanks to the friends who put me in touch with these wonderful resources. Finally, a special thanks to Kim Rouse, who shared her wealth of experience and expertise, guiding me through the intricacies of the publishing process.

Contents

Introduction

This book is about the many choices, large and small, that can help us live more sustainably, benefitting ourselves, our communities and the world around us.

Some of us are already on the path to a sustainable lifestyle, perhaps choosing organic food whenever possible, driving a hybrid car, limiting consumption and waste or investing in renewable energy. Yet while we often view sustainability as synonymous with environmental responsibility, there's a broader definition to consider, one that encompasses economically and socially sustainable choices that also happen to be green. Adopting a holistic approach to sustainability may help us uncover the intrinsic ties between protecting the planet and our health, supporting a greener, more locally focused economy and strengthening our connection to community. As we incorporate holistic sustainability into our everyday lives, we may discover that even simple decisions have the power to effect change in many ways.

A Sustainable Approach to Sustainability

Of course, achieving a holistically sustainable lifestyle is no small feat. And attempting to adopt every suggestion in the following pages all at once would probably lead only to burnout and frustration. On the other hand, we can make a meaningful difference with an incremental approach, gradually but steadily moving from our initial priorities to a wider range of concerns. Each of us will be guided, both in where we begin and how far we go, by our unique goals, values and household budgets. Some will stay focused on issues that affect them directly while others may move toward broader social concerns. Perhaps what matters most is a willingness to take the journey with an open mind.

Why This Book?

Choosing Sustainability won't sit alone in the green living section of online or brick-and-mortar bookstores. As anyone with an interest in the subject knows, there are countless sources of information on topics such as living greener, going local and creating resilient communities. Yet many of those sources either are written by and for professionals and academics or focus almost exclusively on a single aspect of sustainability, referencing the others only as afterthoughts. Many of the former simply aren't that useful for a general audience, while some of the latter may appeal only to those with very narrow interests (fermenting organic heirloom beets, for example). That has left unanswered such important questions as (1) why isn't going green enough? (2) how can localism have a positive impact on both the economy and the environment? (3) what do self-reliance and community resiliency have to do with saving the planet? and (4) how can we easily adopt holistically sustainable choices in our day-to-day lives?

By contrast, this book (1) provides an overview of the "three pillars of sustainability," environmental, economic and social, (2) illustrates how they overlap and reinforce each other and (3) suggests how embracing all three can inform and improve our daily lives…*and* society as a whole. The book also attempts to answer questions such as those just mentioned in a way that will be helpful and immediately useful to a general audience—anyone interested in living sustainably, from the reader taking the first step toward a sustainable way of life to the veteran seeking to expand and deepen a life-long journey.

Why This Author?

Possibly like you, I have long grappled with a desire to live more sustainably, making slow, unsteady progress without much of a roadmap. My casual interest in sustainable living gradually intensified over the past decade, spurred by concerns about extreme weather and other signs of climate change, suspected toxins in our food, water and consumer products, increasing economic uncertainty and frayed community ties.

By early 2011, those concerns had inspired me to begin blogging about sustainable lifestyle choices, focusing on ideas and resources pertinent to my community. What I learned from researching topics for blog posts reaffirmed and deepened my commitment to live as sustainably as possible.

Before long, I was transforming part of my yard into an edible organic garden and diverting the weekly food budget from the supermarket to local farms and organic producers. My husband and I began to tend the lawn and flower garden organically and keep much of our hardscaping water-permeable. We adopted water-conserving habits at home and purchased kitchen and bath fixtures that met the latest water-efficiency standards. We transformed the electric bill into an investment in renewables by selecting a green electricity producer, and we increased the energy efficiency of our old stone house by upgrading to Energy Star appliances and windows, adding extensive insulation and installing a zoned, radiant HVAC system.

The family also has changed its consumer behavior. I've learned to make eco-friendly cleansers and personal care products. We've all placed more emphasis on seeking out products that are green, local or fair trade. And we've increased our efforts to reduce household waste by purchasing less, recycling more, exploring opportunities to reuse, upcycle, donate or swap and keeping the compost piles high, except during months when the ground is frozen solid. We've also taken steps to make our financial lives more sustainable by choosing independently owned local institutions and focusing our charitable donations on local environmental organizations. We've become more engaged in community as both volunteers and activists. And we've reconnected with nature through hiking, kayaking and spending quiet time outdoors. Finally (at least for now), with the publication of this book, I have redirected my writing career to more closely reflect my sustainable values.

As I delve ever deeper into the world of sustainability, I occasionally experience a sense of déjà vu. I remember my mother saying she'd happily return to the days when you might bite into a peach and find a worm because everything tasted better before pesticides. I recall how she bought much of our food from independent local sources—a few butchers, a fish market, the milkman (who presumably worked for a local farm)—and most of our clothing and other household goods from independently owned stores *uptown*. It occurs to me that when I needed to open my first checking account during college, my parents steered me toward a savings and loan, explaining that this type of bank was in business "for people like us." I have wonderful memories of escaping into fields and woods to "commune with nature." And I remember feeling deeply connected to my home town, which though nearly a small city, always felt like a cohesive community where I could be sure I belonged.

So long before "sustainability" entered my vocabulary, I was attracted to something essential about the idea. Protecting the environment and my family's health, localizing our financial lives, embracing self-sufficiency and connection to both nature and community....for me, these ideas simply felt right, obvious, a bit like coming home. Yet while nostalgia may sometimes provide inspiration, becoming sustainable is not about returning to the past. Instead, it can involve combining the best of the old and the new...something that's evident in today's most exciting sustainable ideas.

While my journey toward a more sustainable lifestyle has taught me a great deal, I cannot claim to be an expert at any of the subjects covered in the following pages. That said, perhaps no one individual could be an expert at every aspect of this complex subject. What I can offer are the skills honed over many years of working as a communications professional, researching a wide range of complex topics and writing about them in an informative and engaging manner for a variety of audiences. As I embarked on the task of writing this book—a much heavier lift than any website, brochure or in-depth article produced for past clients—I drew on the "educational marketing" approach that had served me (and my readers) well over the years. The following pages contain as organized, comprehensive, informative and readable a presentation of my research findings as I could muster...and an expression of a lifelong passion.

What This Book Includes...and Excludes

Part I of this book introduces the idea of holistic sustainability and provides a brief history and overview of each of the three pillars. Part II suggests ways to become sustainable environmentally, economically and/or socially in six areas of our lives: what we eat, how we live at home, what and how we consume, how we get around, how we manage our work lives and recreational time and what choices we make regarding our finances. Throughout Parts I and II, the book references not only the broad categories of environmental, economic and social sustainability but also the ideas and strategies associated with today's many sustainably oriented grassroots social movements.

While I have addressed most subjects in some depth, the book does not provide diagrams or directions on such topics as how to build a straw-bale house, convert a gas-combustion car into one that runs on grease, choose a composting toilet or establish a public commons. In other words, unlike the renowned *Whole Earth Catalog*, this book isn't a how-to manual for the sustainably inclined. It is simply a big-picture (360-degree, if you will) view of the choices available to us as we evolve toward greater sustainability.

The Personal Is Political

It would be incredibly helpful if those we elected to office were committed to supporting environmental, economic and social sustainability. But with or without that type of leadership, I believe the decisions we make in our daily lives can be surprisingly powerful. They can help us achieve a lifestyle that more fully reflects our values. They can help us share those values with family members, friends and neighbors. And when combined with the actions of others, they can help move the dial on a host of issues, from increasing the availability of organic food, nontoxic consumer products and electric cars to reducing greenhouse gas emissions, pollution and landfill waste to making our local economies and communities more vibrant and secure.

Using This Book

I encourage you to read this book from cover to cover. But there are two reasonable alternatives. Part I may be skipped by those who prefer to jump straight to the how-to chapters. Or the book may be treated as a reference guide, perhaps stored on a kitchen shelf next to the cookbooks and pulled out occasionally when you are ready to tackle the next sustainable choice. However you proceed, you may want to check out the resources area of my blog, **Sustainable Choices (sustainablechoices.net)**, for sources of more in-depth information, *including those instructions on building a natural home or retrofitting a car to run on biofuel.*

What Is Holistic Sustainability?

The Three Pillars of Sustainability

Sustainability: The ability of any system, including an eco-system, to endure, remain healthy and intact or last indefinitely

▶ **Environmental sustainability:** The ability to protect and heal the environment and ensure its lasting well-being through actions such as reducing pollution, greenhouse gas emissions and waste, protecting open space and native species and preserving nonrenewable natural resources

▶ **Economic sustainability:** The ability to create or maintain an environmentally sustainable economy that provides opportunities for financial and employment stability by promoting local production for local use and prioritizing improved quality of life over perpetual material growth

▶ **Social sustainability:** The ability to support social justice, equality, community-wide well-being and resiliency in the face of change by encouraging the development of both self-reliance and enduring social connections

ENVIRONMENT

SUSTAINABILITY

ECONOMY   SOCIETY

Why It's Time for Holistic Sustainability

From a changing climate that threatens our survival on the planet to a changing economy that is eliminating many types of work to a changing society that has weakened community ties, we are living in an age of profound challenges. Those challenges are environmental, economic and social...and they're surprisingly interconnected. They aren't entirely new, but they have reached a tipping point, demanding our immediate attention if we're going to avoid calamity.

Uncertainty about the future has cast a shadow over our time, particularly since many of us no longer expect our elected leaders to offer much help. But at what may seem like the darkest hour, our personal power has become palpable. Motivated by a desire to "be the change," a growing number of us are taking transformational steps on our own or as part of one or more sustainability-focused grassroots social movements. Through countless day-to-day choices, we're learning to live our values and help ourselves while supporting sustainability for the environment, the economy and our local communities.

What's Unsustainable About the Present?

There's no shortage of concerns fueling today's interest in sustainability. A majority of scientists agree that greenhouse gases (GHGs) from human activities are warming the Earth's atmosphere, raising sea levels and changing the climate in dramatic ways. We're already experiencing extreme weather events and threats to biodiversity, food security and the habitability of coastal regions and islands. Despite the recent oil and natural gas boom, experts believe we are running out of the readily extractable fossil fuels that have powered our economy and our daily lives for generations. Our overconsumption of other natural resources may cause future generations to face scarcity. Our health may be threatened by toxins lurking in everything from our food and water to many of the products in our homes. Our consumer culture continues to produce an unsustainable level of waste. And industrial agriculture may be contributing to climate change, pollution and unhealthy diets while also degrading one of our most precious resources—our soil.

As if that weren't enough, we're also experiencing an economic transition as profound and disruptive as the Industrial Revolution. Rapidly evolving technology and globalization are among the factors leading to growing income inequality and the loss of many types of work. We're increasingly dependent on big, nonlocal businesses, while our local communities lack much-needed investment. And the social isolation of our modern lifestyles has weakened our ties to community, increasing social discord and undermining our ability to address shared challenges and work together for the common good.

As these challenges grow more urgent, impacting our personal lives, our communities and the country as a whole, the ideal of sustainability offers a welcome prescription for change. That change involves protecting the environment, living within the Earth's natural limits and helping to repair the damage already done. It encompasses support for a green, local, human-scale economy. And it encourages a lifestyle that's more self-reliant *and* more intertwined with community.

What Is the Sustainable Future?

Assuming we could adopt a holistically sustainable lifestyle and, in doing so, help address the biggest challenges of our time, exactly what would replace the current state of affairs? Let's take a moment to imagine *perfection*.

What if...

....Green energy became the norm? We would all power our homes and businesses with affordable, non-polluting, non-greenhouse-gas-emitting renewable energy from sunlight, wind or local streams. Our heating and cooling would come from the Earth (geothermal systems), our walls (insulating green building materials) or the same clean energy that turned on our lights. Our homes and businesses would be *net neutral*, producing all the energy they needed and either returning excess electricity to our utility (possibly earning us some extra income), sending it to a community microgrid or storing it in our own solar batteries. The batteries in our electric vehicles also would store excess energy from our homes, and a nationwide network of charging stations would ensure we could always "refuel" conveniently. We might need to use less energy than we do today, but we could be confident that powering our homes, businesses and vehicles would not contribute further to climate change or pollution.

...All agriculture were local and/or organic? A much-revised federal farm bill could support this transition by increasing subsidies to small, independently owned sustainable farms. Local farms (rural or urban), community gardens and our own backyards would provide all of us with affordable access to fresh, healthy, tasty food. Both food insecurity and obesity would decline, along with a wide range of health conditions associated with diet. And the quality of our air, water and soil would improve dramatically, benefiting us, our farmers and the entire ecosystem.

...All consumer goods were nontoxic? The many products in our lives—clothing, bedding, bath towels, cosmetics, furnishings, kitchen implements, toys, cleansers and so on—would be made from healthy ingredients that didn't harm us, the workers who produced them or the planet. The environmental regulations overseeing the manufacture of these products would be far more effective than they are today, so we would no longer feel the need to scrutinize every product choice to protect our health and safety.

...Protecting the environment were "business as usual?" Responsible regulations, combined with reliable demand for sustainable consumer goods, would lead most manufacturers to take steps to reduce air and water pollution, excessive energy use and unnecessary packaging and to preserve natural resources by utilizing rapidly renewable alternatives. We would do our part as consumers, lightening our environmental footsteps by consuming less, producing more at home, upcycling, reusing and recycling as a matter of course. The impact of pollution, development and invasive species would no longer threaten the wealth of native flora and fauna that are essential to a healthy planet. Most development would take place around the urban core, leaving open space intact, while more of our nation's majestic landscape would be set aside as public land. And the development of organic agriculture, renewable energy and clean-tech manufacturing would provide us with the green economy necessary to protect the environment and rebuild the middle class.

...Downtowns made a comeback? Independently owned local shops would meet most of our consumer needs with goods produced locally from locally sourced raw materials. Our support of the local business community, including not only retailers and food venues but also financial institutions, service providers and manufacturers, would yield a variety of local jobs as well as opportunities for entrepreneurs. Increased local tax revenues would support high-quality schools and provide sufficient resources for first responders. And our thriving downtowns would bring us together with other members of the community in a friendly, safe environment to shop, dine, celebrate and be entertained.

...We could all rely on a stable income? Our commitment to support local businesses would help create strong local economies. Within nearly every municipality or region, the employment landscape would include environmentally and socially responsible businesses of all types, including worker cooperatives, community-owned ventures and other enterprises with roots in and a long-term commitment to the local economy. This would make it relatively easy for individuals with a wide range of talents and skill levels to find jobs paying a living wage or more without straying far from home.

...We could choose to slow down and still make ends meet? For those seeking a simpler, slower-paced lifestyle allowing a focus on family or creative pursuits, it would be much easier than it is today to off ramp from the mainstream economy and piece together a livelihood by scaling down, replacing consumption with home production and embracing what sharing enthusiasts refer to as "access over ownership."

...We embraced age-old wisdom and held new technologies to a higher standard? We would place a modern spin on some of our ancestors' ways—growing food without chemicals, eating what's in season, producing more of the goods we need and avoiding unnecessary debt—while weighing the pros and cons of new technologies before adopting them wholesale.

...We could invest in Main Street? We would diversify our investments to include environmentally, economically and socially sustainable businesses with a commitment to our local communities. Our investment dollars would provide a much-needed source of capital to the independently owned businesses that historically have produced the majority of American jobs.

...Community life prospered? Viewing ourselves as members of a community would reduce social isolation, enable us to work with others to address mutual concerns and create opportunities for us to enjoy shared activities and celebrations.

...We knew that our actions mattered? Through personal choices, collective action within our communities and ongoing participation in democratic life, we would gain a greater sense of agency, knowing we could make our voices heard and make a difference in our own lives and beyond.

How Can We Get There?

Helping to address the biggest challenges of our time and improve our own lives in the process may sound like a Herculean task, particularly today. In the not-so-distant past, we believed in our ability to effect change at the ballot box, through our "Yankee know-how" or by working collectively with friends and neighbors. More recently, the pace of change, dysfunction of government and sheer volume of information—and misinformation—have buried some of us in apathy and pessimism while driving others to cynicism and rage. Confidence in "the system" may well be at an all-time low. But what's happening just outside that system should be cause for optimism.

A Quiet Revolution

A sustainability movement that began in academia and policy think tanks decades ago now inspires a wide range of highly energized grassroots social movements. Those movements, in turn, have inspired a small but growing number of us to chart a path toward something new. Unlike political movements of the past, many of today's social movements eschew formal organization, existing solely as loose configurations of individuals with similar views and goals. Embracing a *personal is political* approach, they focus more on what each of us can accomplish through everyday choices than on what government might achieve through laws and regulations. Operating successfully without charismatic leaders, they exemplify small-d democracy, grassroots activism and a local, decentralized approach to change.

While each movement has distinct priorities that can be described as environmental *or* economic *or* social, most have embraced a holistic approach, acknowledging the connections between saving the planet, reimagining the economy and rebuilding resilient communities. These movements ask us to make daily choices individually and with members of our communities that can help address climate change, protect natural resources or decrease pollution and waste. They encourage us to envision a good standard of living as one that brings happiness with much less consumption. And they challenge us to revisit ways from the past—producing what we need at home, sharing or collaborating with neighbors—to become both more self-reliant and more attached to community.

A Holistic Approach to Change

Adopting a holistic approach to sustainability, rather than simply going green, can help us create virtuous cycles that benefit ourselves and countless others. For example, buying local organic food can protect our health while also helping to reduce pollution, slow climate change, preserve farmland and support farmers and a food-based local economy. Similarly, choosing to live without a car may improve our health, lower household expenses and reduce our impact on global warming and pollution while also supporting modes of transportation that are social and rooted in community. While not every suggestion in the following pages spans the three pillars of sustainability, each can bring us a bit closer to the type of lifestyle and society we'd like to enjoy.

As we begin or continue our journey toward holistic sustainability, we may want to explore the ideas of some of the social movements leading the way. Among the most notable are:

▶ **The unofficial (vs. "official") environmental movement.**
The official environmental movement comprises large nonprofit advocacy groups focused on specific issues, such as climate change, sustainable agriculture, environmental toxins, natural resource and open space depletion, protection of endangered species, air and water pollution and reduction of both personal and industrial waste. While these groups continue to play a vital role in fighting for a cleaner, healthier environment, it has become increasingly common to view environmentalism (or going green) as a matter of personal responsibility, informing choices in nearly every area of our lives.

▶ **The many food movements.** Members of the local food movement, the Slow Food movement, advocates of sustainable and organic agriculture and individuals committed to vegetarian or vegan diets are among those seeking a healthier, more eco-conscious approach to the production and consumption of food. Despite varying views and goals, most support a return to non-chemical agriculture, localized food production, fresh whole foods and an epicurean delight in dining. Many activists also support economic sustainability by working to develop local food economies. And they support social sustainability by encouraging community food production and efforts to end hunger.

▶ **The local movement.** Drawing on the ideas of mid-20th-century economists Leopold Kohr and E. F. Schumacher, among others, localists encourage us to support our local economies in as many ways as possible. Many of us already are familiar with the *shop local movement* and the *local food movement*, the latter promoting the benefits of eating food grown or produced locally. But the broader local movement also encompasses such alternatives as banking and investing locally, producing goods and services (e.g., food, energy) locally that we would otherwise need to import from other locations, supporting community-owned businesses and celebrating our connection to the communities in which we live.

Localists believe it's economically sustainable to keep more of our money within the local economy, where it can help support business and job creation and increase the municipal tax base. Localism also can be environmentally and socially sustainable, helping us reduce our carbon footprints, support environmentally responsible businesses and make our communities more resilient in the face of challenges such as climate change.

▶ **The fair trade movement.** A holistically sustainable alternative to free trade, fair trade is promoted by nonprofit organizations (and some for-profit companies) that encourage producers in the developing world to protect the environment, pay workers fairly and reinvest in communities in ways that combat poverty and lead to rising wages and living standards. In return, producers receive fair trade certification, which gives them direct access to affluent consumer markets and the ability to charge a premium for their goods. Many sustainably minded consumers who seek out green or local products also now prioritize imports labeled "fair trade." In addition to giving consumers another way to support the ethical production of goods, fair trade may be a key to leveling the global playing field and reducing the flow of jobs overseas.

▶ **The sharing movement.** Inspired by both the communalism of the 1960s and the online sharing ethos of open-source operating systems and social media, the sharing movement promotes access over ownership and experience over consumption. Sharing enthusiasts seek a more equitable and democratic economy by removing money from many of our transactions. They view sharing as a way to help us spend and consume less so we can live within our means and lighten our environmental footsteps. Since sharing inherently involves working with others, sharing advocates also promote its ability to expand our social networks and foster stronger community ties. Nearly any type of product or service can be shared. Sharing advocates are exploring a diverse range of sharing strategies, including swapping goods, bartering services, joining co-work spaces, co-owning homes and cars and making use of public commons and community gardens.

▶ **Supporters of community resiliency and a post-carbon economy.** These overlapping groups believe that as we gradually run out of carbon-based fuels and choose to protect the environment by adopting renewables, we will need to transform our lifestyles to fit a new reality. Since renewables don't produce quite as much energy as fossil fuels, a post-carbon economy will require conservation and other eco-conscious choices. Those choices will include forms of relocalization, such as relying less on global trade and increasing local production of goods we would otherwise import. Beyond a changing energy picture, community resiliency advocates also raise concerns about a wide range of environmental and economic disruptions likely to transform our lives in coming years. In order for us to survive, thrive and protect future generations, they urge us to work toward both self-reliance and cooperation with other members of the community.

▶ **The DIY/radical homemaker trend.** In recent years, many of us have rediscovered the art of producing at home what we would otherwise need money to buy. By helping us meet more of our needs without outside sources of income, a DIY lifestyle can help us survive a period of joblessness or even choose to prioritize family or creative pursuits over traditional employment. Becoming *makers* also may help us lighten our environmental footsteps by producing eco-friendly replacements for store-bought products and by reducing excess consumption and waste.

▶ **Statewide sustainability programs focused on local community action.** Increased concern about sustainability and resiliency has led some states to create initiatives that encourage problem solving at the municipal or community level. Currently, a dozen states (California, Connecticut, Florida, Massachusetts, Maryland, Michigan, Minnesota, New Jersey, New York, Pennsylvania, Wisconsin and Virginia) oversee programs that utilize "green teams" comprising municipal, business and civic leaders as well as community-based volunteers. By joining green teams, individuals who live in these states can become engaged in addressing concerns of particular relevance to their communities. For example, green teams may help create and support community-based composting programs, community gardens, urban farms, community-scale (distributed) renewable energy generation, local microgrids or programs that work for social and economic justice.

> According to a recent Pew Research study, 75% of Americans are significantly concerned about helping the environment in their daily lives. Still, only one in five report consistently making an effort to live more sustainably.[1]

More information is available at nnsso.com (the National Network of Statewide-Local Sustainability Organizations) and from individual state programs, such as Sustainable Pennsylvania.

▶ **New, ethical business models.** Back in 1994, socially conscious entrepreneur John Elkington introduced the idea that companies could benefit by measuring their "triple bottom line" or "the 3 Ps": profits and losses as well as any impact on "people and the planet." Elkington recognized that doing this could help strengthen brand loyalty among the growing number of socially conscious consumers. Today, many entrepreneurs are embracing Elkington's ideas, creating *benefit corporations* (also called B corporations or B corps) that seek to "do well by doing good." Toward that end, these companies employ *true cost accounting*, evaluating both the tangible costs associated with the production of their goods or services and the hidden costs to society of unintended consequences such as pollution, global warming, disease and poverty.

The Way Forward

It may go without saying that individual choices and loosely configured social movements can't address all that ails us. Achieving meaningful change will require us to elect leaders that truly represent "We the People." We'll need to continually raise our collective voices in protest or consent. And we'll need to support the many organizations that have worked for decades to protect the environment and support workers' rights and social justice. Yet, regardless of what takes place on the national stage from one year to the next, we can make a meaningful difference in the world by embracing lifestyle choices that are environmentally, economically and socially sustainable. The power of those choices already is evident in the dramatic growth of the organic, local and vegetarian food markets, eco-friendly consumer products, green homes and gardens, electric cars, renewable energy, sustainable jobs and community-based economic and social endeavors. In fact, many in the sustainability movement believe that our success at forging a better world *depends on* ordinary people embracing sustainable lifestyles.

This book presents a wide-angle view of three interconnected approaches to supporting a healthier environment, a more secure economy and a renewed sense of connection to community. We can embrace any one of these approaches or all three simply by becoming conscious of how our day-to-day decisions can lead the way to meaningful change. Few readers will agree with or adopt each and every idea suggested in the following pages. But regardless of our different points of view, many of those ideas are likely to seem useful. In fact, what makes a holistically sustainable approach to change particularly exciting is that it renders our usual divisions irrelevant. Simple choices such as eating local food or choosing safer products or buying an electric car or sharing co-work space don't belong to any one social or political group. They embrace and even meld values held dear by many different groups. Most importantly, they give all of us back the power to help improve our lives, our communities and our country, one ordinary decision at a time.

Our Power in Numbers

- Organic food sales climbed to $47 billion in 2016, accounting for more than 5% of total U.S. food sales and representing the fastest growing sector in the U.S. food industry.[2]

- Local food sales increased from $5 billion in 2008 to $12 billion in 2014.[3]

- Electric vehicle sales were up 38% from 2015 to 2016.[4]

- Renewable energy is being adopted at a rapid pace.[5]

- Recycling increased from less than 10% in 1980 to more than 34% in 2012.[6]

- Green home demand is strong and growing.[7]

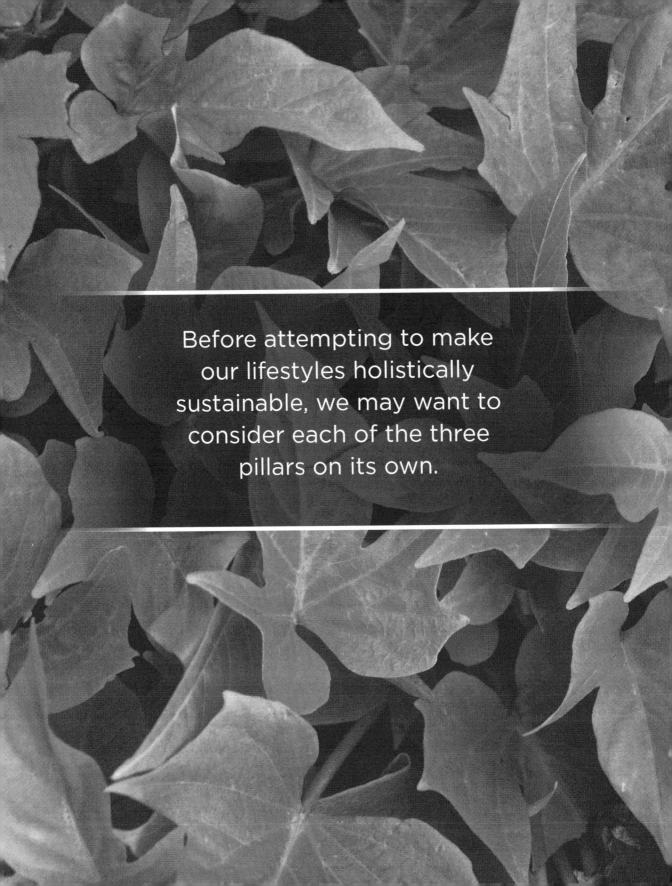

Before attempting to make our lifestyles holistically sustainable, we may want to consider each of the three pillars on its own.

Breaking It Down: Three Paths to Sustainability

Each path to sustainability—environmental, economic and social—can help us address a wide range of concerns.

Environmental Sustainability

For many of us, the most familiar of the three approaches to sustainability is "going green." We probably all have at least some familiarity with a wide range of environmental issues, from protecting endangered species to avoiding toxins in our food to reducing our impact on pollution and waste. Yet it's only natural to become tunnel-visioned, focusing mostly on a concern that has just been reported in the news or on the handful of issues that seem most relevant to our lives. The first step to becoming *holistically sustainable* is developing a broader idea of what it means to be green.

The definition of green has evolved over time. The earliest American environmentalists focused primarily on the twin concerns of *conservation* and *preservation*, responding to the damage done both by settlers who sought to tame the nation's vast wilderness and entrepreneurs willing to exploit our natural resources to the point of depletion. It took until the late 19th century, when the frontier began to close, for these concerns to make their way into national politics. President Theodore Roosevelt (1901 to 1909), a conservationist, supported laws that established limits on the use of natural resources, an approach now referred to as "sustainable development." Preservationists such as Sierra Club founder John Muir believed we should preserve land for its own sake. Though sometimes at odds, these early environmentalists and their colleagues made a profound difference by taking action to reduce the impact of development and setting aside large tracts of land as national parks and monuments.

In the first few decades of the 20th century, environmental concerns remained mostly under the radar,[1] though our collective environmental footprints were fairly light given that many Americans still lived on small subsistence farms and modern technologies with the potential to threaten the ecosystem had not yet become part of our daily lives. After World War II, those lucky enough to benefit from the country's rapid economic growth happily left behind the depravations of the Great Depression and war years and embraced the nation's burgeoning consumer culture with its inter-state highway system, increased car ownership, suburban sprawl, abundance of new products, chemical agriculture and processed, packaged foods. Unfortunately, all of this set in motion an unprecedented period of environmental harm.

Early stirrings of environmentalism arose in the 1950s in response to above-ground testing of atomic weapons, which raised the specter of radiation poisoning and triggered fears of a nuclear winter. But the modern environmental movement wouldn't fully emerge until after the 1962 publication of Rachel Carson's book *Silent Spring*, an indictment of chemical pesticide use that has been admired for both its scientific rigor and beautiful prose. In the years that followed, the worsening of such problems as species endangerment, litter, smog and oil spills—as well as river pol-lution so severe that it prevented fishing and swimming (and, in a few cases, actu-ally ignited fires)—raised the environmental consciousness of a growing number of Americans. By the late 1960s, environmentalists were able to leverage public aware-ness and the protest spirit of the era to launch a national movement that would reframe environmentalism from its original concern with *preserving land* to the modern-day goal of *preserving the planet*.

The movement's potential political power became evident on the first Earth Day, April 22, 1970, when an estimated 20 million Americans[2] participated in environmen-tal protests, cleanups and other events throughout the country. Soon after, Congress created the Environmental Protection Agency (EPA) and passed the most sweeping environmental legislation in the nation's history. (Among the many environmental laws passed around this time was the National Environmental Policy Act (NEPA), which requires federal agencies to assess and report on the potential environmental impact of any proposed, federally funded project.) The nation's new environmental regulatory system soon began to make significant strides, improving air and water quality, protecting land and wildlife and placing meaningful limits on industrial pollu-tion. Eventually, the EPA even banned the chemicals Carson had warned about in her book. But while regulations may have lulled some into complacency, plenty of environ-mental battles remained.

In the decades since the first Earth Day, concerns about acid rain, ozone deple-tion, overflowing landfill sites, nuclear weapons and nuclear power, toxic industrial spills, strip mining, fracking, the clear-cutting of forests, toxins in food and consumer products and, eventually, global warming and climate change each have taken a turn in the environmental spotlight. Those years also have witnessed an evolution of the environmental movement from a collection of ad hoc protest groups into an army of well-established non-profit organizations capable of keeping pressure on regulators and battling polluters in the courts.

As environmental organizations have kept their attention on legal and regulatory action, others have begun diverging from environmentalism to *environmental sustainability*. With roots as far back as the 18th century, the idea of sustainability first became the focus of *ecological economists* and other academics and policymakers in the 1970s. (Ecology, a branch of biology focused on the relationship of organisms to each other and their environments, is one of the scientific underpinnings of environmentalism.) Unlike most environmentalists, these *sustainists* were interested in the connections between environmental, economic and social issues and believed that protecting the environment depended on altering both the economy and society. They raised the concern that a surging world population, combined with a growth-oriented economy, rapidly changing technology, fossil fuel dependence and rampant consumerism, would deplete the Earth's resources while polluting air and water, destroying biodiversity, creating an abundance of waste and contributing to social injustice. Emphasizing the need to lighten our ecological footprints through environmental as well as economic and social choices, sustainists attempted to reframe our idea of success, replacing the pursuit of never-ending economic growth with the quest for an improved quality of life. By the 1990s, sustainability gained traction outside of academic and professional circles and it became more common to view both our environmental problems and their solutions as rooted in daily life. Picking up where the back-to-the-land enthusiasts of the 1960s left off, many turned to a personal approach to saving the planet centered on sustainable living.

Our environmental regulatory system includes:

Institutions, such as:

- The U.S. Environmental Protection Agency
- The National Oceanic and Atmospheric Administration (NOAA)

Laws, such as:

- The National Environmental Policy Act
- The Clean Air Act
- The Marine Mammal Protection Act
- The Endangered Species Act
- The Clean Water Act
- The Ocean Dumping Act
- The Safe Drinking Water Act
- The Energy Supply and Environmental Coordination Act
- The Coastal Zone Management Act
- The Toxic Substances Control Act
- The Eastern Wilderness Areas Act
- The Forest and Rangeland Renewable Resources Planning Act
- The Wilderness Act
- The Solid Waste Disposal Act
- The Land & Water Conservation Fund Act
- The Wild & Scenic Rivers Act

The Building Blocks of Green

So what would it mean today to become holistically green? Among the issues we would need to consider are the following.

▶ **Green energy.** Four interconnected issues that have dominated environmental headlines for many years involve our dependence on fossil fuels.

Climate change and global warming. Climate change (or "global climate change") refers to a cascade of environmental transformations, including *and brought about* by global warming. For example, climate change encompasses shifts in local climate and weather patterns, increased severity of storms, droughts and wildfires, rising sea levels, irreversible salinization of waterways, the increasing prevalence and range of certain pathogens and invasive species and the loss of coral reefs, land mass, polar ice caps and biodiversity. Such changes are triggered directly or indirectly by global warming.

The natural carbon cycle, in which carbon dioxide (CO_2) is released and absorbed in a relatively balanced manner, was disrupted by the Industrial Revolution. Our use of fossil fuels shifted CO_2 from the Earth to the atmosphere, where it began to contribute to global warming. Forests can help reverse this problem by absorbing CO_2 and converting it into biomass through photosynthesis. Soils and oceans also have the ability to absorb excess CO_2.

Global warming is the result of greenhouse gas (GHG) emissions from human activities accumulating in the Earth's atmosphere. It is compounded by the Earth's diminished ability to sequester carbon due to deforestation and damage to soils and oceans. Prior to the Industrial Revolution, naturally occurring GHGs helped keep the climate at a livable temperature by trapping some of the sun's heat as it was reflected off the planet's surface. Excess heat escaped into space. But the consensus among scientists from a wide range of disciplines is that the addition of GHGs from the burning of fossil fuels for electricity, transportation and the manufacture of products, including agricultural chemicals, has tipped the natural balance, setting our climate on the destructive path referred to as "global warming." The Union of Concerned Scientists (UCS) compares the effect of excess heat-trapping gases in the atmosphere to a blanket that holds heat in and warms the planet. According to the Intergovernmental Panel on Climate Change, the average temperature rose about 1.53 degrees Fahrenheit between 1880 and 2012.[3] While that may not sound like much, it's close to a dangerous tipping point—a rise of about 3.6°F—that scientists believe would trigger irreversible harm to our way of life. (The goal of the Paris Climate Agreement is to prevent warming above this level.) Left unchecked, scientists believe that the climate change triggered by global warming has the potential to leave many areas of the world uninhabitable, create extreme weather events, upset biodiversity, increase the risk of infectious disease and seriously threaten natural resources, including food and water. The latter could worsen global poverty and intensify violent conflict between the "haves and have nots."

A 2017 Gallup poll found that concern about global warming stands at a three-decade high in the U.S., with 62% of those interviewed (a record number) saying its effects are happening now and 68% believing that it is caused by human activity.[4]

Global warming also sets off what scientists call "positive feedback loops," changes that beget other changes, speeding up the negative impacts of climate change. For example, as warmer temperatures cause the Arctic tundra's permafrost to melt, it releases methane, a potent GHG, contributing to more global warming. As polar ice caps melt, they reflect less heat, causing more heat to be absorbed by the Earth; that, in turn, speeds up melting. As oceans become warmer and more acidic, they lose their ability to sequester carbon dioxide (CO_2). And since warm water expands, the combination of rising temperatures and melting polar ice caps is raising sea levels throughout the world. That alone threatens the survival of low-lying islands and coastal areas, including some of the world's biggest cities. But rising air and water temperatures also shift the air and water currents responsible for our weather patterns, changing the climate in ways that lead to more damaging weather events, including storms, floods, droughts and fires. Many of us already have witnessed the impact of extreme weather, including loss of life, property damage, destruction of entire towns and disruptions in access to affordable energy, food, water and other resources.

Warmer ocean temperatures and the acidity they cause are among the factors killing off coral reefs. Since coral reefs support a wide range of marine life, their loss may have devastating environmental consequences.

The U.S. remains the world's second-largest contributor to global warming, though significantly behind China.[5] In 2015, we generated about 5,271 million metric tons of energy-related CO_2 emissions from a combination of oil, natural gas and coal,[6] giving Americans a personal carbon footprint about 20 times that of individuals in developing nations.[7] According to studies published in *Nature* in 2009, to avoid catastrophic climate change, global emissions of CO_2 and other GHGs through 2050 would need to remain below 750 billion metric tons. Reaching that goal would require industrialized nations such as the U.S. to cut emissions by more than 90%.[8]

It may be too late to reverse all the damage done by our use of fossil fuels, but we have the technology and know-how to slow global warming and climate change and even begin to reverse them. The answers include reducing dependence on fossil fuels, transitioning to renewable energy sources for electricity and transportation, conserving energy and supporting organic farming and reforestation, which can restore the ability of soils and forests to sequester carbon and reduce its impact on the planet.

Our carbon footprint is equal to the total amount of greenhouse gas emissions generated by such daily activities as driving, powering our homes and businesses and consuming products and foods made with or from fossil fuels.

Peak oil. For decades, oil industry analysts have predicted the era of "peak oil," a time when the world's oil fields will have reached their maximum level of production only to begin a slow but steady decline. A much-touted boom in oil and natural gas production in recent years has brought the peak oil theory under scrutiny. But peak oil theorists say we're actually experiencing two of its symptoms: volatile oil prices and exploration of increasingly expensive and environmentally damaging fuel reserves. Examples of the latter include Canadian tar sands, oil from deepwater wells and nature preserves and the use of fracking for natural gas extraction. As global demand for oil continues to grow, the future holds the very real possibility of shortages and price spikes that could upend our energy-dependent lifestyles and the entire global economy. While the oil and natural gas industries still have plenty of life in them *and* the resources to garner support from politicians and the public, environmentalists view peak oil as an opportunity to transition to renewables that can sustain our energy needs long after the last oil fields run dry.

Renewables. On the positive side, combined with energy efficiency and conservation, renewables including solar and wind can help us meet much of our energy needs. This is not a new observation. In 1952, the Paley Commission told President Truman that, assuming we conducted the necessary research, we could produce a not insignificant portion of the nation's electricity from solar by 1975.[9] While the political power of the fossil fuel industry has dramatically slowed our progress, many believe production of renewables has now passed a threshold that will allow continued growth regardless of events in Washington. Continual development of electric and hybrid cars, along with the necessary charging infrastructure, also has the potential to significantly reduce our need for fossil fuels. The U.S. has been making meaningful progress in transitioning to renewable sources of energy and reducing greenhouse gas emissions from both electricity generation and transportation. Yet, because renewables produce less energy than fossil fuels, our transition to a *post-carbon economy* also will require us to adopt lower-consumption lifestyles.

Distributed energy. Renewables also open the door to localizing and decentralizing how we produce energy. Distributed energy typically consists of solar, wind or other renewables produced by a homeowner, business or community rather than by a utility. Homeowners and businesses that install solar panels or other renewable systems can lower their electricity costs over time. They also may be eligible for federal and/or state tax credits as well as credits or payments from the utility if they supply excess energy back to the grid. When entire communities produce their own energy, they also may be able to install microgrids, large-scale

What About Nuclear Energy?

As of 2015, nuclear energy represented about 19.5% of electricity generation in the U.S.[10] The "No Nukes" movement, most active in the 1970s and 1980s, raised public awareness of the potential dangers of nuclear power; that, in turn, made it more difficult to bring new nuclear power plants online. Nuclear power does not produce greenhouse gas emissions. But disposal of spent fuel rods remains an unresolved challenge. And public trust in nuclear power has dramatically declined in the wake of such accidents as Three Mile Island, in Pennsylvania, Chernobyl, in the former Soviet Union, and Fukushima Daiichi, in Japan.

backup generators that can run on locally produced energy and provide power when the grid experiences an outage. (More information: Chapter 4, Home)

▶ **Conservation and preservation.** As mentioned previously, some of the earliest efforts to protect the nation's natural lands and native species took place around the turn of the 20th century. During his presidency, Theodore Roosevelt created the United States Forest Service (USFS) and put in place the first land use laws. He protected 230 million acres of public land, establishing 150 national forests, four national game preserves, five national parks and 51 federal bird reserves.[11] He also signed into law the Antiquities Act of 1906, which gave presidents the authority to preserve federal lands as national monuments; Roosevelt himself named 18 such monuments.[12] Since our need for land is ongoing, so is the need to balance development with preservation. Today, conservation and preservation are supported in several ways.

Land use law. Direct democracy is in full swing most weekday nights as community planning and zoning boards, along with concerned citizens, weigh in on the desirability of proposed development projects. Land use laws continue to evolve to address such concerns as noise pollution, traffic congestion and wetlands encroachment.

Open space preservation. The U.S. loses about 6,000 acres of open space each day to development.[13] Some states have implemented "smart growth" plans to focus development in existing population centers. Additionally, some states and municipalities are preserving land with zoning laws that restrict development and/or with the public purchase of development rights from land owners (often farmers) ready to sell their properties. Along with nonprofit land trust organizations, these and other open space initiatives have placed millions of acres in preservation in perpetuity. Depending on the terms of the preservation deal, the land may be left as "scenic" open space or used for sustainable purposes, including organic farming, parkland or even green burial.

Biodiversity preservation. A diversity of native flora and fauna makes the environment healthier and more resilient in the face of change by allowing nature to perform vital *ecosystem services*. These services include storage and sequestration of CO_2 by forests, soils and oceans, pollination by bees, air purification by plants and renewal of soil through decomposition. Threats to even one species have the potential to disrupt entire ecosystems.

Protection of forests. Trees perform several important ecosystem services. They sequester CO_2, filter many pollutants that would otherwise contaminate air and water and support soil fertility and biodiversity, creating habitat for a wide range of plants and animals. For many years, clear-cutting of old-growth forests threatened to eliminate forested areas, along with jobs in logging and related in-dustries. Sustainable forestry practices, including selective logging and reforesta-tion, have slowed the loss of the nation's forests. So has the cultivation of rapidly renewable sustainable forests as a substitute for old-growth woods. Sustainable forestry products are now widely available to consumers.

Creation and maintenance of parks and recreational areas. Both the federal government and the states have overseen the creation and maintenance of these public areas for well over a century. Public lands belong to the American people and generally cannot be developed by private companies. It is therefore in our interest to use and enjoy them and, when necessary, fight to protect them. At this time, there are unprecedented efforts underway to undo the protected status of some parks and monuments to make way for development.

Protection of wetlands. Long viewed as undesirable, wetlands are now recognized both for their recreational possibilities and their importance in providing ecosystem services. They create habitat for native plants and water fowl, help reduce flooding and storm damage, remove water pollutants, sequester carbon and help recharge supplies of groundwater. Both national and state wetlands regulations protect these important natural assets from the threat of development.

Protection of native and endangered species. The extinction of many native species has been prevented or slowed by laws such as the Endangered Species Act and the Marine Mammal Protection Act. Environmentalists continue to work to preserve biodiversity and protect endangered species from loss of critical habitat due to development, industrial pollution, other toxins and invasive predators. Meanwhile, naturalists have raised the alarm about the impact of invasive species of plants, insects and animals on our local ecosystems. As awareness of these issues has grown, gardeners have begun choosing native plant varieties while communities have taken mitigation measures to restore habitat for native species.

Protection of natural resources. From logging to extraction of fossil fuels to mining for precious metals, our economy has always relied heavily on natural resources that are not renewable. As the world's population has continued to grow, along with our overuse of nonrenewable natural resources, it has become clear that our ecological footprint is placing the survival of future generations in jeopardy. En-vironmentalists say that footprint, which represents the total amount of land, water and other resources we need to maintain ourselves, already is large enough to place humanity in a state of overreach. Shrinking our enormous ecological footprint will require a significant reduction in consumption and a commitment to alternatives, including sharing goods and resources, reusing products and raw materials until their useful life is spent and substituting nonrenewable resources with rapidly renewable alternatives, such as bamboo or wood from sustainably grown forests.

▶ **Pollution.** Air and water pollution were among the first major issues tackled by the modern environmental movement.

Air pollution. By the late 1960s, more than a century of air pollution from industrialization was threatening human health and leading to the extinction of numerous species, including our national symbol, the American bald eagle. President Johnson famously warned that, left unchecked, air pollution would make it necessary to become "a nation in gas masks."[14] Fortunately, the hard work of environmental activists prevented that fate. In 1970, the Clean Air Act originally passed in 1963 was greatly expanded to regulate additional pollutants. The revised law required industry to install filters to reduce smokestack pollutants, car makers to install catalytic converters to reduce tailpipe emissions and oil companies to phase out the use of leaded gasoline.

> ### The Population Bomb
>
> In *The Population Bomb* (published in 1968), Paul R. Ehrlich and Anne Ehrlich argue that environmental problems stem from overpopulation. They predict that overpopulation will lead to starvation and annihilation of the human race. While their predictions have proved overly pessimistic, the United Nations reports (as of June 21, 2017) that today's global population of 7.6 billion is on track to reach 8.6 billion by 2030, 9.8 billion by 2050 and 11.2 billion by 2100. It is the world's mushrooming population that makes depletion of natural resources an increasingly dire threat.[15]

The Clean Air Act's significant impact was immediately visible to the public because the law also required ongoing monitoring of air quality, something meteorologists continue to report on along with the weather. But even the expanded law wasn't the final word on air pollution. In the late 1970s, Congress banned fluorocarbons from aerosol sprays (e.g., deodorants, spray paints) after scientists determined they were depleting the Earth's protective ozone layer and increasing our exposure to ultraviolet radiation from sunlight. The Montreal Protocol of 1987 called for the phaseout of chlorofluorocarbons (CFCs), used primarily as refrigerants and fire retardants, because they too depleted ozone. CFCs were replaced by hydrofluorocarbons (HFCs), which are considered much more potent greenhouse gases. But the Kigali Accord, a legally binding multi-nation agreement reached in the fall of 2016 (an update to the Montreal Protocol) requires that companies begin developing non-greenhouse-gas-emitting replacements for HFCs over the next few decades. In 1990, concern over acid rain, a by-product of fossil fuels, led Congress to pass a cap-and-trade program, which encouraged industry to reduce (cap) pollutants and sell (trade) credits to companies unable or unwilling to meet regulatory limits. While cap-and-trade helped, environmentalists say that acid rain from Midwestern coal-fired power plants and other sources still migrates east, placing the ecosystem of areas such as the Adirondacks at significant risk.[16] In 2014, the EPA strengthened regulations designed to reduce smog, which harms the environment and human health, particularly impacting the elderly, the very young and those with respiratory conditions (including asthma).[17] Air pollution also is known to harm plants and crops, interfering with photosynthesis, increasing vulnerability to pests and diseases and reducing agricultural yields. The Clean Air Act continues to be amended periodically, reflecting both the concerns of environmentalists and pressure for deregulation by industry and lobbyists.

Water pollution. Before passage of the Clean Water Act of 1972 and the Safe Drinking Water Act of 1974, pollution from sources including industry, power plants, agriculture and sewage treatment facilities had polluted many waterways, contaminating drinking water and making swimming and fishing unsafe. This state of affairs was dramatized when Ohio's Cuyahoga River caught fire in 1969. Regulations helped reduce pollution of lakes, rivers and streams and mandated their restoration for recreational use."[18] As with air pollution, while regulations made a dramatic difference, they didn't solve every problem. Current water pollution concerns include:[19,20]

✓ Runoff of chemical fertilizers and pesticides from agriculture and other sources that is contaminating aquifers, streams and larger waterways and contributing to toxic algal blooms in the Great Lakes and elsewhere.

✓ Inadequate sewage and wastewater treatment in some locations.

✓ Mercury contamination of fish from sources including coal-fired power plants and waste incinerators.

✓ Chemical contaminants from sources including hydraulic fracking for natural gas extraction and illegal dumping of industrial waste.

✓ Chemical contamination from plastic waste.

✓ Oil spills associated with drilling and transporting fuel.

✓ Contamination of drinking water from aging lead pipes and from chemicals and pharmaceuticals leached into groundwater from landfill sites poisoned by consumer waste.

▶ **Toxins in consumer products.** From cleaning and personal care products to clothing, furniture and home décor, nearly all of our household possessions can contain potentially toxic chemicals. The Toxic Substances Control Act, passed during the heyday of the environmental movement, was intended to monitor the safety of chemicals used in the manufacture of consumer goods. But environmentalists believe the law has been largely ineffective and overly friendly to industry. A much-improved recent update to the law may help address this concern. (More information: Chapter 5, Consuming) In the meantime, activist organizations such as the Environmental Working Group, the Pesticide Action Network and the Natural Resources Defense Council continually work to have some of the most harmful chemicals removed from the marketplace and to raise public awareness about potential health risks and the need for tougher regulations. The public has become more attuned to these concerns in recent years, seeking out products that are safer for human health and the environment. At the same time, a new wave of eco-conscious businesses is transforming the marketplace, expanding the sustainable choices available and helping to make them affordable to a broader range of consumers.

▶ **Garbage.** Earlier generations buried their waste in the woods or in old quarries and mines or simply burned it when garbage mounds grew too large. It wasn't until 1965 that the federal government enacted solid waste management legislation in an effort to prevent the spread of disease from open garbage pits. In 1976, Congress passed the Resource Conservation and Recovery Act (amended in 1984), requiring states to either follow federal guidelines for garbage disposal or enact tougher laws of their own. Despite this legislation, by the 1980s, the combination of overflowing landfill sites, air pollution from incinerators and medical waste washing up on beaches along the East Coast raised public concern about the sheer volume of garbage being produced. Today, we continue to generate more than 250 million tons of municipal (household) solid waste a year,[21] which depletes open space by contributing to landfill and increases global warming by releasing methane, a greenhouse gas produced when garbage biodegrades without adequate oxygen. Another 12% of solid waste is incinerated, releasing into the air a combination of nitrogen oxide, mercury, lead, dioxins/furans, carbon monoxide, sulfur dioxide and CO_2.[22]

We have made a significant dent in the amount of garbage we generate, largely due to the growth of curbside recycling and specialty recycling companies. Eco-conscious consumers are choosing products with minimal or recyclable packaging and reducing waste by reusing, sharing, bartering, purchasing pre-used items and upcycling creatively. Additionally, many businesses are adopting *zero waste* or *circular economy* strategies, manufacturing products from recycled materials and recycling old products continuously.

▶ **Agriculture and the food system.** In recent years, a number of books and documentaries have raised awareness of environmental and health problems associated with modern industrial agriculture. In the second half of the 20th century, the pursuit of higher agricultural yields led to widespread adoption of an industrial approach to farming. Even the language of industry became the norm, with farmers employing "inputs" (e.g., chemical fertilizers, pesticides, herbicides), purchasing increasingly hi-tech heavy machinery and delivering "outputs" (i.e., higher yields, often of just a few types of crops). While industrial agriculture has been around for decades, many attribute current problems to changes that took place in the wake of the farm crisis of the 1980s. During that decade, as many family farms faced bankruptcy, agricultural conglomerates and investors began buying up farmland and renting or leasing it back to bankrupt farmers. At the same time, many of the farms that survived the crisis became contract producers for large food and agricultural companies. These arrangements clearly saved many farms from extinction. But critics say they also led to practices that are unsustainable. In particular, concerns have been raised about the potential health and environmental risks of using agricultural chemicals, GMO seed, antibiotics and hormones and of over tilling, abandoning crop rotation and employing monocrop production. Pollution, food-borne disease outbreaks, soil degradation and both obesity and food insecurity also have become part of the conversation about making our food system more sustainable.

A multi-faceted food movement has helped to raise our awareness of problems, change our consumer behavior and slowly bring about improvements in the nation's food industry. More sweeping changes to the system will require reform of the federal farm bill to support organic and sustainable agriculture as the *norm*, not just an alternative to so-called "conventional" farming.

▶ **Environmental justice.** While the environmental movement once focused mostly on issues relevant to affluent Americans, earning it a reputation as elitist, many of our worst environmental problems actually are found in low-income communities, both urban and rural. Highways that cut through neighborhoods can expose residents to high levels of pollution from vehicle exhaust. Aging factories and power plants in urban areas may spew pollutants and contaminate water supplies. Landfill sites and incinerators may be located where citizens have the least ability to protest. Decrepit infrastructure may place residents in harm's way through exposure to lead and other toxins. And lower-income workers both here and abroad may be more likely to face exposure to toxins on the job. The environmental justice movement seeks to expand the role of environmentalism beyond the suburbs to help redress these wrongs and empower at-risk communities to create cleaner, healthier neighborhoods. Their work is an acknowledgement that a more sustainable world must benefit everyone.

Economic Sustainability

Compared with environmental sustainability, the second of the three pillars may be less familiar to some readers. But as mentioned previously, among sustainists, the two concepts are closely linked. For them, *economic sustainability* is about creating a *green economy* that allows us to meet our needs while living within the limits of Earth's resources. In a green economy, both businesses and individuals would act in an environmentally responsible manner, using renewable rather than nonrenewable resources, reducing their contribution to greenhouse gas emissions, pollution and waste and redefining economic success in terms of quality (as in improved quality of life) rather than quantity (as in the never-ending pursuit of greater material wealth). By embracing a green economy, we may be able to overcome the gravest environmental threats of our time, making our lifestyles healthier today while averting the collapse of civilization at some point in the future.

While supporting a green economy is critical, embracing economic sustainability also can be about addressing today's greatest economic threat: the demise of middle class jobs. Regardless of how the stock market performs or whether unemployment numbers and other economic indicators point to a strong economy, many Americans now believe they are facing a jobless future in which only a small minority will remain economically secure. Theories about what's driving our economic anxiety range from denial that there is any problem to hyperbole about humanity reaching the end of paid employment. Somewhere between these poles lies evidence of economic challenges that are transforming today's workplace. Those challenges include globalization and rapid technological change, both of which hold the promise of opportunity while also demonstrating the ability to wreak havoc on many forms of employment.

There may be no single, surefire way to make today's economy work for everyone. But two approaches to achieving economic sustainability—*localism* and *fair trade*— offer us opportunities to stabilize our economic lives while also going green.

> **Qualitative Growth**
>
> Sustainability advocates believe we should replace GDP (gross domestic product) as a measure of economic growth with a Social Progress Index that tracks quality-of-life improvements, such as:
>
> ▸ Modernizing infrastructure.
>
> ▸ Expanding access to and the quality of health care.
>
> ▸ Improving schools and expanding educational opportunities.
>
> ▸ Growing the local economy.

Localism

As described in Chapter 1, supporters of localism believe we can help create a more stable and equitable economy by relocalizing many of our economic activities—shopping, banking, investing, charitable giving, producing essentials such as food and energy—thereby transforming our communities into "local living economies."[23] By keeping more of our money close to home, we can trigger what economists call a "local multiplier effect" (defined on page 39), infusing our communities with the capital necessary to create new businesses and jobs while also increasing the municipal tax revenue available for schools, first responders and local infrastructure. If we extend our localism to the production of goods that would otherwise be "imported" from someplace else—either by making them ourselves or with members of our community—we also can derive the benefits of greater self-reliance and community resiliency. Adopting localism also can help us support a greener economy by reducing the carbon footprint associated with imports and encouraging the growth of businesses that have an intrinsic interest in protecting the local environment.

While contemporary localism is a reaction to an increasingly globalized and fossil-fuel-intensive economy, it draws on ideas developed more than 70 years ago. Localism's earliest proponents were critical of the prevailing post-World War II view that only continual global economic growth could lead us to lasting peace and prosperity. Advocates of growth argued that it would provide nations with the wealth necessary to address social problems such as poverty and inequality, thereby preventing the economic impetus for future wars. In the years immediately following World War II, economic policies focused on growth helped fuel our consumer-driven economy. They encouraged a strong focus on export markets. And they laid the foundation for modern-day globalization, with its large trading blocs (e.g., the European Union) and global trade agreements (e.g., NAFTA).

The emphasis on growth had the desired effect for many years, raising living standards and fostering greater economic and political cooperation throughout Europe. But as early as the 1940s, economist Leopold Kohr foresaw potential downsides. Kohr believed that as businesses, governments and economies grew ever larger, they would become more fragile and vulnerable to failure while leaving everyday citizens increasingly powerless, with little say over decisions affecting their daily lives. Arguing against the "cult of bigness," Kohr suggested that there was an appropriate scale or size for every human enterprise or endeavor. When it came to our economy and government, he advocated for *human scale*, meaning small enough for each member of society to maintain some degree of self-determination.

The Legacy of Kohr and Schumacher

Kohr and Schumacher have been credited with sparking the green movement because they were among the first to question whether mankind could continue on its path of overusing natural resources in pursuit of economic growth. They viewed a simpler, more locally focused way of life as sustainable environmentally, economically and socially.

Kohr's ideas entered the mainstream in 1970 when his former student and colleague, economist E.F. Schumacher, brought them to life in the cult classic *Small Is Beautiful: Economics as if People Mattered*. Like Kohr, Schumacher rejected "gigantism" and spoke of the importance of keeping businesses, economies and government entities human scale, decentralized and locally focused. He criticized the perpetual pursuit of material and financial growth as destructive to the natural environment and suggested that humanity would benefit much more from a focus on qualitative growth, as in improved quality of life for everyone. Concerned that rapid technological change and its use to enhance profits and reduce labor costs would eventually leave many of us without adequate or meaningful employment, Schumacher also encouraged adoption of *appropriate technology* (or *intermediate technology*), meaning technology scaled to the needs and circumstances of a particular situation or community. Schumacher's views resonated with members of the '60s generation, who were already concerned about the environment, population growth, inequality and the ability of a powerful government to send its citizens to an unpopular war.

Kohr and Schumacher have long inspired and been echoed by intellectuals and policymakers from a wide range of disciplines. In her book *The Death and Life of Great*

American Cities, Jane Jacobs explains how small, diverse yet cohesive neighborhoods can sustain vibrant local economies that offer both social and economic benefits to everyone in the community. Poet, farmer and ecologist Wendell Berry has written about the importance of relocalizing our economies in the face of globalization. As a starting point, he suggests rebuilding food-based local economies to help revitalize rural communities devastated by the impact of big business.[24] Ecologist Kirkpatrick Sale has described the value of reestablishing "bioregionalism"—connection to our local environment and natural resources—as the basis for building resilient community-based economies.[25] And localist ideas and values such as community-based economic development, local business ownership and local control and decision-making authority have been popular for years as approaches to addressing entrenched urban poverty.

Eventually, localism began to catch on with a wider audience, initially in the form of *locavorism*, a local food movement inspired by activists such as Berkeley, California, chef and restauranteur Alice Waters. As more of us learned about the benefits of buying food from local farmers and producers, other types of localism also became popular. Restaurants began promoting their locally sourced ingredients. Towns adopted *shop local* campaigns to overcome a weak economy during the Great Recession of 2007 to 2009. The Occupy Wall Street movement encouraged us to move our money to local banks. Localist economists and former financial industry professionals touted the benefits of allowing everyone to invest in the independent local businesses in their communities. And *transition economy* activists promoted relocalization as critical for shifting from a fossil-fuel-based economy to one powered primarily by renewables. As localist ideas like these went mainstream, some began joking that local was the new green.

The Building Blocks of Localism

Localist ideals now inform a wide range of grassroots movements focused on sustainability. With an emphasis on reconnecting us with the town, city or suburb we call "home," these movements (e.g., locavorism, the slow money movement, the transition economy movement) preference local over global, small over big and a definition of economic growth based on happiness and stability rather than increased wealth and consumption. Localism has been criticized as being nostalgic and unrealistic because it restores practices—for example, buying from local shops and banking with community banks—that were commonplace in the past. But localists believe these practices, updated for our own era, are timeless in their intrinsic social and economic value. The tenets of modern localism include:

▶ **The local multiplier effect** (a term coined by economist John Maynard Keynes). Over the decades, as national and multinational chains have supplanted

By "local," localists generally mean as local as possible, recognizing that some actions or decisions are best made at regional, national or even global levels. The key is opting for what is most appropriate.

local "mom-and-pop" businesses, more of our consumer dollars have left our communities, enriching large corporations while leaving us with fewer jobs, declining downtowns and a shrinking municipal tax base. This trend has only accelerated in the age of nonlocal, online retail giants. Localists believe we can reverse the trend by stimulating the local multiplier effect. All purchases or expenditures trigger a multiplier effect by generating additional economic activity. We can put the multiplier effect to work on behalf of our communities by spending more of our money at local, independently owned businesses. Each dollar we spend locally circulates many more times within the community than a dollar spent at a nonlocal business because local business owners and their employees tend to spend much of their income close to home. As noted previously, that can result in more hiring at local companies, more local business start-ups and additional local tax revenue.

Buying virtually anything from independently owned local shops and businesses triggers the local multiplier effect. The economic benefits can be even greater if businesses are able to sell products made locally—by independent artisans, manufacturers or other types of producers—from locally sourced raw materials. Localizing the supply chain can not only augment the local multiplier effect but also help create a network of resilient local businesses. A common example of this is the farm-to-table restaurant that locally sources much of its ingredients, beverages and supplies, helping to create and sustain a variety of small businesses that can, in turn, create new local jobs.

In addition to the economic benefits already mentioned, stimulating the local multiplier effect also may lead to downtown revitalization. That can help increase tourism, encourage support for walkability and the use of other non-vehicular forms of transportation, reduce crime and even enhance our sense of belonging to a cohesive community. Of course, taking responsibility for stimulating the local multiplier effect may require us to forego a bit of convenience and limit our habit of shopping online.

▶ **Import substitution.** At least as far back as the 19th-century, most economists have touted the benefits of *specialization* and *comparative advantage*. In practice, this means that each country or region should produce what it makes best and cheapest (specialize), export those goods (exploiting their comparative advantage over other countries or regions) and import everything else. This approach to the economy and trade has led us to take it for granted that electronics often come from Japan, coffee and chocolates from Central and South America and tulips from Holland. It also set the stage for today's global economy in which we import a vast array of goods that easily could be produced closer to home. While we may pay less for imports, they actually can cost us more in what economists call "externalities." For example, competition from cheap imports has cost many Americans their jobs

Critics argue that localism is anti-trade and anti-globalization. But while localists generally are critical of the current system, many embrace the idea of global trade. Their aim is to transform today's system into something more equitable and ethical by fostering the development of a network of thriving human-scale economies here and abroad.

as companies have cut workforces or moved operations overseas to reduce production costs and become more competitive. Reliance on imports has left us vulnerable to shortages and price spikes in the event that something—weather, war, trade wars—interrupts global trade. Because imports must be transported, they also have increased the fossil fuel consumption and greenhouse gas emissions associated with most of what we buy.

Localists believe there's a better way to run an economy. In E.F. Schumacher's words, "Production from local resources for local needs is the most rational way of economic life."[26] This can mean substituting imports with goods made in the U.S.— or even right in our own communities. When individuals or communities begin producing goods such as food, consumer products and energy (or even electronics, chocolates and flowers) they can realize several sustainable benefits. They can help create stable jobs at new businesses focused on meeting local needs. They can keep the dollars spent on goods and services inside the community, rather than letting them slip away to parts unknown. And they can make their lifestyles truly green by reducing transportation-related carbon emissions and supporting locally owned businesses that may have an inherent interest in protecting the local environment. Once a community becomes more self-reliant, it may still import goods from other places, or even export the goods it produces. But the import-export relationship will be based more on wants than on needs.

▶ **Localized financial relationships.** Like shopping local, relocalizing financial accounts and transactions gives us the power to help stimulate our local economy. Independently owned local banks are in business to underwrite mortgages that benefit homeowners and their communities and originate business loans that support the needs of local business owners. Local investments can help businesses in our communities grow, prosper and hire. Locally owned insurance companies protect personal and business property from a wide range of risks. And locally focused charitable giving can help us have an impact on issues that directly affect us and our communities.

▶ **Locally/community-owned enterprises.** Localists believe a community's economy is more likely to thrive if it supports a diverse range of locally owned businesses than if it relies exclusively on a handful of nonlocal behemoths. While nonlocal companies can be attracted to a town or city by tax breaks and other financial incentives, their commitment to the area may last only until a better offer comes along. By contrast, companies that are committed to local ownership and operation can provide the long-term jobs and economic stability that our local economies sorely need. Some of these companies may spell out their commitment to the community in their corporate charters. For example, they may formally state that they will include local residents on corporate boards, preference local hiring, develop local supply chains or focus sales on local and regional markets. As members of the community, they also may be more inclined to pay workers fairly, protect the environment and give back through charitable donations or volunteer work. Alternatively, members of a community may choose to operate a business, such as a department store, restaurant, solar garden or urban farm, as a community-owned enterprise. Regardless of size or type of business structure, businesses owned by members of the community can provide a sustainable foundation for the local economy.

▶ **Bioregionalism.** Ecologists view localism as a natural, Earth-centered way to manage the economy. According to Kirkpatrick Sale, throughout human history, communities have organized themselves around bioregions, such as forests, coastal areas, river basins or even deserts. The natural resources found in a bioregion generally have served as the basis for a community's food supply and culture as well as for its sustainable local economy. For example, a community with large forested areas might engage in logging as well as related, value-added businesses, such as the manufacture of furniture and other wood products. While global competition has threatened and, in many cases, shut down these types of businesses, growing consumer demand for local, American-made and sustainably sourced goods is opening the door to a new era of bioregional business development. By encouraging us to depend on the local ecosystem, bioregionalism can point the way toward sustainable economic development while also drawing us closer to our natural environment.

▶ **Connection to place.** Suburbanization, along with the replacement of downtown shopping districts (full of independently owned small businesses) with strip malls (lined with national chains), has left many of us living in homogenized communities that lack much connection to the local environment, history or culture. Localists believe that rediscovering and celebrating such connections (e.g., to local food, history, cultural heritage or natural beauty) can enrich our lives in ways that support environmental consciousness, vibrant local economies and stronger communities.

▶ **Human scale.** Like Leopold Kohr, localists reject a cult of bigness (i.e., the preference for ever-larger businesses, economies and government bureaucracies), viewing this approach to organizing society as weak and vulnerable to collapse. Instead, localists promote Kohr's idea of appropriately sized, decentralized, human-scale organizations, such as independently owned small businesses, relocalized economies and community-level governance.

▶ **Appropriate technology.** As mentioned earlier, in his book *Small Is Beautiful*, E. F. Schumacher predicts that continual technological innovation will lead to widespread unemployment. Localism can't reverse the course of a high-tech economy that is rapidly lowering pay scales and replacing entire professions with robots and digital apps. But it can help reemphasize the value of people-centric businesses, such as small, locally owned shops. And it may help encourage us to use technology in ways that empower rather than alienate us. Examples include seeking out platform cooperatives (cooperatively owned online businesses that allow peers to buy and sell from each other without any for-profit intermediaries), scaling down our lifestyles to include only the greenest and most necessary technologies or finding ways to extend the benefits of technology to everyone in the community, regardless of income or resources.

Fair Trade

Of course, we can't rely strictly on a local economy. Global trade has always existed in some form. The question is how to make today's globalization work for all of us. Free trade agreements have allowed our trade partners to sell their goods here without paying import tariffs (and vice versa). The absence of tariffs, along with very low labor and production costs in developing areas of the world, can make imports much cheaper than domestically produced products, rendering American companies less competitive. Critics of free trade argue that it has led many American manufacturers to either pay workers less or offshore their jobs. Free trade agreements also have enabled our trade partners to challenge our environmental laws on the grounds that they represent barriers to free trade.

> **Third-Party Fair Trade Certifiers**
> - Fair for Life (the Fair for Life Social & FairTrade Certification Programme)
> - Fairtrade International (FLO)
> - The Agricultural Justice Project (AJP)
> - Small Producers' Symbol (SPS) (an initiative of the Small Fair Trade Producers)
>
> **Fair Trade Membership Organizations**
> - Cooperative Coffees
> - Domestic Fair Trade Association (DFTA)
> - Fair Trade Federation
> - World Fair Trade Organization (WFTO)

While politicians debate the merits of free trade versus protectionism, proponents of fair trade believe it offers a compelling alternative to both. Nonprofit fair trade organizations offer companies and producers in the developing world the opportunity to earn more for their goods if they meet guidelines for protecting the environment, paying and treating workers fairly and reinvesting in workers' communities. This can help raise the standard of living in poorer countries and begin to level the global playing field, potentially removing the incentive for companies to ship jobs overseas. Some for-profit companies also are choosing to embrace fair trade principals when they offshore manufacturing. In recent years, other companies have decided to reshore jobs to the U.S., recognizing that American workers remain among the most productive in the world. As more consumers demonstrate a willingness to pay a premium for ethically produced and American-made goods, this trend could accelerate.

The Building Blocks of Fair Trade

By triggering a *virtuous cycle* in which businesses strive to improve the well-being of workers, their communities, consumers and the environment (as opposed to a vicious cycle in which businesses pursue a race to the bottom by placing low cost above all other criteria), fair trade can allow for global trade while helping entire communities here and abroad become more sustainable environmentally, economically and socially. Transforming global trade ultimately will require renegotiation of our international trade agreements so that they embrace fair trade ideals. Under the best of circumstances, that will take time. For now, the fair trade concept is being tested throughout the world by a growing number of fair trade companies and organizations that offer fair trade labeling to producers and brands that meet criteria such as the following:

▶ **Paying workers fairly.** Businesses seeking fair trade certification must help alleviate chronic poverty by paying workers a living wage. Fair trade organizations help place more money directly into the hands of workers by guaranteeing a premium price for certified fair trade goods and giving workers direct access to consumers, without intermediaries such as packagers or distributors.

▶ **Protecting workers' rights.** Fair trade organizations advocate for safe working conditions, reasonable hours, nondiscrimination, gender equity and freedom of association. They also are active in banning child labor and other abuses, including slavery.

▶ **Supporting worker development.** Fair trade worker collectives may provide training to help workers develop the production and entrepreneurial skills needed to transition from low-paid employment to better jobs or self-employment. They also may help workers obtain access to the credit necessary to improve their living arrangements or launch their own businesses.

▶ **Strengthening workers' communities.** Fair trade organizations encourage workers or businesses to support social stability by setting aside a portion of income or profits to invest in workers' communities. Investments in areas such as health care, water purification and education can help lift everyone out of poverty.

▶ **Encouraging environmental stewardship.** Fair trade organizations seek to protect the environment and the environmental health of workers and consumers by requiring companies to act in an ecologically responsible manner and by working to assure transparency and traceability in the supply chain. Companies may be required to conserve natural resources, reduce and remediate the effects of pollution, support reforestation, remove toxins from production processes, use renewable energy or minimize waste. In the case of food, producers may be asked to grow crops organically and/or avoid GMOs.

Social Sustainability

As we take steps to become more sustainable environmentally and economically, we may be drawn toward a variety of grassroots movements and ideas that also support *social sustainability*. Less precise a term than "environmentalism," "localism" or "fair trade," social sustainability can be defined broadly as the ideal of a peaceful, healthy, democratic and inclusive society, unscathed by environmental harm, economic exploitation or political corruption. The focus of those promoting social sustainability ranges from social justice and equality to quality education, health care and employment to grassroots democracy and good governance. Such social benefits can result from environmental and economic sustainability. For example, a green, localized economy may improve health by reducing pollution, improve schools by increasing local tax revenue, increase opportunities for individuals to find stable, meaningful employment by keeping money in the community and increase civic involvement and political participation by encouraging local, human-scale approaches to governance.

Activists, community organizers and elected representatives may be in the best position to work for the type of social sustainability described above. As individuals, we can help create a green, socially sustainable society by embracing two other values—*self-reliance* and *community resiliency*. Both ideals have deep roots in our nation's history. They hark back to the frontier ethic of rugged individualism on the one hand and community barn-raising on the other. Of course, well into the 20th century, many Americans had little choice but to be self-reliant, growing their own food and making most of what they required for daily life. Many also relied on cooperation with neighbors to tackle large tasks, obtain access to resources and address concerns that affected the entire community. Out of necessity, those who came before us were less dependent on a paycheck, more skilled at the living arts and more closely connected to members of their communities than most of us are today. Necessity also led these earlier generations to live in greater harmony with nature, staying attuned to the seasons, consuming and discarding less and reusing as much as possible. All of that changed dramatically during the economic boom that followed World War II, when Americans happily embraced good jobs and the proliferation of mass-produced consumer goods. In the decades that followed, most of us (with the exception of those suffering chronic poverty) have taken for granted that our jobs would provide the income to, at the very least, meet basic needs. For those with more expendable income, conspicuous consumption soon became the norm. A high-consumption lifestyle transformed us from producers and protectors of the Earth to consumers complicit in the depletion of natural resources. It also made us dependent on others for employment and income, increased our risk of debt and financial insecurity and distanced us ever further from the potential helpmates next door, members of our immediate communities.

It wasn't until the late 1960s, when environmental consciousness was on the rise, along with disdain for consumerism and a conventional, suburban lifestyle, that some began to revisit the importance of both self-reliance and connection to community. Inspired by frontier-era self-sufficiency as well as early 20th-century Socialism, these sustainability pioneers rejected consumerism for DIYism, explored cooperative ownership in place of private enterprise and embraced direct democracy as an alternative to large, unresponsive bureaucracies. Experiments with these ideals included moving back to the land to farm organically, living off-the-grid in the earliest solar-powered homes, participating in consumer or worker cooperatives and engaging in community organizing or grassroots politics. Such experimentation fell out of favor by the 1980s and remained on the fringes for the next few decades. But in recent years, ideas about self-reliance and community resiliency have once again begun to resonate, this time among those seeking a sustainable response to a threatened environment, a challenging economy and a disappearing sense of community. Some even suggest that it's time to trade in an increasingly fragile American dream, one that leaves us on our own in the pursuit of the best job, the highest pay and the most consumer rewards, for a new definition of "better off" that values a simpler but more personally fulfilling path marked by less consumption, more creativity and greater connection to those around us.

The Building Blocks of Social Sustainability

Grassroots movements focused on self-reliance and community resiliency have become wellsprings of creative strategies for sustainable living. While some individuals may focus exclusively on either self-reliance *or* community resiliency, given the overlap between the two pursuits, it's practical to consider them together. Prescriptions for forging a more socially sustainable world by increasing self-reliance and community resiliency include:

▶ **Replacing an extractive economy with a productive one.**
Advocates of social sustainability encourage us to transition away from the consumerism that requires extraction of nonrenewable natural resources. Replacing rampant consumption with eco-friendly home- or community-based production can help us achieve that goal while also reducing the pollution, greenhouse gases and waste associated with the lifecycle of consumer goods. This transition also can enable us to become more self-sufficient, relying less on outside income and more on ingenuity and creativity. Individuals can adopt this approach to sustainability by becoming makers or DIY enthusiasts, producing anything from food, clothing and furnishings to an entire home or renewable energy system. Other opportunities to reduce extractive consumption include reusing and upcycling as well as engaging in various forms of collaborative consumption, such as sharing, swapping, bartering and tapping the unused value of existing assets (all discussed

below). At the community level, we can replace extractive consumption with production by communally growing and distributing food (e.g., via community gardens, urban farms, community foraging, community kitchens, community-supported agriculture or seed and harvest swaps) or developing community-scale renewable energy (e.g., with solar gardens or microgrids).

▶ **Replacing financial forms of capital with social capital (our connection to others).** This is the goal of many sharing advocates, who believe that by removing money from the equation, we can create more democratic, equitable ways of obtaining and distributing goods and services, enabling everyone to meet basic needs even when income is limited. As just mentioned, sharing can help us reduce extractive consumption and become more self-reliant. It also can bring people together around shared needs and facilitate transactions in which the currencies of exchange are trust and cooperation, two important forms of social capital. Creating and leveraging social capital can enable us to live more simply, rely less on traditional forms of currency and forge the social connections necessary for stable, resilient communities. Nearly all of us already share online via open-source software platforms or social media sites. We also may want to consider sharing any item or service for which access is just as good as—or even better than—ownership. This may include such consumer goods as special occasion clothing, recreational items and tools, services such as childcare or transportation, or space, such as a room, a home or an office. Swapping, buying collectively with others and joining a community "library of things" are other ways to engage in sharing. We may even wish to barter services, an alternative that can support a broader effort to create a solidarity economy (discussed on page 48).

▶ **Fully utilizing assets.** Sustainability theorists have suggested that rather than continually buying new goods that have built-in obsolescence, we should be able to lease the products we want or need. This could help reduce excess production and consumption and encourage the manufacture of better-quality products. A variation on this idea has become popular within the sharing movement. Seeking income in the absence of a paycheck, some individuals are using the social web to extract the untapped value of their homes, offices or vehicles by "sharing" them with friends, neighbors or strangers. Many personal assets are never fully utilized; for example, studies show that most cars sit idle about 95% of the time,[27] while many of us have spare rooms in our homes or workplaces that rarely get used. Since renting out existing assets may reduce the need to manufacture additional vehicles, erect new buildings or eliminate more open space, this strategy can be environmentally sustainable. As with other forms of sharing, it also can support social and economic sustainability by strengthening community ties and reducing the cost of living.

▶ **Supporting a solidarity economy.** Combining the best aspects of capitalism and socialism, a solidarity economy (also referred to as a "social economy" or "the next economy") is made up of organizations and businesses committed to social justice, community control, equality and sustainability. In a solidarity economy, shareholders may be replaced by collective owners, members or users, while boards of directors are replaced by democratic employee-manager teams and hierarchical salary structures give way to employee-owner profit-sharing. The various forms of sharing described previously can play an important role in building a solidarity economy. Non-profit organizations, B corporations, social enterprises, labor unions and municipally owned enterprises all may be part of the mix. Other ways we can support social sustainability by helping to create a more egalitarian, democratic and secure economy include:

Going co-op. Inspired by England's 19th-century Rochdale cooperative, which established such cooperative principals as open membership, democratic (i.e., one member, one vote) governance and a commitment to the communities in which they operate, cooperatives are businesses or organizations owned and collectively managed by workers or members. Popular during the Great Depression of the 1930s and then again in the late 1960s and early 1970s, cooperatives are becoming prevalent today among individuals seeking greater control over their work lives. Beyond the natural food groceries most of us associate with the term "co-op," there are many other types of consumer co-ops (e.g., REI and Cabot Creamery), as well as platform cooperatives, producer cooperatives (e.g., Land O'Lakes and the United Cranberry Growers Cooperative) and financial co-ops (e.g., credit unions and loan funds that provide capital to other cooperatives). There are even large, corporate conglomerates run cooperatively, such as Spain's highly successful Mondragon Corporation.

Platform Cooperatives

Platform cooperatives are online or app-driven sites that allow individuals to buy or sell products or services from each other on a peer-to-peer basis, without any for-profit intermediaries. The platforms are owned and democratically managed collectively by producers and users. Sharetribe (sharetribe.com) offers open-source technology for creating a platform cooperative.

Participating in time banks. Bartering can help individuals obtain services they otherwise couldn't afford while developing marketable skills and building both personal and professional networks (i.e., social capital). This can be useful in communities where work and income are scarce, either historically or due to a temporary downturn in the economy. It also can offer benefits to retirees who want to stay active and share a lifetime of skills while reducing their cost of living. Bartering of skills (and goods) often occurs informally between friends and neighbors. But some communities have taken the step of creating nonprofit *time banks* that enable a wider population to barter services in a fair and systematic way.

Creating commons. Public commons were once a typical feature of European village life. Commons also flourished in Colonial America, serving a variety of purposes. Boston Common, for example, provided space for military training, cattle grazing and burial grounds before becoming a hub of civic and social life for modern-day Bostonians. Today's resiliency advocates celebrate commons for their potential to bring community members together around shared interests and needs. Public parks reclaimed as commons (for example, when community members pay for repairs not available from public funds) may allow members of a community to garden or forage collectively, participate in educational or physical fitness programs, enjoy celebrations, social gatherings and entertainment or explore resiliency strategies through information shares or swapping and bartering events. Commons also can take the form of cooperatively rented spaces, such as community kitchens, seed or tool libraries, libraries of things, makerspaces or co-work spaces. Even courtyards and sidewalks are being appropriated as commons for purposes ranging from urban farms and community gardens to *pop-up libraries* (tiny lending libraries often housed in movable kiosks) and *little free pantries* (small storage containers stocked with free food for those in need).

Now that we've considered these three paths to sustainability, we can ask ourselves what holistic sustainability might look like for us. The answers will vary widely from one person to the next as we pick and choose from ideas like those in the following pages.

How Can We Create a Holistically Sustainable Lifestyle?

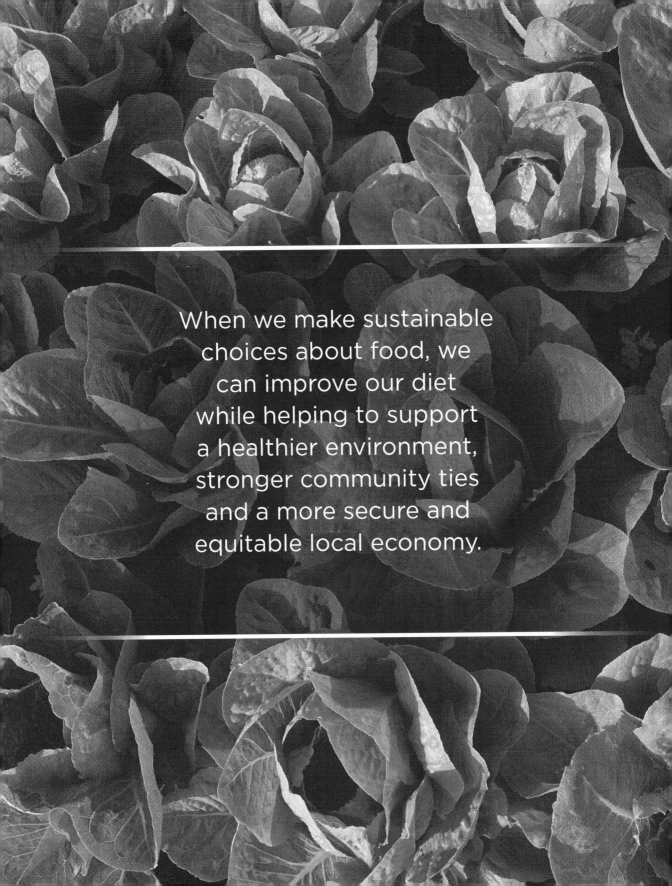

When we make sustainable
choices about food, we
can improve our diet
while helping to support
a healthier environment,
stronger community ties
and a more secure and
equitable local economy.

Food

For many of us, a sustainable lifestyle begins with food. That's not surprising given the central role it plays in our lives as a source of sustenance, good health and enjoyment. Food also has a history of serving as a catalyst for change, bringing us together around shared concerns for the planet, the economy and the communities we call "home."

Interest in eating sustainably has exploded in recent years as we've learned about the failings of our industrial food system. From the organic, local and Slow Food movements to vegetarian and vegan diets, a quiet revolution has been taking place around what and how we eat. That revolution has given rise to a new generation of sustainable farmers, edible gardeners, artisanal food entrepreneurs and farm-to-table restauranteurs. It's also created a burgeoning consumer market for healthy, non-industrial food.

We may begin our journey toward a more sustainable relationship with food focused on one particular concern: improving our health *or* protecting the environment *or* recharging our local economy and community. But once we get started, we can easily find ourselves making choices that are not just environmentally *or* economically *or* socially sustainable but rather some combination of all three. Each of the following choices can provide a jumping-off place for achieving a *holistically* sustainable diet.

> **Six Approaches to Eating Sustainably**
>
> ▸ Organic
> ▸ Local
> ▸ Slow
> ▸ Vegetarian/Vegan
> ▸ Self-reliant
> ▸ Communal

Organic

A majority of American consumers now purchase some organic food on a regular basis.[1] Eating organic food whenever possible can help us protect both the environment and our health. But as we begin to seek out organic choices, it's important to understand exactly what that label means. There are three broad categories: (1) food certified as organic by the USDA (United States Department of Agriculture), (2) food certified as organic by alternative certification programs and (3) food from farmers who are committed to sustainable agriculture but have opted not to seek formal certification.

USDA organic certification guidelines went into effect in 2002, when the agency's National Organic Program (NOP) began implementing the Organic Foods Production Act of 1990. While several states had their own organic certification programs as far back as the 1970s, the NOP superseded them, establishing a federal standard for organic food production. The USDA organic program's overarching goal is to ensure that food is produced in a way that is environmentally sustainable, protecting both human health and natural resources. To achieve that goal, organic farmers must follow the USDA's organic guidelines. (The guidelines can be reviewed at usda.gov/organic. certification.) For example, the NOP prohibits the use of:

✓ Most synthetic chemical fertilizers, pesticides, herbicides and fungicides, the fossil-fuel-based agricultural inputs responsible for about 40% of the energy used in the nation's food system.[2] As a last resort, farmers may use certain "allowed synthetic substances" listed on the NOP's National List.

✓ GMO seed for either produce or feed crops.

✓ Growth hormones and prophylactic antibiotics.

✓ Irradiation and sewage sludge.

Additionally, under the NOP:

✓ All livestock feed must be 100% organic and contain no animal by-products.

✓ Livestock must have access to the outdoors as weather permits, and ruminants must have access to pasture for grazing.

✓ Manure must be managed in a way that doesn't cause soil, water or crop contamination.

NOP guidelines do not address the labor conditions of farmworkers, the proximity of farms to consumers (i.e., whether they are local) or the use of fossil fuels for energy and/or transportation. They also do not ban the CAFOs (concentrated animal feeding operations), hog confinement pens and poultry mills common throughout industrial farming.

As of 2016, there were nearly 22,000 USDA-certified organic farms, ranches and other food producers operating throughout the country.[3] Farms shifting to organic processes over a required three-year period may identify themselves as "transitioning organic" prior to receiving official certification. Farms that meet USDA guidelines but have less than $5,000 in annual sales can label their products "organic" without paying for certification. Farmers, ranchers and other food producers may qualify for various levels of organic certification.

In addition to the USDA organic program, there are at least two recognized nonprofit certification programs: Certified Naturally Grown (CNG) and Demeter Certified Biodynamic. These programs address some issues not covered by USDA certification, such as fair labor practices and humane treatment of livestock. There also are many farms committed to sustainable agricultural methods but unwilling to pursue USDA certification due to the time and costs involved, discomfort with government oversight or the belief that the USDA guide-

There are four levels of USDA organic certification:

1. **100% USDA-Certified Organic** (bearing USDA organic seal): 100% of ingredients must be organic.

2. **USDA-Certified Organic** (bearing seal): At least 95% of ingredients must be organic.

3. **Made with organic ingredients** (no seal but may list organic ingredients): At least 70% of all ingredients are certified organic.

4. **Some organic ingredients** (no seal): Less than 70% of ingredients are certified organic.

lines aren't as rigorous as their own practices. Some farms also are adopting *regenerative agriculture*, which combines organic practices with a focus on restoring the soil and its power to sequester carbon dioxide (CO_2). With non-USDA-certified organic, consumers must decide for themselves whether they trust a farmer's claims. But since many of these farms are small, family owned and local to their customer base, there often is ample opportunity to learn exactly what a particular farmer means by "sustainable agriculture." It also may be possible to learn a farm's status (e.g., sustainable, low-impact or transitioning sustainable) by reviewing our state's agricultural directory or contacting the state organic farming association (e.g., NOFANJ, the NJ branch of the National Organic Farming Association).

Whether certified or not, organic food generally offers many benefits over "conventional" alternatives.[4]

▶ **Reduced exposure to chemicals.** Conventional farming employs fossil fuel-based fertilizers, pesticides, herbicides and fungicides made from a wide range of synthetic chemicals. According to the EPA, farmers may use only those chemicals the agency has deemed safe for human consumption. But the Environmental Working Group (ewg.org) and other critics of chemical agriculture caution that ongoing exposure to chemicals may pose a range of health threats, increasing risks of certain cancers as well as neurological, autoimmune and reproductive disorders. Health concerns can be greater for young children. We may be exposed to agricultural chemicals in several ways: (1) as residue on the surface of some types of produce, (2) in produce that absorbs chemicals systemically and (3) in the meat and fat of livestock exposed to chemicals in feed.

Organic farmers do not use synthetic chemicals, relying instead on *integrated pest management* strategies (e.g., companion planting, crop rotation, composting, minimal tilling and planting off-season cover crops) and the type of targeted, low-impact biological inputs used for generations before the introduction of synthetic chemicals.

▶ **Reduced exposure to growth hormones and antibiotics.** Nonorganic farms give cattle growth hormones to make them grow faster. While the USDA and FDA claim that growth hormones do not pose risks to human health, independent studies suggest possible links to a variety of health issues, including hormone imbalance and certain cancers. Antibiotics have been given to livestock to encourage growth (though this practice was recently banned) and to counteract unhealthy conditions in the crowded CAFOs, confinement pens and poultry mills where most commercially raised livestock spend their days. It has been estimated that the use of antibiotics for livestock accounts for about 80% of all antibiotic use in the U.S. That overuse of antibiotics has been linked to the rise of life-threatening antibiotic-resistant strains of bacteria in both animals and humans.

USDA-certified organic farms are prohibited from using either growth hormones or prophylactic antibiotics. Noncertified farms that are committed to organic, sustainable agriculture typically do not give livestock growth hormones or antibiotics.

▶ **Reduced exposure to GMOs.** Until the emergence of genetically modified seeds in the 1990s, farmers typically collected seeds from their highest-quality plants to use the following season, filing in with seeds purchased from various suppliers. When GMOs were introduced, the stated intention was to help farmers produce hardier plants—more resistant to disease, insects and other threats—and ultimately realize higher yields. That benefit would result from GMO seeds having a higher tolerance for being treated with synthetic agricultural chemicals. Some seeds, such as varieties of feed corn, have even been genetically modified to contain pesticides that are released as plants develop. Today, a large percentage of commodity crops (e.g., corn, soybeans, canola, sugar beets) are grown from GMO seed. About 80% of all nonorganic processed foods contain GMO crops, often in some laboratory-modified form, such as high-fructose corn syrup. The FDA even approved a genetically modified breed of salmon in 2015.

There are several common criticisms of GMOs. The original claim that they would reduce the need for pesticides and other chemicals has not panned out. According to the Non-GMO Project and the National Academy of Sciences, farmers actually have been increasing their use of chemicals, leading to more resilient pests and weeds that require still greater use of chemicals. The National Academy of Sciences conducted tests on the safety of GMOs in 2000 and 2004. While those tests didn't identify any unique risks to human health from eating GMO foods, the Academy did express concern about the potential for exposure

---

to allergens and toxins. They were particularly concerned about the potential health risks associated with increased exposure to certain herbicides. Environmentalists believe increased use of chemicals has endangered honey bees, monarch butterflies and other beneficial species while also posing risks to human health. Environmentalists and other scientists also have concerns about the potential for GMOs to threaten the biodiversity essential to a healthy ecosystem.

GMO labeling requirements were signed into law in 2016, and many companies will be required to label their products as of 2020. But labels are expected to read "bioengineered" rather than "GMO," and since there will likely be a significant number of exemptions, it is possible that not all GMO foods (or foods that contain GMO ingredients) will necessarily be labeled as such. Up until now, a few states have required GMO labeling and some food brands have voluntarily labeled their products "non-GMO." While waiting for federal labeling requirements to go into effect—and perhaps even afterwards—our options for avoiding GMOs include buying products labeled "Non-GMO Project Verified" or choosing USDA-certified organic food, which cannot contain GMOs.

▶ **Nutritional benefits.** While improved nutrition isn't a stated goal of organic farming, there is some evidence that it may be yet another potential benefit. Studies have found that organic, pasture-raised hens (which eat insects, worms, grubs and greens, rather than genetically modified feed) contain higher levels of omega 3 fatty acids, cancer-fighting carotenes and vitamins A, D and E than hens raised on non-organic farms. Organic hens also have lower levels of omega 6, a nutrient linked to cardiovascular disease and type 2 diabetes, and lower levels of cholesterol. Organic dairy and meat also have been found to contain higher levels of omega-3 fatty acids than their conventionally produced counterparts. And organic crops appear to be higher in antioxidants and other potentially beneficial compounds.

▶ **Cleaner air.** Critics say conventional agriculture contributes to air pollution by spraying crops with chemicals from crop duster planes and employing CAFOs, which are a source of volatile organic compounds and other pollutants. Manure from CAFOs also releases methane, a potent greenhouse gas. Industrial farms also contribute to greenhouse gas emissions through the use of fossil fuels for transportation and chemical inputs. While organic farms do not use crop dusters, some larger organic livestock farms employ CAFOs. On organic produce farms, the only air pollution generally is from the tail-pipe emissions of farm vehicles.

▶ **Cleaner water.** Stormwater runoff from conventional farms is considered the nation's largest *nonpoint source* of water pollution, with contaminants including sediments, salts, herbicides, pesticides, pharmaceuticals and nutrients from fertilizers, such as nitrates and phosphates. (As opposed to *point source* pollution, which comes from identifiable sources, such as industrial wastewater or sewage treatment plants, nonpoint source pollution has many possible sources. We all may contribute to it by improperly disposing of trash, oils, animal waste or chemical pesticides and fertilizers.) Critics say that runoff is a particular problem on industrial farms because their agricultural practices weaken soil structure, contributing to top-soil erosion. The water pollution caused by agricultural runoff has been linked to massive fish kills, contaminated drinking water, toxic residues in fish sold for human consumption and dead zones in the Gulf of Mexico, the Great Lakes and elsewhere. (The term "dead zone" refers to any aquatic area, such as an ocean or a lake, where nutrients from runoff produce an abundance of algae that, in turn, absorb excess oxygen, depriving marine life of an adequate supply.) The EPA attributes no less than 75% of water pollution in rivers and streams to the impact of agriculture. While all agriculture can produce some runoff, organic farming greatly reduces the problem by eliminating chemical contamination and the unsustainable practices that lead to soil erosion.

▶ **Healthier soil.** Healthy soil is essential to food production, providing the water and nutrients crops need to grow and thrive. Industrial agriculture is criticized for harming soil in a variety of ways. Farms that grow commodity crops, such as corn, soybeans and sugar beets, often practice monocrop production, growing just one type of crop. According to organic farming advocates, that depletes the soil of nutrients, making it weaker, more prone to erosion and less fertile. Industrial farms also are criticized for degrading soil by over-tilling, which decreases the infiltration of rainwater into the ground, and for failing to rotate crops annually or allow fields to lay fallow periodically. All of these practices fly in the face of farming techniques employed successfully since biblical times. According to a Cornell University study, those practices also are responsible for 1.7 billion tons of top soil being blown away or washed away from farmland annually. Sustainable Table reports that, over the past four decades, 30% of the world's arable land has lost its fertility due to soil erosion. According to a study published by *Science*, it's estimated that erosion of agricultural soil (and the related loss of water) costs the U.S. economy more than $37 billion a year.

Protecting soil gets to the heart of what is meant by *sustainable*. The fates of Ancient Rome and the Dust Bowl-era Midwestern U.S. paint a clear picture of what can happen when we don't take our responsibility to the soil seriously. Industrial farms can remediate soil problems by applying more chemicals. But sustainable agriculture advocates believe it's only a matter of time before this chemical arms race becomes ineffective. By contrast, organic farmers help reduce soil erosion and build healthy, productive soil by eliminating synthetic chemicals, reducing or eliminating tillage, growing a diverse range of crops, rotating crops, letting fields lay fallow and planting cover crops off season. Organic farmers also help preserve or restore soil quality by fertilizing with compost (organic matter), which slowly releases the nutrients necessary for healthy crops.

▶ **Land stewardship.** In addition to protecting the air, water and soil through sustainable agricultural methods, organic farmers act as good stewards of the land in several other ways. They help protect native flora and fauna by eliminating chemicals from the environment. USDA-certified farmers who purchase land that previously was farmed with chemicals are required to restore fields to their natural state using such methods as planting grasses that absorb chemicals and help cleanse the soil. Farmers also must protect buffer areas between productive fields and adjacent waterways.

▶ **Remediation of global warming.** While oceans take first place in sequestering the planet's CO_2, soil comes in second, holding four times as much carbon as all of the world's plants and trees combined. Soil that is not sprayed with synthetic chemicals naturally contains certain beneficial fungi to which CO_2 molecules bond. That allows the soil to act as a natural *carbon sink*, absorbing CO_2 from the atmosphere. But scientists, including those at the Rodale Institute, say that the soil's ability to sequester carbon is being undermined by industrial agricultural practices. They have calculated that "practical organic agriculture, if practiced on the planet's 3.5 billion tillable acres, could sequester nearly 40 percent of current CO_2 emissions."[5] Studies by Rodale and the Conservation Technology Information Center (CTIC) also point out that organic farming has less impact on climate change than conventional farming because it eliminates the fossil fuels associated with synthetic inputs.

▶ **Increased yields.** A common argument against organic farming is that it can't possibly "feed the world" because it produces lower yields. According to the Rodale Institute, only organic farms that mimic conventional farming practices, such as over-tilling and monocrop production, underperform chemical agriculture. Rodale's research shows that, over several decades, "true" organic farming has matched the yields of chemical farming and, for corn, exceeded it by roughly 30% in years of drought. Other studies provide further evidence that organic farming can meet or exceed the yields achieved by conventional agriculture.

▶ **More ethical treatment of livestock.** Industrial livestock farms raise large populations of animals in conditions that many have described as environmentally harmful, cruel and unhealthy for consumers. Livestock often live almost entirely indoors in extremely cramped conditions and have little if any time to graze or exercise. In addition to banning the use of growth hormones and prophylactic antibiotics, USDA organic standards improve living conditions for livestock by requiring grazing time, although critics say those standards are too vague. Noncertified farms committed to sustainable agriculture generally manage livestock in more traditional ways. That can mean raising much smaller herds or flocks than typical on industrial farms, while letting cows graze, pigs slop and chickens and other fowl live truly *free range*.

Choosing Organic Food

As a new generation of farmers trained in soil science and conservation methods has embraced organic production, the quality of organic food has increased dramatically. And while organic food can still cost more than nonorganic, consumer demand has grown so substantially in recent years that it's had a noticeable impact in reducing prices. That's important, since the point of creating a more sustainable world is for *everyone* to benefit, not just those who can afford healthier choices.

Depending on the household food budget, there are several ways to include organic food in our daily diet.

▶ **Buy locally produced organic food.** This may include food certified by the USDA or alternative certifiers or noncertified food from a farmer or producer we trust. If any of these options are available and affordable, they can offer the best of two worlds: We can reduce our exposure to synthetic chemicals, antibiotics, growth hormones and GMOs while also enjoying the freshness and nutritional value of in-season, local food—and the many other benefits of buying local. Some national food chains now sell organic food from farms local to their customers. Many small, independently owned family farms sell organic produce, dairy, meats and poultry directly to consumers through farm stands, farm-owned grocery stores, farmers' markets and community-supported agriculture (CSA) programs.

▶ **Buy private label USDA-certified organic food.** Many supermarkets and other retail chains sell their own line of organic foods. These private-label lines go by various names, but provided the products are labeled "USDA organic," consumers can feel confident that they meet the USDA's organic standards. (Note that private-label lines may produce both organic and nonorganic products. Some USDA-certified organic products are sourced outside the U.S and bear the label "Quality Assurance International," which is a certifying entity accredited by the USDA organic certification program.) Private-label organic products tend to cost less than other organic choices, making them an affordable alternative for those on a budget. Because private-label brands provide a large market for organic farmers and producers, over time, they may help drive down the price of all organic foods.

▶ **Buy organic when it matters most.** Another budget-conscious way to choose organic is to focus on select items. Some nonorganic foods are considered more likely than others to expose us to harmful levels of synthetic chemicals.

Scientists at the Environmental Working Group (EWG) review published research to determine the relative safety of nonorganic foods. Based on this review, EWG provides consumers with a list of produce items that are particularly toxic when grown conventionally. Produce items may be added to this "Dirty Dozen" list if the pesticides used on them are considered particularly harmful or if the produce absorbs chemicals systemically, so that rinsing off chemical residues isn't enough to make them safe. The complete Dirty Dozen list (which includes more than a dozen items and is updated periodically) is available at ewg.org.

Beyond produce, it's also important to consider our consumption of all types of animal protein from nonorganic farms. Conventional livestock feed is treated with pesticides. Animals can accumulate these chemicals in their tissue and fat. Consequently, eating beef, pork, chicken or even dairy products can expose us to chemicals as well as to growth hormones, antibiotics and GMOs. We can further reduce our exposure to GMOs by avoiding nonorganic packaged and processed foods made with food additives derived from GMO crops, such as corn and soybeans. Finally, we may want to prioritize organic for foods that we eat frequently. Since it's probably our net exposure to toxins that really matters, frequently consumed foods may pose a greater risk to our health than those we eat only on occasion.

▶ **Grow an organic edible garden.** One of the most cost-effective ways to afford organic food is to produce it ourselves. Whether we have a fertile plot of land or a windowsill, it's possible to grow organic vegetables simply by switching to organic seed, soil and fertilizers and using integrated pest management practices instead of commercial sprays. While becoming an organic farmer takes significant know-how, the small scale of most home gardens makes it relatively easy to adopt organic practices. For novice gardeners, a good place to start is with foods frequently eaten and/or those on the Dirty Dozen list. (More information on organic gardening: Self-Reliant, pages 78 to 79)

Sustainable Pet Food[6]

Pet food can be unsustainable in at least two ways: (1) Much of it is made from the by-products of nonorganic human food, potentially exposing animals to all of the hazards of chemical agriculture and (2) most pet food is highly processed, with natural nutrients stripped out, only to be replaced by additives and preservatives. Fortunately, there are healthier alternatives, including USDA-certified organic pet food, brands with a guarantee from the Association of American Feed Control Officials (AAFCO), which oversees the inclusion and identification of nutrients, and pet foods that specifically identify the sources of protein among the first ingredients and that use vitamins, rather than chemicals, as preservatives.

Sustainable Seafood[7]

Fish can offer an excellent source of lean protein and provide us with many health benefits. But consumers face significant challenges when it comes to identifying exactly which types of seafood are sustainable for us and the planet. Concerns include:

Environmental health. Fish and other seafood may be contaminated by the chemical by-products of industry and agriculture that have polluted our oceans, lakes, rivers and streams for the past century. Two of the biggest culprits are PCBs (polychlorinated biphenyls) and mercury. Though banned in 1977, the PCBs used for decades in a wide range of manufacturing processes remain buried in river beds and estuaries, where they continue to be ingested by migrating fish. Mercury released into the air from coal-fired power plants and other sources accumulates in the oceans and other waterways, where it can contaminate seafood at every level of the food chain. Swordfish, shark, king mackerel and tilefish are among the fish known to have particularly high levels of mercury. Farmed fish also present a range of concerns, potentially exposing us to toxins, antibiotics and pesticides.

Irresponsible fishing. Globally, seafood is under tremendous pressure from overfishing and irresponsible catch methods that harm dolphins and other marine life, often referred to as "bycatch." According to the FAO (the Food and Agriculture Organization of the United Nations), as reported by World Wildlife Fund, 53% of the world's fisheries have been fully exploited and 32% have been overexploited or depleted or are recovering from depletion.

Threats to biodiversity. Farmed fish can threaten biodiversity if and when they escape into the wild and breed with naturally occurring species.

The Natural Resources Defense Council and other environmental groups have provided the following recommendations for those who wish to buy only sustainable seafood.

1. **Buy local.** As with any local purchase, this reduces the carbon footprint associated with transportation and supports the local economy. Community-Supported Fisheries (CSFs) in some coastal and waterfront communities allow customers to purchase shares of future catch up-front and receive an allotment on a weekly or monthly basis.

2. **Buy American.** While our standards are far from perfect, they generally are much higher than those of many countries that export large quantities of fish.

3. **For wild fish, look for the Marine Stewardship Council label.** The council certifies that seafood was caught in a sustainable manner that didn't harm marine life or contribute to overfishing.

4. **Look for the Food Alliance or Aquaculture Stewardship Council labels** for farmed fish and farmed shellfish.

5. **Look for the FishWise low mercury card** at the fish counter.

6. **Choose fish caught by hook and line or with pots and traps.** These methods reduce the possibility of killing or harming other marine life.

7. **For frozen fish, look for shelf-stable, flexible pouches,** which don't contain BPA and are considered environmentally sustainable.

8. **Eat smaller fish.** Because they are at the low end of the aquatic food chain, they have less opportunity to accumulate pollutants than larger fish. They also are far more abundant.

9. **Learn about the risks of specific types of seafood** at rodale.org or nrdc.org.

10. **Buy from retailers that have made a commitment to source seafood sustainably.**

11. **Download the Monterey Bay Aquarium's Seafood Watch app,** which lets shoppers look up the latest information on the sustainability of specific types of fish before they make a purchase.

Sustainable Beverages

We can make sustainable choices about most of the beverages we drink.

Water

Water is a healthy *and necessary* beverage choice. But there are two concerns we may want to consider:

The impact of plastic water bottles, which may harm us and the environment, exposing us to BPA and other chemicals, while requiring fossil fuels for production and transportation and contributing significantly to landfill waste and ocean pollution.

Toxins in water. Water safety is carefully managed in the U.S. But not all contaminants are tracked and monitored. The Flint, Michigan, lead pipe crisis and the recent discovery of groundwater contamination from PFOA (perfluorooctanoic acid) and chromium-6 have raised new concerns about contaminants in drinking water.[8] If we're concerned about our water (e.g., if it changes its taste, color or odor), there are several ways to get assistance.

- ✓ Local water utilities are required by the EPA to monitor quality, address some types of contamination and make quality information available to the public in the form of Consumer Confidence Reports.
- ✓ Municipal public health department and planning offices should have information about local water conditions.
- ✓ Our state's Department of Environmental Protection can offer assistance and information.
- ✓ The EPA's Safe Drinking Water Hotline (epa. gov/safewater) can provide assistance.
- ✓ The Environmental Working Group (ewg.org) offers safety updates and information about researching local water conditions and choosing appropriate filters.
- ✓ Private water-filtering companies can test well water for some impurities. Some municipalities regulate well water quality.

We can help protect our well or municipal water supply by conserving water and avoiding the use or inappropriate disposal of household and garden contaminants, such as motor oil or pesticides.

Milk

Certified organic milk should be free of synthetic chemicals, growth hormones, antibiotics and GMOs.

Coffee and tea[9]

Industrial coffee plantations may use a lot of water, threaten biodiversity and contribute to deforestation and water pollution from synthetic agricultural inputs. By contrast, organic and fair trade coffee is produced in the traditional "shade-grown" manner, with coffee planted amidst other types of trees, providing plants with protection from the sun. Working *with* the ecosystem helps conserve water, improve soil conservation, support biodiversity, reduce weed growth, reduce the use of chemicals and restore native habitat. Some organic shade-grown coffee growers are certified as Bird Friendly by the Smithsonian's Migratory Bird Center because they provide sanctuary for migrating birds. Shade-grown plantations also may meet fair trade criteria. There are also organic and sustainably grown teas, some of which are fair trade certified.

Non-alcoholic beverages

Numerous companies now sell certified organic and all-natural sodas and juices.

Wine, beer and other alcoholic beverages

Many alcoholic drinks are now made from plants (e.g., grapes, hops, barley, rye) grown without synthetic chemicals. The Sonoma, California, wine region has even committed to becoming fulling sustainable by 2019. Wines are available with varying degrees of USDA organic certification. Fully organic wines (labeled "100% organic") must be made from organically grown grapes and contain no nonorganic ingredients or added sulfites. (Some sulfites are naturally occurring.) Wines can be described as having organic ingredients if at least 70% of the ingredients are organic; added sulfites are allowed. Local breweries and microbreweries, searchable at beertown.org, also offer organic and artisanal choices. Organic home brewing information is available at breworganic.com.

Know the Lingo

Demand for healthy, sustainable food has led to more variety *and* more bogus marketing claims. As we seek out better choices, it's important to scrutinize labels and learn to separate the wheat from the chaff.

Unsustainable choices (i.e., the fakes). Terms such as "green," "natural" and "farm fresh" are ubiquitous. But they're often nothing more than marketing hype. Only the ingredients (if they're listed) will tell the real story. If many of those ingredients are unfamiliar or difficult to pronounce, chances are there's not much that's green, natural or fresh about the product. Skepticism also is in order for two other categories: mass-produced foods bearing the description "organic" but lacking a reputable certification label, such as "USDA organic," and products described as "local" that don't identify their place of origin.

Sustainable claims. The only federally regulated food labels are "USDA organic" and "natural" for meat, the latter indicating only that the meat contains no food additives. Labels from nonprofits, such as fair-trade organizations and the Marine Fisheries Council, generally are recognized as reputable. The sustainability of locally produced food, even if not labeled, often can be verified by speaking directly with farmers and/or other food producers.

Labels galore. Somewhere between federally regulated guidelines and marketing hype are a wide range of fairly reliable labels. These include:

- **Sustainable agriculture:** Agricultural methods that protect the environment and human health and support economic profitability and social and economic equity

- **Regenerative agriculture:** Organic agriculture that protects and rebuilds soil to support food security and sequester carbon

- **Non-GMO Project Verified:** A nonprofit that certifies that foods were produced with no more than .09 percent genetically modified seed or feed

- **Certified Naturally Grown (CNG):** A private, nonprofit certifier promoting USDA National Organic Program (NOP) standards, with peer review of participating farmers and transparent process open to the public

- **Demeter Certified Biodynamic:** A "whole-farm" organic certification approach requiring humane treatment of livestock and the setting aside of 10% of land to promote biodiversity

- **Certified Humane Raised and Handled:** Livestock raised humanely, from birth through slaughter, without prophylactic antibiotics, growth hormones or cages, crates or tie stalls

- **AJP (The Agricultural Justice Project):** Seeks empowerment, justice and fairness for all food workers, from the farm to retail, awarding Food Justice Certification (FJC) label to farms and food businesses that meet their standards

- **Grass-fed:** Indicates only that most of a cow's diet is grass

- **Free-range:** USDA-regulated label indicating that poultry had access to the outdoors, though time and space may be limited

- **Cage-free:** Uncaged flocks, able to roam buildings, rooms or other enclosed areas, with unlimited access to food and fresh water

- **Pasture-raised:** Livestock allowed grazing time, but grass diet may be supplemented by grains or other feed types

- **Natural:** Minimally processed meat with no artificial ingredients

- **Fair trade:** Certification of producers that meet standards for environmental responsibility, fair labor practices and community reinvestment

- **Rainforest Alliance Certified:** Certification for coffee, cocoa, tea, nuts and fruits grown in a manner that reduces water pollution, prevents soil erosion, protects habitat and human health, reduces waste and improves livelihoods

- **Food Alliance Certified:** Certification for food producers that meet guidelines for soil and water conservation, fair working conditions, reduced pesticide use, animal welfare and habitat conservation

Local

Local food can be a sustainable choice both environmentally and economically. Eating local can reduce our carbon footprint, help preserve open space and strengthen our connection to community, all while providing us with food that's fresh, tasty and full of nutrients. Perhaps more than any other sustainable food choice, local also holds the key to creating a human-scale alternative to today's vast global economy.

Demand for local food has grown dramatically in recent years, a trend well-documented by the USDA.[10] In 2005, chef and food activist Jessica Prentice coined the term "locavore" to describe consumers interested in knowing the sources of the food on their plates and keeping those sources local. But the local food movement, which advocates relocalizing our diet in as many ways as possible, actually has roots back in the 1970s. Like any movement, this one sprung from the ideas and actions of a wide variety of groups and individuals. One such individual was restaurateur and food activist Alice Waters, who championed the value of choosing fresh, seasonal, local and organic ingredients for her now legendary Berkeley, California, restaurant Chez Panisse at a time when few others were thinking about the benefits of local food. Her decision helped create a web of successful food businesses in and around Berkeley and inspired other chefs and consumers to begin seeking out local food.

In recent years, locavorism and support for local, food-based economies have gotten a boost from numerous books and films that illuminate unsavory aspects of nonlocal, industrial food production and raise awareness of sustainable alternatives. Interest in local food also seems to have grown in response to both an uptick in extreme weather events and increased economic insecurity following the Great Recession of 2007 to 2009. Worries about climate change and skepticism about the mainstream economy may have been just the right mix of ingredients needed to push the local food movement into the mainstream.

But what exactly is local food? Some define it in terms of the distance traveled from producer to consumer, with suggested limits ranging from 100 miles up to 400 miles. Others assert that, while distance is a factor, local is much more about the opportunity for a direct relationship between food producers and consumers. That can encompass anything from growing our own food in a backyard or community garden to purchasing food from local farmers, ranchers or packaged food and beverage producers at farm stands, farmers' markets or CSAs.

While local is a sustainable quality, local food isn't necessarily sustainable in the sense of protecting our health, animal well-being, the environment or the rights of farmworkers. On the other hand, it does offer such sustainable benefits as:

▶ **A lighter carbon footprint.** This is one of the most talked about benefits of eating local. But the local farm stand may not be any closer to our home than the supermarket. The real difference lies in the distribution chain. The food we buy from local farmers has far fewer miles on it than most of what's available from nonlocal sources. And that means it takes less fossil fuel to get from the farm to our plate.

While our ancestors ate local food out of necessity, advancements in transportation, packaging and refrigeration gradually helped make nonlocal food the norm. The food chain has been lengthened further in recent years by globalization and the declining cost of container shipping. The ease and low cost of transporting food on container ships has increased the distance between farmers and consumers. It also has made it economical to ship food to multiple locations around the globe—for inspection, processing, packaging—before sending it on to its final destination. According to the USDA, as of 2013, about 19% of our food came from outside the country.[11] While the amount of nonlocal food from domestic sources varies widely, a 2013 Worldwatch Institute study found that, on average, food travels within the U.S. between 1,500 miles and 2,500 miles from farm to table.[12]

As we've gained year-round access to tropical and out-of-season foods from across the country and around the world, the combined impact of food processing, packaging and transportation via refrigerated jumbo jets, cargo ships and trucks has made fossil fuel an ever-larger part of our annual diet. Shifting to local food can help us take a stand against the globalization of the food supply and significantly reduce oil use and our impact on global warming.

▶ **Support for local farmers.** Less than 2% of Americans earn their living as farmers,[13] and many are small-scale producers that struggle to stay afloat. As interest in local food has grown, many small farms have begun to meet that demand. Today, more than 140,000 farms sell directly to consumers (DTC) through groceries, farm stands, farmers' markets, CSAs and other venues.[14] According to a report from the marketing arm of the USDA, farmers earn more by selling DTC than by wholesaling, partly because consumers who seek out local food are willing to pay a premium for attributes such as "local" and "organic." Even farm-to-institution sales (e.g., sales to hospitals, schools, restaurants) can offer farmers a better deal than wholesaling to national food chains.[15] The USDA estimates that DTC local food sales amount to more than $6 billion a year.[16] So when we buy local, we're not only placing fresher, tastier food on our plates but also making a meaningful difference in the survival of the nation's small farms.

▶ **Reconnection to our local foodshed.** For thousands of years, humans ate the foods indigenous to their local ecosystems (or *food sheds*), regions distinguished by their flora and fauna, climate and geology. Similar to growing native plants, producing foods that are local to our ecosystem is a way of supporting and protecting that system. Sustaining ourselves from the local food shed also can increase our appreciation of how we fit into, benefit from and impact the local environment.

▶ **Preservation of open space.** Over the past 25 years, America has lost 23 million acres of farmland to development, according to a report from the American Farmland Trust.[17] The economic challenges of farming, combined with appreciating land values and ever-growing demand for housing, have led many family farms to sell out to developers. When we commit to purchasing food from local farmers, we not only help them survive and thrive but also make farming a viable enterprise for future generations. That may make it easier for farmers to either pass along their farms to their children or sell their land to up-and-coming young farmers. Along with open space initiatives and land trusts, buying local food may be one of the best tools we have for protecting what remains of the nation's rural landscape.

▶ **Food safety.**[18] A series of widespread foodborne disease outbreaks in the 1990s and early 2000s spurred Congress to pass the Food Safety Modernization Act (FSMA) of 2011. Three underlying factors in the disease outbreaks may have been (1) unhealthy conditions on CAFO farms, (2) consolidation within the slaughterhouse and meatpacking industries and (3) the globalization of the food supply. For example, because much of our meat is processed by just a handful of slaughterhouses and meatpacking firms, contamination in one plant can quickly spread across the country. Meanwhile, with so much food coming from abroad, often without reliable date and origin labeling, it can be difficult to locate the source of an outbreak once it begins. FSMA imposes measures intended to address these problems. But we can protect ourselves further by buying food from local farmers who have a natural interest in monitoring quality since they eat what they produce and depend on the trust of a small number of consumers.

▶ **The local multiplier effect.** As described in Chapter 2, shopping local triggers a multiplier effect that can help support a strong local economy. Buying local food from farmers and small-scale food producers, often the first form of localism we adopt, can help farms and food businesses succeed. When enough members of a community make a commitment to buy local, it may help create or expand a local food economy that has the potential to produce stable jobs as well as opportunities for entrepreneurs.

The Local Multiplier Effect in Action

When a land trust organization wanted to know the economic impact of its seasonal farmers' market on the local economy, it hired an economic policy institute to study the situation. It turned out that shoppers spent about $650,000 at the market during one spring/summer season. That produced a local multiplier effect as well as a *downstream* effect. The latter refers to what consumers spent at local shops and restaurants after being drawn into town by the farmers' market. All told, the economic impact of this one market totaled $2.6 million, including more than $20,000 in municipal and state sales tax revenue.[19]

▶ **Community cohesiveness and resiliency.** Obtaining more of our food from local sources strengthens social connections (with farmers, other food producers, fellow shoppers), increasing our sense of belonging to a cohesive community. Preferencing local food may also open the door to enriching experiences, from exploring local and regional foods to sharing gardening tips and recipes to donating time and food at local food pantries. As discussed later, in Communal, supporting local food also can play a vital role in making a community more resilient in the face of environmental or economic challenges that have the potential to disrupt the national or global food supply.

▶ **Freshness.** For obvious reasons, local food tends to be fresher than food shipped a great distance. Freshness offers two distinct benefits:

Nutrition. Since produce is most nutrient-rich when it's fresh off the vine, local is inherently the most nutritious choice. Foods harvested at a distance from their destination, such as strawberries grown in California for shipment around the U.S., are picked prematurely so that they won't spoil before arriving at the supermarket. Despite modern refrigeration and speedy delivery, these foods can reach peak ripeness during transportation, arriving at the supermarket already past their prime. The early stages of decay can further diminish both taste and nutrient value.

Taste. As locavores know well, freshness makes local food tastier than nonlocal choices. When we're able to enjoy fresh fruit, vegetables, grains and other healthy foods, we may be less attracted to those loaded with salt, sugar and fat.

Choosing Local Food

Our opportunities to source food locally may include:

▶ **Buying directly from local farms.** As mentioned previously, the USDA reported that as of 2012 about 7.8% (144,530) of America's farms sold directly to the public through farm stands, pick-your-own operations, CSAs and other venues.[20] Many small, independent farms, ranches and packaged food and beverage producers have become sophisticated marketers, selling their own goods and cross-marketing those of other local businesses. Some farms also are inviting customers to enjoy "pop-up feasts" that showcase their bounty, particularly at harvest time.

▶ **Shopping at farmers' markets.** According to the USDA, there were more than 8,200 farmers' markets throughout the country in 2014, up 180% from 2006.[21] Farmers' markets offer a great opportunity to gain access to farm-fresh local and organic produce, dairy and meats, even if we don't live in the vicinity of any farms. Many farmers' markets have become social hubs for the communities they serve, offering entertainment for all ages, educational information and opportunities to connect with and learn about other sustainable, community-based goods and services.

► **Buying from local artisanal producers.** Consumer demand for fresh, local and organic food has inspired a new generation of entrepreneurs. Small-scale producers of artisanal foods (i.e., foods that are made using traditional methods or are handcrafted rather than mass-produced) are selling locally sourced and organic varieties of everything from ice cream, cheeses, breads and packaged meals (e.g., potpies, shepherd's pies, macaroni and cheese) to condiments, herbs, jams and jellies. Also on the rise is artisanal production of alcoholic beverages, including not only microbrew beers and local vintage wines but also hard ciders, whiskeys and gins distilled using traditional and handcrafted methods. Many artisanal food and beverage companies produce and retail their goods at the same location. Some participate in farmers' markets and *small holding* days, which are fairs promoting small-scale food producers. Many also are enjoying success distributing their products to retailers both in local markets and beyond.

► **Finding sustainable out-of-season options.** The local food movement encourages us to eat seasonally. But the increasing prevalence of year-round greenhouses, including hydroponic and even aeroponic growers, is making local produce more widely available regardless of season. Of course, local meats, dairy, grains and packaged foods also may be available year-round. When buying out-of-season imports, we can look for those labeled "fair trade."

► **Participating in community gardens.** Community gardens, garden sharing arrangements and urban farms (all described in more detail in Communal) can be transformational in places with few other local food choices. Community gardens, which are popular everywhere from small towns and suburbs to cities, apartment buildings and senior housing communities, bring people together to pool resources and grow their own food. Garden-sharing arrangements are allowing city dwellers who have edible gardens to share both the labor and the harvest with members of the community who want to garden but lack their own plot of land. Urban farms are helping residents of *food deserts* (areas that lack access to supermarkets or other sources of affordable food) learn to grow their own food while improving their economic situation by acquiring horticultural and business skills.

► **Eating at restaurants that source locally.** It's increasingly trendy for restaurants to describe in elaborate detail the origins of the food on their menus. This was parodied well in the first episode of the spoof *Portlandia,* when a waitress assured her customers that the chicken they planned to order had lived a wonderful free-range life. But over-the-top restaurant marketing aside, local ingredient sourcing is playing an important role in localizing our diets. According to a survey of chefs by the National Restaurant Association, local sourcing is one of the hottest trends driving menu planning.[22] That's helping to make restaurant food fresher and more nutrient rich while providing additional income to local farmers and small-scale food producers. Even some fast food chains are going sustainable, seeking out sources that are local, organic or both.

▶ **Using online and mobile local food locators.** Many of us simply lack convenient (or obvious) access to local food. Local Harvest's geographic locator (localharvest.org) can help us identify any local or organic food sources in or near our community. The Greenease app (greenease.co) can help consumers in some areas of the country locate restaurants and other food businesses that source locally and/or offer other sustainable benefits. And the Locavore app (getlocavore.com) can help us locate farmers' markets and other sources of in-season local food.

▶ **Choose fair trade, which offers the benefits of local for nonlocal foods.** Climate change may one day make it possible to grow coffee, cocoa and bananas here in the U.S. (Let's hope not!) But for the foreseeable future, foods like these won't be produced close to home. If we want to make sustainable choices about foods that are only available as imports, the best bet is to look for products that are certified fair trade. It's becoming more common to find fair trade foods at national supermarket chains and other retail outlets. Unlike organic certification, fair trade guidelines aren't regulated by the federal govern-

---

Organic and Local: Making Choices

When considering organic and local food, there are two common questions: (1) how to afford these choices and (2) whether one is better than the other. Organic and local food may cost a bit more. But because organic food may be better for our health, it could end up reducing future health care costs. And since local food should be fresher than non-local food, it may save us money by eliminating the need to replace an item that has rotted prematurely. As for choosing between them, if we can't find local food that's also organic, some possible tradeoffs include:

1. Choosing organic for its health benefits when it matters most, such as for produce on the Dirty Dozen list or foods we eat frequently. (More information: Organic, pages 60 to 61)

2. Choosing local food in season to enjoy its fresh taste while supporting the local economy and reducing our carbon footprint. Some choices, such as poultry, meat and prepared foods, may be available year-round, regardless of our local climate.

3. Changing with the seasons (unless we live in a warm climate with a year-round growing season). In warmer months, we may be able to grow organic produce and buy local food, some organic, some not. When the garden is spent and local farms close for the winter, organic food from the supermarket may be the best choice around. On the other hand, as more local farms adopt sustainable practices and organic farmers add year-round production via hoop houses, greenhouses, hydroponics and aeroponics, our options may continue to improve throughout the year.

ment. But the fair trade label is intended to verify that food was produced in an environmentally responsible manner and that farmers/producers were paid and treated fairly. While fair trade agricultural products aren't always organic, many fair trade organizations prohibit GMOs and promote sustainable, chemical-free (or reduced chemical) agriculture.

▶ **Support the farm to school movement.** For many years, federally subsidized school lunch programs have required school districts to purchase agricultural surplus from large, national suppliers. Critics say that much of that food is processed commercially into unhealthy, "kid-friendly" meals. Since the late 1990s, the Farm to School movement has worked to change this system to increase school children's access to quality, locally sourced food while supporting the livelihood of small-scale farmers. Today's federally administered Farm to School program (which received a boost from the Healthy Hunger-Free Kids Act of 2010) provides eligible schools with grants and technical assistance to help them establish farm-to-school programs that source from local farmers. We can support the movement by encouraging our local schools to opt for locally produced food for their cafeterias.

Slow

The international Slow Food movement was founded by Italian writer and activist Carlo Petrini in 1986. What began as an organized protest against the proposed opening of a fast-food restaurant in Rome grew into a widespread movement against the modern industrialized food system. Like locavores, members of the Slow Food movement emphasize the value of local and regional fare and view food as a catalyst for broader social and economic change. The movement's "Slow Food International Manifesto" decries the industrial mechanization of modern life, with its emphasis on speed and efficiency. The movement's goal of creating a "better, cleaner and fairer world" is predicated on making high-quality, healthy food available and affordable to everyone.

In the U.S., the Slow Food movement is represented by the nonprofit organization Slow Food USA, which lobbies around such issues as the globalization of the food supply chain, the industrialization of farming and the proliferation of GMOs. Slow Food USA also works to promote sustainable food alternatives including organic, local and regional foods, preservation of heirloom seeds, small-scale food production and food gardening.

While Slow Food is an activist organization, at its core, the movement is about our personal relationship with food. It encourages us to take time out from our fast-paced lives and make dining a more creative, social and pleasurable experience, celebrating fresh local ingredients, regional tastes and direct contact with those who produce what we eat. Whether or not we wish to participate in the movement, we can embrace Slow Food values by:

▶ **Avoiding fast food.** Its name being an obvious play on the term "fast food," the Slow Food movement frowns on mass-produced meals and supports the use of fresh, local ingredients, artisanal or individualized food preparation and slow-paced, epicurean enjoyment of meals.

▶ **Making food shopping a pleasurable experience.** Unlike routine supermarket shopping, browsing at a farmers' market, shopping at a farm-owned grocery store or picking up the weekly allotment at a CSA tend to be more relaxed, social experiences, allowing us time to chat with farmers and other shoppers we've come to know. These venues also give us access to a wide range of fresh, local ingredients that may inspire us to cook more creatively, seasonally and healthfully.

▶ **Prioritizing whole foods.** Countless studies have demonstrated the health benefits of whole foods, which are those that exist in nature—fruits, vegetables, legumes, beans, grains, meats, seafood and even cocoa and coffee beans—and that have not been altered or adulterated through commercial processing.

▶ **Eating seasonally.** A throwback to a time (not all that long ago) when there was no alternative, prioritizing what's in season can help ensure that the food we eat is as fresh and nutrient-rich as possible. When we change our diet according to the seasons, we can enjoy the fresh taste and nutritional value of whatever our local farms have harvested recently, often at affordable prices. We also can reduce our carbon footprint by avoiding out-of-season imports, such as tropical fruit from South America in the middle of January.

▶ **Eating regionally.** The Slow Food movement celebrates the regional and local foods that embody a community's culture and traditions. By embracing regional cuisine at restaurants or in our own kitchens, we can enjoy tasty fare while also supporting small-scale local food producers and helping to keep local food traditions alive. That, in turn, can help make our local communities more economically and socially resilient.

▶ **Cooking and eating at home.** According to a study published in the *Journal of the American Academy of Nutrition and Dietetics*, eating at restaurants can significantly increase our calorie intake.[23] While many restaurants and food takeout services now offer fresh, local, organic and otherwise sustainable ingredients, we usually have more control over the source and preparation of our food when we cook it ourselves. Cooking at home also tends to make us more aware of the quality of ingredients, which can lead to healthier choices and better-tasting meals.

▶ **Making the meal a social occasion.** The Slow Food movement conjures images of good friends sharing a leisurely feast in a transformative setting…

perhaps a terrace overlooking the Mediterranean. While we can't approximate that experience at every meal, we can move away from a utilitarian relationship with food toward a more social and sensory one.

Vegetarian/Vegan

A vegetarian or vegan diet can be healthy and environmentally sustainable. A quick scan of today's food landscape, from packaged and frozen meals to restaurants and other food businesses, suggests that interest in going meatless is on the rise. According to a 2015 Harris Poll conducted for the Vegetarian Resource Group, about eight million American adults consider themselves vegetarians, with roughly one million of those identifying as vegans.[24] Several surveys also find that many Americans are moving toward a vegetarian diet, eating fewer meals containing meat.[25] While vegetarians and vegans site a variety of motivations, many express concern with the unsustainability of the modern industrial food system. Avoiding (or at least reducing consumption of) meat and other animal-derived foods can be sustainable in several ways.

▶ **Ethical treatment of animals.** The belief that it's unethical to kill animals for human benefit has always been a primary motivation for vegetarians. Scott Nearing, whose lifestyle (with his wife, Helen) inspired the back-to-the-land movement of the 1960s and 1970s, spoke of not wanting to participate in the "slaughter industry." Some of those who stopped eating meat during the 1960s counterculture years were influenced by the vegetarian practices of Hindus and Buddhists. Many of today's vegetarians and vegans share those ethical concerns. Others are reacting to what they perceive as mistreatment of livestock and the environment on industrial farms.

▶ **Health.** Over the past few decades, research has continued to point to the health risks associated with processed and fatty meats. Meats high in saturated fats have been linked to elevated levels of cholesterol, hypertension, obesity and cardiovascular disease. Research released in 2015 linked consumption of red meats and processed meats to increased risks of certain gastrointestinal cancers. Processed meats also have been associated with increased risk of weight gain, stroke, heart disease and diabetes.[26] Additionally, meat has been the source of numerous foodborne disease outbreaks.[27] And meat produced on nonorganic industrial farms may increase the suspected health risks associated with exposure to synthetic chemicals, antibiotics, growth hormones and GMOs.[28] While lean, non-processed meats provide a good source of protein, important vitamins and minerals, many scientists and health professionals support the idea that the healthiest diet is one comprising primarily fruits, vegetables, nuts, legumes and whole grains.

Beyond these personal concerns, vegetarian and vegan diets also can make a difference environmentally.

▶ **Inefficient use of resources.** A key reason for today's widespread concern with sustainability is that the world's rapidly growing population places us at risk of running out of natural resources. Over the next few decades, it will become increasingly important to use land, water and other natural resources more efficiently. Because raising cattle for meat requires a great deal of land, fuel and other resources compared with other types of food production, sustainability advocates warn that relying on meat as a primary source of protein will become increasingly unsustainable.[29]

▶ **Deforestation.**[30] A rapidly growing world population, increased consumption of meat in developing nations and demand for meat by large, multinational food companies are among the factors leading to millions of acres of old-growth forest and jungle being cleared to make room for cattle. Slash-and-burn methods are particularly damaging, with the remnants of trees burned after clear-cutting. Deforestation is linked to air and water pollution, desertification, flooding and loss of biodiversity. It also contributes to global warming by destroying forests that can help sequester CO_2. The Amazon rainforest has borne a particularly heavy price, with an area about the size of Italy deforested for cattle ranching just between 1993 and 2013. Some progress has been made as a result of a decades-long movement to save the Amazon. Non-governmental organizations (NGOs) have pressured meat-packers and others in the industry to sign *zero deforestation agreements* and support only those ranches committed to reducing deforestation. Unfortunately, there is recent evidence that deforestation actually is on the rise. We can do our part to support land preservation, conservation and biodiversity by moderating our consumption of meat.

▶ **Global warming.** Environmentalists believe that reducing the need for cattle grazing by lowering demand for meat could help address global warming in two distinct ways. First, because trees act as natural carbon sinks, absorbing CO_2 from the atmosphere, any action that slows deforestation has the potential to help mitigate the impact of global warming. Second, reducing demand for meat could help lower production of the greenhouse gases that contribute to global warming. According to a 2006 report from the Food and Agriculture Organization (FAO) of the United Nations, livestock production contributes about 18% of global greenhouse gas emissions (a higher percentage than transportation), including 9% of CO_2, 65% of the nitrous oxide associated with human activity and 35% of methane.[31]

▶ **Pollution.** Minimizing CAFO farming also could help reduce water pollution caused by runoff of antibiotics, growth hormones and manure.[32]

It's unlikely that a majority of us will completely stop eating meat and/or all animal-derived food products. But vegetarians and vegans, along with those who moderate meat consumption or eat meat only from small-scale, local farms, can help reduce the environmental impact associated with industrial livestock farming.

Self-Reliant

Not everyone has a green thumb or a willingness to add "feeding the hens" to their list of daily chores. But a growing number of people are opting for a relationship to food that's sustainable in the sense of fostering self-reliance. The modern-day interest in eating self-reliantly draws on old practices, such as gardening and canning, to meet today's challenges, both environmental and economic.

Producing some of our own food offers a wide range of benefits. It can reduce the need for outside income, giving us the leeway to forge more family-centered or creative lifestyles and helping us feed our families even during periods of unemployment or underemployment. It can provide us with a backup food supply if extreme weather, natural disasters or other out-of-the-ordinary events trigger food shortages or a spike in prices. It can help us take a stand against the excessive consumption that's depleting the world's natural resources. And it can place us in a position to share with friends and neighbors or members of the community struggling with food insecurity.

We can produce our own food by growing fruits and vegetables in an edible garden, processing garden bounty (e.g., by canning or freezing), foraging, hunting, fishing or raising livestock. The ins and outs of many of these activities have been addressed by countless books, blogs and YouTube clips. Here are just a few starting points.

▶ **Grow an organic edible garden.** Edible gardening, also referred to as "foodscaping," has become increasingly popular in recent years. Growing food at home can help us spend less on food, gain affordable access to fresh, healthy choices and reduce the impact of our diet on climate change. Once we've decided to embark on edible gardening, it's relatively easy to commit to organic methods. In addition to making organic food affordable, growing without chemicals can benefit the ecology of our yards, communities and local watersheds by keeping aquifers free of toxic runoff and making our gardens more drought resistant. (More information: pages 78-79)

▶ **Harvest and process.** Even if we can't garden year-round, we may be able to enjoy our backyard bounty throughout the year by acquiring some age-old food-storage skills.

   Put up jarred and canned goods. Depending on what we grow, we can jar or "put up" jams, jellies, preserves, pickles, pickled veggies, ketchup, mustard, vinegar or oils. Some techniques, such as pickling cucumbers, are relatively straightforward. Others may require us to learn the basics of fermentation and safe storage.

Process culinary herbs. There are several ways to turn culinary herbs into fresh, fragrant spices that are full of flavor and will last throughout the winter. Freshly cut herb bouquets can be tied into bundles and hung to dry for about a week in a cool, dark place. Alternatively, herbs can be spread out on wire or mesh trays, suspended so they have access to circulating air. Herbs also can be dried in the oven at a low temperature. But since this uses energy and speeds a natural process, it's the least sustainable method. Once dry, herbs can simply be crumbled into a bowl and checked for any stray branches or seeds. For loose, leafy herbs, there is no need to process further. The herbs can be stored in glass jars for later use. If a powdered form is preferred, the crushed leaves can be pulverized using a mortar and pestle or a blender.

Freeze. It's relatively easy to transform our late harvest bumper crops into months of frozen stock. Tomatoes can be turned into marinara for future use. Batches of pesto can be prepared by blending basil leaves with olive oil and freezing the mixture in ice cube trays. Berries can be frozen, first on trays, then in small containers, and taken out as needed for winter's pancakes and cereals. Roasted squash can be blended and then stored in the freezer for a vegan meal of soup on a cold autumn night.

Create a root cellar. Dry, cool places in a house, barn, garage or other outbuilding may provide the right conditions for storing a variety of fruits and vegetables throughout the winter.

▶ **Forage.** From dandelions and wild onions to mushrooms and berries, our backyards (even in suburbia) can yield a surprising amount of food. Obviously, it's important to learn how to identify edible plants to avoid accidental poisoning.

▶ **Raise bees.** Those willing to learn the art of beekeeping can enjoy a variety of benefits. Bees can provide a reliable supply of natural honey, which is considered far more nutritious and flavorful than nonlocal, store-bought honey. In addition to its culinary uses, homemade honey can help relieve allergies by exposing us to a source of local pollen. Bees also can provide us with royal jelly, which is considered an immune system booster, as well as beeswax for candles. And raising bees assures that we'll always have local pollinators available to improve our garden's productivity.

▶ **Fish and hunt.** Vegetarians and vegans will want to skip this bullet. Some may even be offended by its inclusion. But fishing and hunting can have as much to do with self-reliance and low-consumption living as gardening organically or raising free-range chickens. Time-honored traditions in many families, fishing and hunting (yes, responsibly) also are good ways to know where our food comes from and to be involved in the process of procuring it. According to the U.S. Fish & Wildlife Service, the funds raised from hunting licenses often help support conservation.

▶ **Harvest seeds.** Seed-harvesting enthusiasts point out that even with the availability of organic and heirloom varieties, the best way to know the source of our food is to grow it from our own seeds. Harvesting and cultivating seeds begins with allowing some of the hardiest plants in the garden to go to seed. Collected seeds need to dry out before being stored in clearly labeled glass jars and set aside in a cool, dark, dry location until the following spring.

▶ **Raise livestock.** Backyard chicken coops have become increasingly common in recent years, even in cities. In fact, raising poultry is one of the more ubiquitous examples of our growing concern with self-reliance. Both economic self-sufficiency and an interest in healthy, sustainable food are strong motivators for small-scale chicken farmers. For some, chickens also provide an entrée to permaculture, an ecological approach to land cultivation that encourages activities that offer multiple benefits to us and the environment. (More information: Explore permaculture) Chickens, particularly if raised organically, are a good example of permaculture because they give us two sources of protein while also helping out in the garden, eating non-beneficial insects and providing a natural source of fertilizer. As noted previously, some studies have found that sustainably produced eggs are lower in cholesterol and higher in omega 3 fatty acids, cancer-fighting carotenes and vitamins A, D and E than their conventional counterparts.[33]

Undertaking chicken farming requires research and hard work. Not all municipalities allow it, so it's important to check local ordinances before purchasing a flock of chicks. While chickens are the most popular type of backyard livestock, some households also are adding a few goats, pigs or cows to their menageries.

▶ **Explore permaculture.** Rooted in the field of ecology, permaculture encourages self-sufficiency through sustainable design of gardens, farms, buildings and even entire communities. Permaculture's core principals are to (1) care for the Earth, (2) care for people, (3) reinvest in systems that support both and (4) do all of that with the least possible amount of money, energy, labor and/or other resources. Those goals can be accomplished by putting natural systems to work for us. For example, when it comes to producing our own food, a permaculture approach might include watering plants with greywater and captured rainwater, employing companion gardening to protect and nurture crops and raising chickens which, as noted above, provide multiple benefits to us and the land. A more in-depth view of permaculture is available from the book *Permaculture One* by Bill Mollison and David Holmgren.

Organic food gardening involves these steps:

1. **Test the soil for contaminants and nutrient imbalances.** Soil testing kits are available from state agricultural extension services, which also perform soil analyses. If soil is contaminated with chemicals or heavy metals (for example, lead from flaking paint on older homes), it's important to seek professional guidance about possible remediation. Raised garden beds may be a good alternative to planting directly in the ground. Beds may be lined with a barrier material and then filled with clean top soil. If soil tests show a need for added nutrients, such as nitrogen or phosphorus, organic options are easy to find online or at garden stores.

2. **In addition to adding nutrients, as needed, treat soil with compost prior to planting.** (More information: Composting Basics)

3. **Purchase organic seeds or starter plants grown organically or spray-free.** Both are becoming much easier to find at nurseries and garden centers as well as online and from seed and plant catalogs.

   ✓ If starting from seed, there is no need to use fertilizer until plants emerge. Some seeds must be started in containers indoors, while others can be sowed directly in the ground. Seed packets may offer instructions on when and how to plant, thin, transfer and harvest. Many seed companies offer organic, non-GMO and heirloom varieties. Some have taken the Safe Seed Pledge, a voluntary commitment not to sell GMO seed. Other good sources of sustainable seeds include local seed libraries and the seeds we harvest from our homegrown plants.

   ✓ If starting with plants, it's important to add an organic fertilizer, such as seaweed emulsion or fish emulsion. Organic fertilizers do not contain petroleum-derived ingredients or contaminants that may be present in synthetic fertilizers, such as cadmium, lead, arsenic and dioxins.

4. **Lightly water newly planted seeds and plants each day until they are established.** For seeds, that can mean until the plants emerge. For young plants, two weeks often is ample time. Plants may need additional watering if the weather is dry or very hot. Most gardening guides recommend watering in the early morning or the evening to avoid rapid evaporation from sunlight. That not only allows us to use less water but also makes it easier for plants to absorb the moisture they require.

5. **Combat disease, insects and other pests with integrated pest management techniques, including:**

   ✓ Little to no tilling. This prevents weeds from reseeding and helps prevent soil erosion and runoff.

   ✓ Companion gardening. This involves growing a group of plants together that are mutually beneficial, mimicking how plants grow in the wild. Plants may help each other grow and/or combat diseases and pests.

   ✓ Mulching with leaf mulch or organic compost, which help reduce weeds and maintain soil moisture levels.

   ✓ Hand weeding, which replaces the need for weed killers.

   ✓ Planting an off-season cover crop, such as clover or buckwheat, to restore soil nutrients and reduce weeds.

   ✓ If necessary, using biological (versus chemical) pesticides, fungicides and herbicides, such as insecticidal soap and bacillus thuringiensis (B.t.).

6. **Go beyond veggies.** Herbs are relatively easy to grow and make wonderful ground covers that may be perennial. They can be prepared for culinary use simply by cutting, drying in a cool dark place and crushing or crumbling the fully dried leaves. (More on drying herbs: Process culinary herbs, page 76) Starting a strawberry patch is one of the easier ways to add fruit to the garden. Strawberries are perennial, bear fruit within one or two years, make attractive garden borders and fit into a variety of companion gardening schemes. Berry bushes also are easy to grow, producing fruit in the first or second year and self-pollinating, which makes it possible to have an abundant supply of berries without purchasing a large number of plants. Fruit trees take a bit more expertise but are worth the effort for anyone interested in having affordable access to fresh organic apples, pears, peaches or plums.

7. Extend gardening into the winter months, turning raised beds into mini hoop houses by covering them with translucent plastic sheeting or window pane glass, or, if the garden is large enough, constructing full-size hoop houses or a greenhouse.

8. Embrace small. Organic food gardening can be small-scale, consisting of a few containers on a windowsill or balcony. Those not tied down to one residence or location can even create a portable organic garden by planting in light containers that are easy to move around.

Composting Basics

Compost can enrich our soil and keep it moist while also combatting plant diseases and pests. There are three parts to composting: (1) making a compost pile, (2) collecting compostable scraps and (3) applying compost to the garden. As with any gardening topic, there is no shortage of information on the best way to compost. Here are a few highlights.

1. **Make a compost pile—or buy a composter.** While store-bought composters are readily available, many gardeners find homemade versions preferable as they provide the pile with good exposure to air, water and sunlight, all of which play an important role in brewing healthy compost. A composting structure can consist of a three- or four-sided enclosure made from materials such as old wooden pallets, fencing or chicken wire attached to metal or wooden posts. The foundation of the compost pile (in either a homemade structure or a store-bought composter) should comprise carbon-rich "browns," such as raked leaves, branches and dried straw or grass clippings. Only after this mixture has decomposed (which may take several months) can nitrogen-rich "green" compost scraps (described in #2) be added. The scraps should be well mixed into the existing pile to encourage decay and keep away animals.

    Composting experts recommend a ratio of three parts brown to one part green. Over time, this mixture will allow for aerobic decomposition, the process of microbes and bacteria breaking down the composted waste and producing rich, dark humus. The process is helped along by heat. Steam rising up from the compost pile is a sign that we're on the right track. Heat not only facilitates decomposition but also kills harmful bacteria and further discourages animal intruders.

2. **Collect "green" scraps.** The kitchen compost bucket can keep a significant amount out of the weekly trash while helping us accumulate greens for our compost pile. While some gardeners eschew anything but eggshells and coffee grounds in their compost, others mix in fruit and vegetable scraps, teabags, stale bread and coffee filters. Animal products, such as meats and cooked eggs, should not be composted.

3. **Apply the compost.** A compost pile started at summer's end should be ripe in time to prep the garden in early spring. Compost is ready for use when it looks and smells like fresh soil. The pile should be about as moist as a wrung-out sponge. All that's needed is a few shovelfuls in each garden bed. Mature compost will help maintain a healthy moisture level in the soil. It also will help rebalance soil, maintaining proper pH levels and adding nutrients that may have been expended during the previous growing season. Other benefits of compost include suppression of plant diseases, remediation of soil contaminants and control of weeds. While we tend to associate composting with edible gardening, it's just as beneficial for growing flowers, shrubs or other ornamental plants. Much more information on composting is available at howtocompost.org.

Community Composting

City dwellers and others unable to compost at home may have access to community-scale composting programs. Increasingly prevalent, particularly in large cities that are committed to reducing the impact of organic waste on global warming, these programs allow residents to send their food scraps to a central composting location. The compost may be turned into biogas for heating and transportation or returned to members of the community for gardening purposes.

Communal

Food can be a lever for community resiliency in numerous ways. We can help make our communities more economically resilient by buying from local farmers and food producers. Buying from local producers also can help strengthen our connection to community, as can sharing meals and participating in community gardens or urban farms. Growing food as a community can help us become more resilient in the face of food shortages caused by economic, climate or weather disruptions. It also may help us address food insecurity related to poverty, creating a surplus that can be donated to food pantries and helping those in need learn to provide for themselves. Here are a few possibilities.

▶ **Share a meal.** Support for a sharing economy, where access and relationships trump ownership and consumption, can be expressed by weaving some communal dining into our schedules. Whether it's a weekly group dinner with vegan friends, a celebratory harvest at the community garden, a potluck meal, a progressive dinner (with each course eaten at a different home) or a meal served at the local food pantry, sharing food is a wonderful expression of community and a way to build resiliency through enduring social connections.

▶ **Share the food shopping.** Buying food in bulk with housemates or friends can lower our household food expenses and make healthy, organic and local choices more affordable. It also may help reinforce social ties and inspire other forms of sharing. And when a group collectively purchases and shares bulk bags of grains, oats, beans or other foods, it can reduce the waste that results from the purchase of smaller, single-use food packages.

▶ **Start or participate in a community garden or urban farm.** Whether we're concerned with forging community or feeding a community in need, cooperatively tilling the soil may be part of the solution. In some areas of the country, a communally plowed plot of land may be the only available source of fresh local food.

Community gardening has become popular in recent years as more of us seek out affordable sources of healthy food, a greater sense of community and opportunities to make our towns or cities more resilient. There are community gardens in rural areas that otherwise lack access to fresh local food because all the farms exclusively grow commodity crops. Community gardens grace the suburbs, where most residents have been used to relying solely on supermarkets and national retail chains. And there are community gardens in cities, located everywhere from public parks and commons to strips of land along sidewalks to the rooftops of high-rise apartment complexes. Regardless of setting, such gardens offer a common benefit: the opportunity for individuals without land of their own to grow food for themselves, their families and their neighbors.

People of all ages and abilities can participate in community gardening and learn from each other. Older residents may pass along a lifetime of gardening skills while children learn to recognize that the food on their plates is the bounty of Mother Earth. Avid gardeners often take the lead, while novices participate as much as possible, gaining new skills along with access to the food they help grow. Of course, organizing any group of people can have its challenges. To avoid conflict, community gardens often establish rules from the start. That may include deciding whether one individual will serve as the group's leader, or if the garden will be treated as community property or be divided into sub-plots for each participating gardener.

Urban farming is a larger-scale form of community gardening that typically makes food available for sale through a farmers' market or other venue. In low-income urban areas, where fresh food often is as scarce as jobs, farming an abandoned plot of land can deliver much-needed food, enable us to build stronger community ties and help participants develop valuable job skills. Detroit, Michigan, has embraced this idea, with social entrepreneurs and activists working alongside resident-farmers to transform empty and derelict lots into modern-day Gardens of Eden. The same type of process is taking place in many other areas of the country, with urban farming viewed as a key to ending food deserts, creating food security and expanding economic opportunity to all.

One potential downside of urban farming is that soil contamination can be more widespread in cities, particularly if they were once home to industry. This makes it particularly important to have soil tested before planting and follow any recommendations provided for growing food safely. Raised garden beds can be a solution if soil is too contaminated for use. Another alternative is rooftop gardening. In addition to offering all the other benefits of urban farming, rooftop gardens can help purify the air, insulate buildings, provide habitat for local wildlife and control stormwater runoff.

▶ **Start a food forest.** A variation on community gardens, food forests are essentially public commons (parks or other publicly owned open spaces) where the harvest from trees or other plants is available for free. For example, a community might designate an area of a public park for the cultivation of nuts, fruit-bearing trees, mushrooms or other native plants that can be foraged for food. Rather than an individual laying claim to a portion of the cultivated land, anyone can visit the forest and take what they need. Obviously, some ground rules may need to be defined at the outset of this type of project. More information is available at fallenfruit.org.

▶ **Share a garden.** Backyard garden sharing connects individuals who have gardens with those who want to grow their own food but don't have a place to do so. This can take a variety of forms. The website sharedearth.com, a sort of Match.com for would-be gardening partners, connects landowners with gardeners and farmers in need of land. In towns and suburbs, some sharing enthusiasts are turning private gardens into neighborhood resources. This works best where homes are relatively close together and neighbors can easily access each other's yards. (Getting along well with neighbors obviously is another prerequisite.) Some of these neighborhood sharers reposition edible gardens to extend across the lawns of their neighbors. Others swap access to the bounty from their gardens or fruit-bearing trees for babysitting services, lawn mowers or other pooled neighborhood resources. (More information: Chapter 4, Home)

▶ **Start or support a community kitchen.** Cooperatively owned and/or run, community kitchens allow individuals or groups to prepare food on a larger scale than possible in most residential kitchens. Farmers may use a community kitchen to transform harvested crops into value-added products (e.g., sauces, jams, potpies) that can be sold for additional income. A community kitchen can be used to develop other types of small-scale food businesses, teach culinary skills or prepare catered meals. Volunteers in the community might use the kitchen to bake pies for fundraisers or to feed families in need.

▶ **Participate in a crop swap.** One drawback of producing some of our own food is that we often end up with a bumper crop of one item and not quite enough of another. Arranging to swap excess harvest with other members of our community can round out everyone's diet and ensure that food isn't wasted. A crop swap also can enhance community resiliency, making everyone more food secure.

Crop swaps can be as casual as a group of fellow gardeners agreeing to meet occasionally to exchange eggs for squash. Or they can take the form of regularly scheduled events open to anyone in the community who has homegrown or home-prepared food to swap. Organizing a larger, more official crop swap involves choosing an accessible location and a regular schedule, establishing guidelines for what can be swapped (e.g., organic produce, homemade condiments), displaying items in an organized manner and deciding on a process for swapping that is orderly and fair.

▶ **Participate in a seed exchange or seed library.** Historically, farmers and many gardeners collected seeds at harvest time to plant the following season. That practice began to fade away when packaged, store-bought seeds became widely available. It has all but disappeared on the nation's largest industrial farms, which now rely primarily on seed that is mass-produced and often GMO. Concern about the risks to food security and biodiversity in the age of GMOs has led many smaller-scale farmers and gardeners to recommit to collecting, storing and preserving seeds from the year's harvest. Some communities have created seed libraries, either through existing public libraries or newly established nonprofit organizations, which allow members to exchange seeds in an organized manner. In addition to preserving heirloom and other non-GMO seeds, some seed libraries help educate the broader community about their mission and encourage sustainable, edible gardening.

A popular example of the sharing movement, seed libraries have proliferated in recent years, with several hundred of them now active throughout the country. But as this movement grows, so do legal battles in states that have laws prohibiting seed swapping due to concerns about the potential for unregulated seed banks to become vulnerable to contamination or even agri-terrorism. Seed-sharing activists have challenged such laws in court and have already won some victories, including passage of the 2016 California Seed Exchange Democracy Act. But communities interested in starting seed libraries should first consult state authorities to ensure that they aren't violating existing laws.

▶ **Donate food.** Food insecurity, the state of not having enough to eat on a regular basis, surged during the last major recession and remains historically high, leaving many Americans in dire circumstances. In 2007, about 26.5 million Americans were eligible for SNAP (the federal food aid program formerly referred to as "food stamps"). By 2014, that number had grown to nearly 47 million, an increase of approximately 57%. While an improved job market has helped reduce SNAP participation, a drop in the number of recipients also has been linked to discontinuation of waivers given to states during economic downturns to allow them to extend the duration of benefits eligibility.[34] When SNAP recipients run out of assistance before the end of the month, they often turn to their local food pantries. That places food pantries on the front lines in addressing hunger. But, despite generous contributions by community members, many have had trouble keeping an adequate supply of food on their shelves.

Donating to food pantries is one of the most direct ways we can help reduce hunger in our communities. Most pantries accept donations of canned and packaged foods. Increasingly, many are accepting fresh, local produce. Some organizations encourage gardeners to set aside part of their harvest specifically for donations. An example of this is the Share the Harvest program run by Philabundance, a nonprofit organization that helps address hunger in the Philadelphia, Pennsylvania, area. We can locate local food donation opportunities at ampleharvest.com. We also can help address hunger by employing a sharing movement idea, working with members of our community to create little free food pantries. This involves erecting storage units about the size of a mailbox in parks or other public areas to be stocked anonymously and accessed by anyone in need. While no substitute for actual food pantries, these mini pantries can help broaden community awareness of hunger, encourage a practice of giving and sharing, and provide immediate relief to those in need when other resources are not available. More information can be found at littlefreepantry.org.

Besides donating food, we may be able to volunteer for organizations in the community that collect surplus harvest from farmers and deliver it to pantries. If we can afford to do so, we also may want to realign our annual donations (or planned gifts) to focus on local organizations involved in addressing hunger.

▶ **Start or join a food co-op.** A food co-op is a cooperatively-owned food store, run collectively by members who pay dues and/or volunteer their time. According to the Rochdale Pioneers Museum, the first known food co-op was founded in Rochdale, England, in 1844, by unemployed weavers seeking an affordable source of food. Many of today's most well-established co-ops date from the late 1960s, a time when there was growing interest in both "health food" and more communal, democratic ways of organizing business and society.

Co-ops have become increasingly popular in recent years as sources of sustainable, organic and local food and proponents of community resiliency. Members gain affordable access to healthy food through a discount on their purchases. Some co-ops also offer members opportunities to invest (sometimes with potential returns in the form of dividends) in the store's expansion or in other cooperative ventures, such as daycare centers, food assistance programs or other services or programs that respond to the needs of the broader community. (More information on investing in co-ops: Chapter 8, Money) A few co-ops have even opened stores in food deserts with the express aim of addressing the local need for fresh, healthy food. Information on starting a food co-op is available from numerous sources, including the Cooperative Grocer Network (grocer.coop) and the Food Co-Op Initiative (fci.coop).

▶ **Join a CSA (community-supported agriculture) program— or a community-supported ranch or fishery.** Many farms run Community-Supported Agriculture programs that allow customers to buy shares of the future harvest at the beginning of the growing season and receive weekly allotments later on. Some CSAs require members to provide a few hours of labor as partial payment for their shares. CSAs offer members an affordable way to access fresh local and organic food. They offer farmers a predictable income stream that alleviates some of the uncertainty endemic to farming. By forging a bond between farmers and consumers, CSAs also help strengthen community ties and instill a deeper appreciation of the value farms provide. According to the last published USDA Census of Agriculture, there were 12,617 CSAs in the U.S. as of 2012.[35] (Compilation of data for an updated census is underway.) In addition to produce, CSA shares may provide members with dairy, meats or other farm products. In some areas of the country, the same model is used for ranches and fisheries. There are even community-supported restaurants that sell shares to the public to raise capital and repay investors with food. (More information: Chapter 8, Money)

▶ **Reduce food waste.** When our mothers told us to clean our plates, they were onto something inherently sustainable. Concern about food waste has grown recently as more of us become aware of shocking statistics, such as that the U.S. wastes about 70 billion pounds (or 40%) of edible food each year.[36] Much of that food ends up in landfill, contributing to methane emissions as it decays. Besides not eating what's placed in front of us, there are numerous other ways that we waste food each day. According to the Natural Resources Defense Council, roughly 27% of the produce grown each year goes to waste because it doesn't meet the food industry's criteria (or our consumer expectations) for being "saleable."[37] Restaurants are under particular pressure to reject all but the most perfect ingredients. Even food donated to pantries sometimes undergoes scrutiny for freshness and aesthetic standards that may have little to do with whether an item is edible and nutritious. Such perfectionism is widespread at a time when (as discussed previously) a large number of Americans are food insecure.

Farmers are now donating their seconds to food pantries. We can do our part to reduce food waste by filling our plates only with what we intend to eat, storing food properly in the refrigerator, eating leftovers, composting food scraps, making food from scraps (e.g., stocks for soups and sauces) and eating produce that is still fresh even if it's no longer photogenic. Increasingly, it's also possible to dine at restaurants and purchase from food businesses that make meals from food waste.

Doing More

In a perfect world, it wouldn't take so much effort to eat well, assure that everyone has enough food and prevent our diet from harming the environment. Besides making thoughtful choices about what we eat, we can help bring about a more sustainable food system by supporting or advocating for issues such as the following:

▶ A better farm bill;

▶ An end to food deserts;

▶ More funding for food pantries and other services or efforts to end food insecurity;

▶ Reform of laws that ban seed libraries;

▶ Ordinances that allow for local, domestic and community-based food production; and

▶ Open space preservation.

Becoming more sustainable at home can help us protect the environment and our health, support the local economy and reconnect with our community and natural surroundings.

Home

Our home can play an important role in keeping us healthy and safe, supporting our chosen lifestyle and allowing us to give tangible form to sustainable values. The words "sustainable home" may conjure images of high-priced, cutting-edge architecture (the type featured in magazines such as *Dwell* and *Metropolis*) or back-to-nature shacks devoid of creature comforts. But making our home life more sustainable doesn't need to be expensive, extreme or complicated.

Depending on our household budget, goals and preferences, we can explore the environmentally, economically and/or socially sustainable choices that fit our personal idea of home. There are seven areas to consider.

1. **Building, renovation and maintenance.** We may be able to make sustainable choices about our home's location, design, construction, building materials and upkeep.

2. **Utilities.** Decisions about electricity, heating, air-conditioning and water all offer opportunities for greater environmental responsibility.

3. **Furnishing.** We can decorate with an eye toward consuming less, protecting our health and supporting the local economy.

4. **Cleaning.** Sustainable cleaning alternatives can be budget-friendly, healthy and safe for the environment.

5. **Greenscaping.** We can become good stewards of the Earth whether we have ample acres or a few potted plants.

6. **Housemates and neighbors.** Sharing living space can help us build community, reduce expenses and lighten our environmental footsteps.

7. **Retirement living.** This may be the right time to scale down, drive less and share more.

Building, Renovation and Maintenance

While there's obviously a big difference in scope between building, renovating and maintaining a home, each offers opportunities to get to the heart of what makes home-life sustainable.

Greening the blueprints

If we have the resources to build, we may literally be able to green our home from the ground up. An eco-friendly home can help us conserve resources, including water, electricity and building materials. It can decrease our exposure to allergens and toxins and reduce our impact on the environment and climate. It may enable us to reconnect with our natural surroundings or the local community. And whether we spend a great deal to build the home or find cost-effective alternatives, over time, our green home will most likely reduce our living expenses by substantially lowering energy costs and potentially reducing the need for furnishings or even a household car.

There are many examples of innovative green dwellings, ranging from yurts to underground structures to straw-bale homes and tree houses. For a more *inside the box* approach to building an eco-conscious home, we can draw on guidelines like those developed by the U.S. Green Building Council, the recognized thought leader in the field of environmentally responsible building.[1] Tenets of green building include:

▶ **Finding the right location.** The real estate adage "location, location, location" is particularly relevant when it comes to building a green home. Perhaps most importantly, building green means avoiding environmentally sensitive areas, such as prime farmland, wetlands or endangered species habitat. A green home may be built on an infill site, such as the former location of a factory, shopping mall, parking lot or housing development. It may take the form of a repurposed space in an existing, nonresidential structure, such as a warehouse or school. Or it may be part of a high-density development where homes are clustered to allow for more open space and recreational area.

For those seeking the privacy and beauty of a pristine site in the woods or countryside, the key to finding a green location is situating the home where it will benefit most from the landscape's natural features. How a house sits on a property can affect the amount of natural light it receives, whether it benefits from prevailing winds or passive solar heat and if plantings will be able to provide year-round protection from excessive heat or cold. The location of a home also may impact opportunities to produce renewable energy. For example, a home situated in an open field may be a better candidate for solar than one located in the woods.

Similarly, a home's location may determine the practicality of installing a geothermal heating and cooling system or a domestic wind turbine.

Our home's location also may influence us to adopt other sustainable lifestyle choices. If we live in or near a beautiful natural setting, we may be more inclined to spend time outdoors, reconnecting with nature. If we live in or near a walkable town, we may drive less (reducing transportation-related greenhouse gas emissions), shop at more local stores or become more involved in the local community.

▶ **Downsizing.** With green building, small really is beautiful.[2] In fact, scaling down is so central to building green that it's probably fair to say that there's no such thing as a green McMansion. A home that's just the right size for us and our family should cost less to build and maintain than a larger house and use less energy, since it will have less space to heat, cool and light. It's also likely to require fewer building materials and furnishings, reducing our impact on natural resources, pollution, global warming and landfill waste. Our right-sized home may even reduce the amount of time we need to spend on mundane tasks such as cleaning and maintenance and allow more time for family, creativity or other personal pursuits.

▶ **Designing green.** In addition to size, elements of green home design may include:

An open or flexible floor plan that allows space to be used in multiple ways, eliminating the need for extra rooms.

Ample windows or skylights that help maximize natural light, reducing the need for electric lights while also supplying plenty of fresh air.

Eco-conscious roofing. A white or light-colored roof can keep a home cooler, reducing the need for air-conditioning. A green roof can double as gardening space while increasing insulation, controlling stormwater runoff, improving air quality (particularly important in urban settings) and acting as a carbon sink.

Connection to the environment. This can involve taking advantage of a site's natural features (e.g., sunny fields, shady glades, trees, streams) or incorporating elements of the landscape (e.g., a hill, a mountain range, a cave) into the home's placement, design or construction. It also can take the form of "vernacular building," an approach supported by sustainability advocates who believe that, along with food and energy, construction is an ideal business to localize. Vernacular builders may use materials indigenous to the area or materials grown or produced by farmers (e.g., bamboo, straw, clay). They also may hire local workers and construct a home in accordance with local customs and traditions.

▶ **Choosing green building materials.** Green building materials can offer several environmental benefits.

Reduced waste. Home construction, remodeling and demolition account for about 30% of the nation's solid waste stream.[3] Much of this "C&D" (construction and demolition) waste can be recycled. But we can help reduce the amount of waste created by building smaller structures and choosing biodegradable building materials.

A healthier home environment. Eco-conscious building materials can reduce our exposure to allergens, carcinogens and other potential toxins.

Increased energy efficiency. (More information: Becoming energy efficient)

▶ **Becoming energy efficient.** According to the U.S. Energy Information Administration, our homes account for about 21% of total U.S. energy consumption and about 20% of CO_2 emissions.[4] A green home can simply be more energy efficient than a typical home. Or it can be net-zero, meeting all its energy needs from renewable sources and producing no carbon emissions. A home can even be net positive if it does all of that *and* produces excess energy that can be delivered back to the grid. Some aspects of energy efficiency were mentioned in the preceding bullets; others are addressed in more detail in Utilities.

We can *build* energy efficiency into a home's design in two ways.

A net-zero home can be a component of a "carbon neutral lifestyle." It's possible to use sites such as carbonfund.org or terrapass.com or apps such as oroeco.com to track any carbon emissions associated with our homes, transportation habits and other lifestyle choices. We can then offset those emissions with donations that support reforestation, energy efficiency or renewable energy production.

Green building materials can be high-end and expensive or low-cost and alternative, such as:

Natural framing and wall materials: Stone, straw bales, sandbags, lumber from sustainably managed forests

Alternative framing and wall materials: Recycled composites, insulated concrete forms (ICFs), salvaged materials

Flooring made from natural, rapidly renewable or recycled materials: Stone, bamboo, cork, sustainably grown wood, wood re-milled from old floors or wood furnishings

Eco-friendly roofing: Clay tiles, metal (which may be made from recycled materials and by recyclable), slate (which is natural and highly durable) or shingles made from sustainably harvested trees, reclaimed wood or recycled materials such as plastic, rubber or wood fiber

Alternative kitchen and bath cabinet options: Made from salvaged or composite materials or constructed of wood rather than pressboard or particle board, which may be treated with formaldehyde

Nontoxic, non-polluting "wet" materials: Old-fashioned milk paints or paints, varnishes, grouts, joint compounds, caulks and sealants that meet the latest low-VOC or no-VOC (volatile organic compound) requirements

Materials obtained locally: Natural materials, such as stone, slate, granite, wood, earth, bamboo, straw or clay, or locally reclaimed or recycled materials, all of which can reduce the greenhouse gas emissions associated with the production and transportation of non-local materials

1. Choosing sustainable materials and finishes, such as:

Framing lumber wide enough to allow for insulation that exceeds current building codes with respect to R-value. The rating refers to the insulation's "resistance to heat transfer" or the amount of heat that can escape through a home's walls. A higher R-value means less heat loss and better insulation. Other building materials, such as windows and doors, also have R-value ratings.

Alternative building materials that provide superior insulation, reducing the need for heat and air-conditioning. (More information: below and page 90)

Eco-conscious insulation materials.[5] All insulation contributes to energy efficiency, helping us stay cooler in the summer and warmer in the winter without using more air-conditioning or heat. But the most common types of insulation (e.g., spray foam, fiberglass and mineral wool) aren't eco-friendly. Foam contains HCFCs (hydrochlorofluorocarbons) that can damage the ozone layer, while fiberglass and mineral wool may be associated with health risks. Alternative materials that can make our homes energy efficient without posing potential harm to us or the environment include soybean foam insulation, wool, cotton, recycled plastic and cork. All of these materials are available as packaged insulation products. Denim and other recycled materials offer additional alternatives. Some national clothing chains, such as Madewell and J. Crew, now collect customers' used denim jeans and send them to companies that produce insulation from the recycled fibers.

Energy-efficient windows. This can include dual-glazed, Energy Star-rated alternatives, which provide good insulation, reducing heating and cooling costs while increasing sunlight and blocking ultraviolet rays.

Very Alternative Home Building Materials

Unconventional alternatives to traditional building materials include:

Straw bales from local farms, used in place of cinder blocks or wood framing. Straw bales offer an eco-friendly, nontoxic, energy-efficient and acoustic option adaptable to creative design. The straw-bale building blocks are plastered with earthen, lime or cement-lime plaster.

Adobe, an ancient building material consisting of clay, sand and water. Adobe is natural, affordable, durable, energy efficient and can be molded into any desired form.

Cob, a mixture of clay, sand, straw and soil. Cob can be shaped as desired, is long-lasting, energy efficient and inexpensive.

Cordwood (logs) from local trees. Unlike traditional log cabins, with cordwood homes the rounded ends of the logs face outward, forming the surface of walls. Gaps are sealed with sawdust or other natural materials. Cordwood homes are strong, durable and energy efficient.

Rammed earth, another ancient building material, consisting of earth, sand, gravel and clay. Rammed earth homes are affordable, durable, noncombustible and thermally balanced.

Shipping containers left over from the global transport of goods. Containers are being transformed into beautiful homes with versatile designs. Repurposing shipping containers diverts a significant amount of waste from landfill.

Solid core, heat-transfer-resistant doors. This includes Energy Star-rated products that seal tightly to help homes maintain the desired temperature throughout the year.

Interior and exterior window shades and canopies to shade southern and western exposures.

Energy-efficient appliances. (More information: Renovating and maintaining a home, below)

2. Installing sustainable systems, such as:

Solar or wind to power the HVAC system.

A renewable heat source, such as a geothermal system or a wood burning stove that burns pellets. (More information: Utilities)

An energy-efficient HVAC system. As compared with forced-hot-air systems, radiant (water-fed) heating systems are more energy efficient, producing heat more evenly. Adding several heating zones can increase energy efficiency by allowing us to vary programmable thermostat settings, as needed, in different parts of the house. Regular maintenance can help keep nearly any HVAC system running more efficiently.

Renovating and maintaining a home

While most of us will never live in a new platinum LEED-certified dwelling, renovating or maintaining a home may be the greenest options of all, since they don't require additional land and may allow us to reuse building materials and fixtures. If the household budget is relatively small or we're currently renting, greening our home may seem impractical and out of reach. But not all eco-conscious choices are expensive, and some can help us lower household expenses, making our financial lives more sustainable. Alternatives for renovating or maintaining a home sustainably include:

The U.S. Green Building Council and LEED-Certification

Established in 1993, the U.S. Green Building Council is credited with creating the first organized set of criteria for building in an environmentally sustainable manner. That criteria, known as LEED (Leadership in Energy and Environmental Design), can guide architects, engineers and builders in creating buildings that are energy efficient, healthy and compatible with the local environment. Buildings can earn LEED certification—certified, silver, gold or platinum—depending on the degree to which they incorporate LEED criteria. A green home, with or without LEED certification, uses water, electricity and other resources in an efficient manner, reduces waste and enhances the health of residents. While most homeowners don't pursue LEED certification, the guidelines can provide a useful starting point when considering a green home project. More information can be found at usgbc.org.

▶ **Conducting a home energy audit.**
Before embarking on renovations, it can be helpful to assess how our home currently uses energy. A professional home energy auditor may help us find ways to conserve energy or switch to a renewable system.

▶ **Applying green building standards when possible.**
Some green building ideas can be applied when updating an existing home. For example, a renovation may provide opportunities to open up the floor plan, knocking down interior walls to reconfigure living space without adding to the home's footprint. We may be able to increase natural light or passive solar heat by updating to energy-efficient windows. We can block wind shear, potentially reducing heating costs, by strategically planting new trees and shrubs. We may be able to upgrade to a renewable energy system, fully or partially, for example, by installing a solar-powered system for the entire house or a solar thermal system just for heating water. And we can choose eco-conscious finishes, such as low-VOC paints and floors made from cork or bamboo.

▶ **Considering green additions.** If adding one or more rooms is part of the renovation plan, the addition could present opportunities to further green our home. The new rooms may make it possible to install a renewable energy system if the addition is located on the south-facing side of the house and is structurally able to support solar panels. South-facing additions, such as sun rooms, also can increase passive solar heat in the winter while potentially providing space for year-round indoor food gardening.

▶ **Refurbishing.** Updating our home's existing features lets us renovate without depleting natural resources or adding to landfill waste. Options include refinishing floors or covering them with new flooring materials, resurfacing or repainting kitchen cabinets, restoring nonworking fireplaces or simply repainting the walls.

▶ **Insulating.** A significant amount of heat and air-conditioning can be lost due to inadequate insulation and gaps in the attic, walls, doors and windows. We can reduce our energy use, carbon footprint and utility bills while making our homes more comfortable by taking steps such as:

Tiny Homes

Those open to a more off-beat approach to reducing their ecological footprints and/or their living expenses may opt for tiny homes. Tiny home owners often express a desire to live sustainably or to prioritize experience over possessions. While tiny homes vary widely, reflecting the creativity and aspirations of individual owners, most comprise no more than a few hundred square feet and many sit on wheels, enabling a mobile lifestyle. Some tiny home enthusiasts participate in the building of their homes in order to save money and gain a better understanding of what they will need to live comfortably...and what they can do without. While not all tiny homes are built green, their scale automatically reduces the use of land, building materials and household possessions. Some tiny home dwellers take sustainability further, living off the grid with the aid of solar panels, wood stoves, composting toilets and small, energy-efficient appliances.

Adding or improving insulation in the attic and walls. (More information on eco-conscious insulation alternatives: Becoming energy efficient, page 91)

Plugging holes, cracks and gaps in the walls or foundation.

Caulking and weather stripping doors and windows.

Adding insulation around outdoor spigots and wiring as well as indoor electrical outlets and switches.

Sealing cracked or disconnected ductwork so that heat and air-conditioning are distributed more evenly.

Blanketing the hot-water heater and insulating hot-water pipes with foam or fiberglass sleeves to retain heat, potentially making it possible to lower the boiler's temperature setting.

Placing a glass screen in front of the fireplace during months when it is in use to prevent the home's warmth from escaping up the chimney along with flames and smoke from the fire.

▶ **Replacing old appliances with energy-efficient models.** Most new appliances offer greater energy efficiency than older models. The best choices are those with the Energy Star label, the official stamp of approval for energy efficiency from the EPA and the U.S. Department of Energy. According to the Green Home Guide, each Energy Star appliance in a home can shave $50 a year off the electric bill.[6] Of course, using less electricity also reduces carbon emissions.

▶ **Keeping up with routine maintenance.** In addition to warding off the need to make major repairs or purchases, we can increase energy efficiency, lower household expenses and reduce natural resource depletion by maintaining our home's appliances, roof, well and plumbing as well as its septic, heating and electrical systems.

Renting Sustainably

The sustainability of a rented space will depend mostly on choices only the landlord can make. But that doesn't mean renters are powerless to take some positive steps (with the landlord's approval, as appropriate). For example, renters can:

▶ Conserve electricity, heat, air-conditioning and water, whether or not they pay the utility bills.

▶ Use eco-friendly paints, paint strippers, caulks and sealants.

▶ Buy eco-friendly furniture and furnishings. (More information: Furnishing)

▶ Recycle and compost waste.

Hiring Green Contractors

Nearly any qualified contractor can help us build a home with some green features. But it's also possible to find architects, engineers and builders that focus specifically on green building. Some are even certified by the U.S. Green Building Council or other green building advocacy groups. We can search geographically for green contractors at greenhomeguide.com. Alternatively, we can interview candidates to gauge whether they are willing and able to help us realize our personal idea of a sustainable home.

Utilities

We can become more sustainable with our use of electricity, heat, air-conditioning and water by (1) replacing fossil-fuel-based sources of energy with renewables and (2) adopting conservation methods.

Electricity: Switching to Renewables

According to the EPA, electricity produced from fossil fuels is responsible for about 30% of annual greenhouse gas emissions.[7] It also produces pollutants, such as sulfur dioxide, which contributes to acid rain, and nitrous oxides, which contribute to smog.[8] About one-third of electricity in the U.S. is produced from coal, which emits significant greenhouse gases.[9] Obtaining electricity from renewable sources can help us reduce the greenhouse gas emissions associated with powering our homes. It also can help us support increased production of renewables, enabling them to become an ever-larger portion of the country's net energy supply. Our alternatives include:

▶ **Purchasing electricity from renewable producers.** If we live in a state with a deregulated electricity market, we may be able to choose a renewable energy supplier. Deregulation, which began in the 1990s, was intended to increase competition in energy markets and pass along price savings to consumers. It also ended up opening the door for new companies that produce renewable energy. While utilities in deregulated states continue to own and maintain the grid, they must allow customers to purchase electricity directly from their chosen energy suppliers. Customers can select suppliers based on price or the type of energy a company produces.

Switching to a renewable energy supplier allows us to directly impact the amount of renewable energy being produced throughout the country. Consumer choice of renewables in deregulated states is among the factors that have enabled renewable energy to climb from 9.2% of all U.S. energy in 2006 to about 13.5% in 2015.[10] That percentage actually is higher in a handful of states, particularly those with large-scale hydroelectric generation. In Idaho, for example, renewables represent 88% of state energy production![11] The growth of renewable energy has helped the U.S. make meaningful progress in reducing its greenhouse gas emissions. According to Yale Climate Connections, as of 2013, U.S. carbon dioxide (CO_2) emissions had dropped 12% over a five-year period, down to 1996 levels.[12]

States with Deregulated Electricity Markets

In addition to the **District of Columbia,** the following states have deregulated electricity markets:

Connecticut	New Hampshire
Delaware	New Jersey
Illinois	New York
Maine	Ohio
Maryland	Oregon
Massachusetts	Pennsylvania
Michigan	Rhode Island
Montana	Texas[13]

We can begin the process of switching to a renewable energy supplier by visiting our state's energy department website. The site should allow us to locate a list of renewable energy suppliers doing business in the state and compare suppliers by price and the energy mixes they offer. Once we're ready to select a supplier, we can go directly to the company's website or contact them by phone.

Regardless of which energy supplier is selected, it's helpful to understand these four points.

1. We can shop around for competitive rates, but while the cost of solar continues to drop, renewable energy may still cost a bit more per kilowatt hour than nonrenewable power.

2. Since energy is fungible (i.e., no matter where or how it is produced, it gets mixed in with all the other energy supplying the grid), the electricity we purchase won't necessarily be delivered to our home. Instead, our purchase will represent an *investment* that helps fund the production of additional renewable energy. (More on the financial aspect of investing in renewable energy: Chapter 8, Money)

3. The utility with which we already have an account will continue to distribute our electricity, maintain and repair our power lines and send us a monthly bill.

4. Renewable suppliers may receive certification and verification from independent third parties confirming that the power being produced is indeed from renewable sources.

We can learn which fuels our local utilities use by visiting the EPA's Power Profiler tool at epa.gov and typing in our zip code. The EPA site provides a graphic breakdown of all the sources of power in our area. We also can plug in our average monthly electricity usage to find out how much we are contributing to carbon emissions. Or we can use the site to find renewable energy suppliers. Even those who don't live in a deregulated state may be able to invest in green energy by purchasing renewable energy "credits" from a supplier in another state.

▶ **Installing solar panels.** Producing our own renewable energy is an excellent way to green our electricity usage. Among those pursuing this option, solar is by far the most popular choice. Nearly half a million American homes had solar panels as of 2013[14] and growth in residential solar systems has soared ever since. Solar power is an inexhaustible source of electricity that produces no greenhouse gas emissions or other forms of pollution. According to the Union of Concerned Scientists (UCS), "just 20 days of sunshine contain more energy than the world's entire supply of coal, oil and natural gas [combined]."[15]

A residential solar energy (photovoltaic) system works by connecting solar panels that are installed on a south-facing roof or an array in the yard to the home's electrical system. The panels, made of photovoltaic cells, convert energy from sunlight into direct current (DC) electricity. A device called an "inverter" then converts the direct current into alternating current (AC), the type we need to turn on the lights and power the appliances. The power is carried to the home's breaker panel, allowing it to electrify the household. An online energy monitor allows homeowners to track the amount of energy being produced and used, while a smart utility meter measures excess energy returned to the grid as well as any power derived from the grid when the solar system isn't producing the amount of energy required for the home.

Since power generation declines at night and in inclement weather, most homes don't obtain all of their energy from a photovoltaic (PV) system. The amount of power a system generates depends on factors such as the average daily sunlight in the location, the number and quality of PV panels and their positioning on the roof or ground-mounted solar array. (While sunlight is important, PV panels are designed to produce power even on cloudy days.) The home's energy usage also is a factor, with more energy-efficient homeowners able to meet more of their needs with solar. Professional installers can help homeowners determine how to obtain the maximum amount of power from their system. With a suitable system, favorable climate conditions and reasonable energy conservation methods, it is possible to produce all the energy the average home needs. Consumers also can now look into three new alternatives: thin film (TF) panels, which are less noticeable on a roof than traditional PV panels, Elon Musk's new roof tiles, which double as solar panels, and the space-efficient "smartflower," which maximizes solar collection with panels that rotate to remain 90 degrees from the sun.

The vast majority of residential PV systems today are "grid-tied," meaning they are connected to the utility's infrastructure, allowing the home to both receive power from and return power to the grid. That allows homeowners to sell excess energy back to the utility. (Unfortunately, some states have allowed utilities to not only stop paying homeowners for excess energy but actually charge them for it.) But it also means that during a power outage, when the grid goes down, so does the residential solar system. Grid-tied systems must shut off automatically during power outages to avoid electrocuting utility workers.

Non-grid-tied systems are available, but they require battery storage that can significantly increase the cost of the system. Until recently, battery storage capacity also was a limiting factor. But innovations such as Elon Musk's Powerwall batteries and the smartflower's batteries are expected to produce the paradigm shift necessary to make renewable energy for our homes and vehicles efficient and affordable. Ideally, we'll be able to store excess solar energy in these advanced batteries and then use the stored energy to power our electric vehicles and keep the lights on whenever the PV system isn't producing an adequate supply of energy.

The prevalence of PV systems has grown exponentially over the past decade and they have become more affordable thanks to consumer demand, the declining cost of producing panels, the increased efficiency of panels, the reduced cost of kilowatt hours, attractive financing alternatives and incentive programs from the federal government, some states and utilities. Since 2006, households that have installed PV systems have been eligible for the solar Investment Tax Credit (ITC). According to a solar industry group, tax credits have allowed solar to grow at a compounded annual rate of nearly 60%.[16] Concern that the ITC would sunset at the end of 2016 triggered a boom in the installation of residential systems through that year. The credit ultimately was extended for another five years, representing a major boost to renewables. Energy analysts have predicted that an additional $25 billion in tax credits during the extension period will produce $38 billion in solar investment as well as another $35 billion in wind investment. Besides doubling U.S. solar production and greatly expanding wind generation, that level of investment is expected to be enough to finally make renewables consistently competitive with fossil fuels even without further subsidies.[17]

Since the ITC was created in 2006, the cost of installing a PV system has dropped by more than 90%.[18] In some states, the cost of a kilowatt of electricity produced by solar also has plummeted, nearing or reaching parity with a kilowatt produced from fossil fuel sources. Many states have further boosted solar production by enacting *renewable portfolio standards* that require in-state utilities to increase the percentage of energy derived from renewables within a prescribed period of time. States have encouraged progress toward those goals by offering consumer incentives, such as SRECs (solar credits), which homeowners and businesses can sell (either directly to utilities or to solar installers, financing companies or other intermediaries) to partially defray the cost of installing a system. Utilities have done their part by offering customers rebates and competitive loans to cover the costs of installation. And solar installers have helped consumers afford this choice by offering the option to lease a system instead of buying it outright. The leasing company, which receives any available tax credits or rebates, maintains the system and charges customers for the energy used. Leasing can be a good solution for nonprofit organizations, schools, religious institutions and government entities, since they don't pay taxes and, therefore, do not need tax credits.

PV System Information Checklist

✓ Information about current federal and state tax credits, grants, loans, utility rebates and other incentives is available at epa.gov as well as from state websites, the Database of State Incentives for Renewables & Efficiency (dsireusa.org), utility company websites and PV system installers.

✓ Permitting requirements are available from municipal offices.

✓ Online solar calculators can provide data on the productivity of solar arrays in our area, helping us gauge whether the option is effective enough to warrant the investment.

✓ More information on installing PV systems is available at homepower.com.

▶ **Creating or joining a community-scale renewable energy project, such as a community solar garden.** There are many ways to organize, finance and structure this type of project. A solar garden can consist of an array of panels on a local site that is well-suited to year-round energy production. It also may comprise collective ownership of solar panels located on municipal buildings or on private homes and businesses throughout a community. Consumers can subscribe to a solar garden simply to obtain household power. In doing so, they can reduce fossil fuel use and, over time, lower the household utility bill. Some subscribers may choose to become initial investors, paying for electricity needs up-front in order to help fund the development of the solar garden. Subscriber-investors may be paid back through a credit on future electric bills; they also may be eligible for the federal ITC or for state tax credits. Solar gardens also may be financed by community banks, energy cooperatives, local businesses, foundations or finance companies that specialize in renewable energy projects. In some cases, a solar garden may be owned for a period of years by investors or by the municipality before reverting to subscribers, who may organize themselves into a limited liability corporation (LLC). Whatever form a solar garden takes, producing renewable energy locally, as a community, can offer benefits such as:

> **Municipal Utilities**
>
> Taking community-scale renewable energy one step further, some municipalities form their own utilities. For example, in Santa Fe, New Mexico, where some residents were frustrated with their utility's rates and lack of support for renewables, there was interest in the creation of a municipal energy company. The first proposed step was to install solar panels in new developments. Proponents believe a locally controlled utility would prove both fiscally and environmentally beneficial, supporting the growth of renewables, increasing energy efficiency, lowering household utility bills, keeping more money within the community and creating quality jobs.

Enhancing energy resiliency. If a solar garden is used to power a local microgrid, it can help make a community more resilient in the face of uncertain energy costs or weather events that interrupt the power supply. (More information: Distributed Energy and Community Microgrids sidebar, page 100)

Reducing the carbon footprint of the entire community.

Providing an affordable source of renewable energy to homes, businesses, schools and other public buildings.

Keeping the money spent on electric utilities within the community.

Creating local jobs.

Offering financial rewards in the form of investment returns and/or tax credits.

Helping a community come together to solve a challenge and, in doing so, recognize the power of working together.

▶ **Installing wind turbines.**[19] Wind turbines are small electric generators that produce electricity from air currents in a process that creates no greenhouse gas emissions or other pollutants and can reduce or eliminate household energy costs. Wind is now the leading source of renewable energy produced by utilities (and actually provides nearly all of the energy for Kodiak Island, Alaska). Few homeowners currently power their homes with these systems, however, since the turbines require an abundant, relatively constant source of wind not available in most residential settings. Residential wind turbine systems also can pose a number of other problems and challenges. They can kill birds and disrupt migration paths. Installation costs can be high. And output can be interrupted due to "turbulence," the effect of trees, roof lines and other tall structures blocking the wind. Turbulence also can lead to wear and tear on the system. Industry experts recommend that homeowners only consider wind turbines if they (1) own at least an acre of land, (2) can mount the turbines about 80 feet to 120 feet off the ground to reduce turbulence (assuming their municipality will issue permitting for towers of that height), (3) can mount turbines relatively close to the home to reduce energy loss during transmission and (4) can count on average wind speeds of at least 12 mph.

A professional installer can assess a site and help a homeowner determine whether wind turbines are feasible. A typical five-kilowatt turbine can produce 8,000 kilowatts a year with 12 mph average winds, providing 100% of the average home's electricity usage.[20] Both grid-tied and off-grid systems are available. Some smaller systems are paired with solar panels.

▶ **Installing a residential micro hydroelectric system.** While not very common, micro hydroelectric systems can offer a relatively inexpensive and constant source of renewable energy. The ability to install this type of system depends on having an adequate supply of water (such as a stream) on the property and a topographical drop-off that allows the water to be pressurized by gravity. Approvals must be obtained from the municipality and, often, also from state

Distributed Energy and Community Microgrids

Homeowners, businesses and communities that generate their own solar, wind or other renewable energy are participating in what is known as decentralized or "distributed" energy production. While most remain grid-tied, it's increasingly feasible to get off the grid and onto a community-owned microgrid. Used by universities, hospitals and government agencies for many years, microgrids are small-scale, free-standing localized power grids. Like backup generators, microgrids generally remain connected to the utility-owned grid until a power outage occurs. During an outage, the microgrid switches to another source of energy, in this case, renewables. This can help make a community more energy resilient. Microgrids also can be used to absorb small sources of renewable energy produced by homes and businesses that cannot easily be integrated into the grid. They may even be able to operate completely independent of the grid. By encouraging local production of renewable energy, a microgrid can help a community reduce dependence on fossil fuels while potentially lowering its energy costs.

environmental agencies. Many states don't allow these systems because they can have environmental impacts that need to be evaluated. Assuming that such a system is allowed, a licensed vendor can help a homeowner determine its feasibility and cost-effectiveness.

Electricity: Conserving Energy

The EPA's Household Carbon Footprint Calculator (www3.epa.gov/carbon-footprint-calculator) can help us measure the carbon emissions associated with our home. We can reduce our carbon footprint and the electric bill by conserving electricity through both obvious and not-so-obvious tactics. For example, we can:

✓ Turn off lights when we leave rooms.

✓ Use motion sensors or timers for outdoor lights so that they will turn on only when needed.

✓ Unplug appliances and electronics when we leave the house for any length of time, since they use some electricity as long as they are plugged in.

✓ Replace incandescent light bulbs with energy-efficient LED bulbs. Compact fluorescent bulbs, a transitional alternative now being replaced by LEDs, should be used only in light fixtures at least a foot away from us to prevent exposure to ultraviolet rays.

✓ Maintain appliances (e.g., change filters regularly) to keep them running efficiently.

✓ Adjust settings on computers and devices (e.g., lower screen brightness and disable screen savers) to reduce power usage.

✓ Lower the temperature on the hot-water heater and use less hot water (e.g., wash clothes in cold water whenever possible). According to the U.S. Department of Energy, hot-water heaters represent the second largest home energy expense.[21]

✓ Dry clothes on a clothesline.

✓ Run the dishwasher and washing machine at off-peak hours. Utility companies can provide information about local peak and off-peak periods. We also may want to experiment with running the dishwasher's quick cycle to further reduce energy consumption.

✓ Use manually powered appliances, such as carpet sweepers instead of vacuum cleaners or hand whisks instead of motorized mixers.

✓ Replace obsolete appliances with Energy Star-rated models.

Heating and Cooling: Switching to Renewables

When it comes to heating and cooling our homes, renewable alternatives include:

▶ **Geothermal.** A geothermal system utilizes geological conditions below the Earth's surface that keep the temperature between about 40°F and 60°F year-round. In the winter, a geothermal system generates heat by pumping water or antifreeze first through a network of underground pipes, then into a compressor in the home that heats the water to about 120°F. Warmed air then travels through the home's ventilating air ducts. In the summer, the system reverses itself, removing heat from the house and depositing it underground. The system also can be used to provide hot water throughout the year.

According to the EPA, geothermal systems are "the most energy efficient, environmentally clean and cost-effective"[22] sources of heating and cooling available to homeowners today. But not all homes have the conditions necessary—for example, the type and density of rock beneath the ground—for an effective residential geothermal system. Installation costs also can be prohibitive, though they vary from one local market to the next. While these factors may prevent residential geothermal systems from becoming widespread, their popularity has grown substantially in recent years thanks to increased consumer interest in renewable energy alternatives and the availability of federal tax credits.

▶ **Wood-burning stoves.** These have long been a popular and affordable substitute for traditional heating. But in the past, the use of wood could produce harmful indoor air pollutants, such as nitrogen oxides, carbon monoxide, sulfur oxides and fine particulates. Newer, EPA-certified stoves are clean burning and efficient because they allow for complete combustion. Alternatives to consider include catalytic stoves, advanced combustion stoves and stoves that burn wood pellets. Professional installers can help homeowners find alternatives that are clean, affordable and efficient at heating the home. The National Fireplace Institute lists certified professionals in the field.

Heating and Cooling: Conserving Energy

Whether or not we're responsible for paying utility bills, it makes environmental sense to reduce our use of heat and air-conditioning. In addition to the energy-saving ideas mentioned previously in Building, Renovation and Maintenance and later in Greenscaping, we can conserve by:

In colder months:

✓ Pulling up shades or opening curtains in the sunniest rooms to increase passive solar heat.

✓ Wearing extra layers of clothing rather than immediately turning up the thermostat.

✓ Setting ceiling fans to run clockwise at a low speed to pull colder air toward the ceiling and push warm air downward.

✓ Ensuring our home is well-insulated. (More information: Building, Renovation and Maintenance)

In warmer months:

✓ Installing awnings and closing blinds or shades during the day to reduce solar heat gain.

✓ Installing an attic fan, which can pull heat out of a house quickly and efficiently, using far less energy than air-conditioning.

✓ Setting ceiling fans to run counterclockwise to create a cooling downdraft.

✓ Making use of window and oscillating fans and cross breezes when possible.

✓ Grilling instead of using the kitchen stove, especially on the hottest nights.

✓ Wearing lighter clothing, rather than immediately lowering the temperature on the air-conditioner.

Year-round:

✓ Switching to a programmable thermostat, which allows programming of day and night temperatures for each day of the week. That can assure we have heat or air-conditioning when we need it most while saving energy and money when we can be comfortable with less.

Water: Switching to Renewables

We can reduce both the fossil fuel use and expense associated with heating our home's water supply by installing a renewable water heating system. Alternatives include:

▶ **Solar thermal systems.** Substantially less expensive than PV systems that power an entire home, these systems absorb heat energy from sunlight and use it directly to heat water.

▶ **Geothermal systems.** As noted previously, households that have installed geothermal heating and cooling systems can rely on them to heat the home's water year-round.

Water: Conserving Resources

Using water thoughtfully can help ensure that there will be enough for us, for future generations and for wildlife and their habitat. In addition to preserving this precious natural resource, water conservation can reduce the need to build new community wells, water and wastewater treatment facilities, dams and reservoirs, all of which can have negative environmental impacts.

While water conservation has always been important, it may soon become a matter of urgency. Environmental scientists warn that climate change is likely to lead to water shortages as extreme weather patterns produce lengthy droughts, reduce the annual snowfall needed to replenish streams and rivers each spring and cause lakes and reservoirs to dry up and become irreversibly salinated. We don't need to wait for future events to unfold to grasp the impact of a long-term, widespread water shortage. A historic drought has plagued the West Coast, Southwest and parts of the Midwest in recent years, with ramifications including extensive wildfires that have destroyed thousands of homes as well as crops and cropland. The drought's impact on farmers was felt nationwide, with rising food prices and sporadic shortages. But with so much of our food coming from other parts of the world, it has been easy to overlook even a crisis of this magnitude. As a consequence, many of us in unaffected areas of the country have remained fairly oblivious of the need to conserve water.

Even so, a long-term study by the U.S. Geological Survey (USGS) found that we are using less water today than at any time since 1970. Much of the decrease is attributed to technological advances that have allowed industry and agriculture to reduce water usage even while increasing productivity.[23] Consumer adoption of newer, water-saving home fixtures has helped as well. (More information below) According to the USGS, the average American currently uses about 80 gallons to 100 gallons of water a day.[24] Water usage dropped a bit from 1980 to 2005, then fell about 13% between 2005 and 2010.[25] We can help ensure this trend continues by taking the following steps:

▶ **Monitor water usage.** If we have public water (as opposed to a private well), we can review the water bill to track our usage at different times of the day or year. There may be a peak water usage period in the mid- to late summer. In addition to helping us gauge when it's most important to reduce water usage, our bill may lead us to take note of and fix any faulty plumbing or leaks. Conserving water can have the added benefit of helping us use less electricity, thereby reducing our carbon footprint and lowering the utility bill.

▶ **Choose WaterSense or other water-saving toilets, showerheads and faucets.** Whether we're selecting fixtures for our new 100% green home or simply replacing what's broken, it's relatively easy to find affordable fixtures that use much less water than older models. Toilet flushing represents about 27% of household water use.[26] Switching to low-flush toilets that meet the Department of Energy's requirement to use no more than 1.6 gallons of water per flush (versus the 3.5 gallons to 5 gallons common with older models) can save the average household more than 26,000 gallons of water a year.[27] (All new toilets are low-flush.) Another option is a dual-flush toilet, which allows us to choose the amount of water used for each flush. The EPA's WaterSense brand showerheads reduce average water use from 2.5 gallons per minute to no more than 2 gallons a minute.[28] WaterSense sink faucets reduce water usage from 2.2 gallons per minute to 1.5 gallons per minute, saving the average household about 700 gallons of water a year.[29] The EPA's WaterSense calculator can help us determine how much water we would save by installing WaterSense toilets, showerheads and faucets. Energy Star dishwashers and washing machines reduce water as well as electricity usage, helping to lower utility bills.

► **Add a composting toilet.** A completely waterless alternative, composting toilets use the natural processes of decomposition and evaporation to recycle human waste in a sanitary and eco-friendly manner. Liquid waste evaporates while solid waste is converted into usable fertilizer for the garden. While not likely to catch on with the majority of homeowners, composting toilets work well in tiny homes and are ideally suited to off-grid living.

► **Moderate water usage.** We can reduce our water usage by fixing any plumbing leaks, showering instead of bathing, taking shorter showers, installing faucet-head aerators, which reduce water flow, washing only full loads of clothes in an Energy Star-rated washing machine and washing full loads of dishes in an Energy Star-rated dishwasher rather than washing dishes by hand. The latter can reduce our household water use by about 5,000 gallons a year.[30] We also can conserve water by turning on the faucet only when necessary, such as when rinsing after brushing our teeth. We can reduce the need to run water while waiting for it to heat up by insulating the hot-water heater and pipes. And we can take steps to reduce water use in our yards. (More information: Greenscaping)

► **Use less soap.** Since most laundry, dishwasher and dish soaps are highly concentrated, even using the manufacturer-recommended amounts may be overdoing it. Excessive soap produces an abundance of suds, requiring extra water for rinsing. In addition to causing us to waste water, the extra suds can damage dishwashers and washing machines and leave soap residue on dishes and clothes.

► **Recycle.** We can harvest and reuse water by installing rain barrels in the yard for gardening needs, diverting greywater from the house to an irrigation system or using the nutrient-rich water leftover from cleaning fish tanks for our household plants. (More Information: Greenscaping)

Furnishing

When it comes to furnishing and decorating a home, there are several ways to approach sustainability. We can protect our health and the environment by choosing furniture made from nontoxic, natural, renewable or organic materials. If we're replacing older furnishings, we'll want to find sustainable disposal alternatives, such as recycling or donating. (More information: Chapter 5, Consuming) We can support resilient economies and responsible business practices by buying furnishings that are made locally, regionally or by certified fair trade producers outside the country. And we can reduce the financial and environmental impacts of consumption by repurposing existing furnishings or buying pieces that are pre-used, antique or upcycled in creative ways.

▶ **Choose healthy, eco-friendly soft furnishings.** Pillows, blankets, mattresses, sofas and rugs are among the household possessions we most associate with safety and comfort. It can be unsettling to learn that some of those furnishings may be exposing us to potentially toxic chemicals. Mattresses, pillows

Sustainable Furnishing Labels

Artisan-made: The nonprofit Aid to Artisans (ATA) helps create economic opportunities for artisan groups around the world by linking them with new markets and buyers.

Craftmark-certified: Part of the All India Artisans and Craftworkers Association, the Craftmark organization enables artisans from India to certify their products as authentically handmade and helps them gain access to consumer markets around the world.

FSC-certified: The Forest Stewardship Council establishes industry standards for responsible forest management. FSC-certified paper and wood products come from well-managed, sustainably harvested forests that adhere to stringent environmental, economic and social standards.

Greenguard: This nonprofit organization certifies that products do not off-gas volatile organic compounds.

CRI Green Label Testing Program and Green Label Plus: Certification from the Carpet and Rug Institute verifies that carpets, cushions and adhesives emit only very low levels of VOCs.

GOTS-certified: Global Organic Textile Standard (GOTS) certification of cotton and other fabrics assures that producers meet sustainable criteria regarding everything from labor standards to the harvesting of raw materials to manufacturing, packaging and labeling. GOTS prohibits GMOs as well as heavy metals and other known toxins and carcinogens and requires growers to use organic agricultural methods.

Handmade: This refers to any original product made by an individual, rather than by machines or mass-production processes.

Nontoxic: This refers to products that do not contain known toxins or carcinogens.

OEKO-TEX Certified: This global testing and certification system sets guidelines for the human ecological safety of products such as bedding and towels.

Rapidly renewable: This refers to any natural resource, such as jute, bamboo, hemp, bankuan or abaca, which regenerates in a short period of time.

Reclaimed or recycled: This refers to products made from previously used materials that would otherwise end up in landfill.

Sustainably sourced: This refers to products produced with sustainable forestry products or other renewable natural resources obtained without harming the environment.

and sofas may contain petrochemicals and other toxins that can irritate skin and emit toxic (though often unnoticeable) fumes associated with respiratory complaints and other health concerns.[31] The latter is an example of "off-gassing," the release of volatile organic compounds (VOCs) into the air. Quilts, crib bumpers and other items containing cotton batting may expose us to toxins from cotton, one of the most chemical-intensive agricultural crops.[32] Sofas, other upholstered furnishings, curtains and rugs may be drenched in a range of chemicals, including flame retardants and stain blockers, which studies have linked to health concerns including reproductive and developmental abnormalities and certain cancers.[33] Furnishings that contain formaldehyde may be another ongoing source of off-gassing.[34] Carpets can trap off-gassed chemicals and toxic particles, increasing our long-term exposure. And some furnishings may expose us to potentially toxic fabric dyes made from petroleum-based industrial chemicals.

Fortunately, growing consumer awareness of these potential hazards has led to both improved regulations and a wider range of eco-friendly alternatives. Since 2013, manufacturers have no longer been required to apply flame retardants to upholstered furnishings provided that they find other ways to meet fire-safety regulations. Many also have stopped using known toxins, such as formaldehyde and stain blockers that contain perfluorinated chemicals (PFCs),[35] and have replaced polyurethane foam cushions with eco-friendly alternatives such as down feathers or natural latex from rubber trees. It's increasingly easy to find organic and nontoxic mattresses and pillows as well as upholstery fabrics, sheets, towels, blankets and other textiles for the home that are made from bamboo, certified organic cotton, rapidly renewable hemp or sustainably produced wool. It's also possible to find sheets, towels and other household textile products that are unbleached or dyed with natural, plant-based colorants. Many national furniture chains and small, independently owned stores have begun to carry nontoxic soft furnishings. We can locate retailers that sell green home furnishings at Earth 911 (earth911.com) or at the website of the Sustainable Furnishings Council (sustainablefurnishings.org). Certification labels such as those in the sidebar on page 106 can help us verify whether an item meets our expectations for sustainability.

▶ **Choose sustainably produced wood furniture.** With wood furnishings, the main environmental issue is protecting old-growth forests. Sustainable manufacturers rely on wood from young forests with rapidly renewable varieties of trees grown exclusively to supply the furniture industry. Trees grown in sustainable forests take less time to mature than the hardwood varieties traditionally used for furniture. And sustainable forests are continually planted with new trees to replace those that have been harvested. Sustainably produced wood furniture is now widely available both at specialty shops and national home-furnishing chains. We can verify that furniture is made from sustainable forestry products by looking for the certification label from the Forest Stewardship Council (FSC). Another sustainable alternative to old growth woods is bamboo. Rapidly renewable, it grows quickly, requires no irrigation, fertilizer or pesticides, reduces soil erosion and pollution and absorbs CO_2.

▶ **Buy locally made, American-made and/or artisanal home decor.** As with any local purchase, buying furnishings from independent local shops, artisans or artists triggers a multiplier effect that can strengthen the local economy. Buying goods that were produced locally from locally sourced raw materials can be even more beneficial. That might include an artisan-made table produced from locally salvaged wood or a rug handcrafted with wool from locally raised sheep. In addition to helping us support the local economy and reduce our carbon footprint, furnishing with local, artisan-made goods can lend our home a unique, personalized look and feel. If it's not possible to furnish our entire home with goods from nearby, we can seek out the next best options: regionally made or "Made in the U.S.A."

▶ **Buy fair trade.** Buying a unique item from a far-off land won't help our local economy. But if the product is certified fair trade, our purchase will still be sustainable. As with other types of fair trade goods, this label on furnishings should indicate that products were made in a safe and environmentally responsible manner, that workers were paid and treated fairly and that profits were reinvested for the benefit of workers' communities. Ten Thousand Villages was the pioneer in making fair trade items available to U.S. consumers. Today, there are numerous fair trade organizations and retailers offering furnishings and other goods online, at national home-furnishing chains and at independent local stores that recognize fair trade as an important sustainable choice.

▶ **Restore and refinish.** Refurbishing our own furniture (or our flea market finds) reduces trash by turning it back into something useful. It also reduces the need to deplete natural resources, such as wood from old-growth forests, for the production of new furniture. This type of upcycling can offer a creative outlet while helping us spend less and achieve a lower-consumption lifestyle.

If we're moving into our first home just as our parents or grandparents are downsizing, they may have some family relics to get us started. Other great sources of "gently used" furniture or bona fide antiques include garage sales, flea markets, antique and used furniture shops, Goodwill shops and, of course, eBay and other online sources. Reuse centers are a recent entry into the world of restored and upcycled furnishing, selling both furniture ready for repurposing and the creative materials needed to get the job done. Of course, when our retro furnishings were new, they may well have contained harmful chemicals. Since many chemical residues break down and dissipate over time, it's possible that decor from our grandparent's era may have aged into being green.

Cleaning

Once we've made our home as safe and eco-friendly as possible, we'll want to keep it clean without undoing all our hard work. That may be a challenge given the ingredients often found in household cleaning products. According to the Environmental Working Group (EWG) and other environmental organizations, cleaning products often contain nonbiodegradable ingredients that pose a long-term threat to the environment, polluting at every point in their lifecycle, from manufacture to household use to eventual disposal. Many of the ingredients in cleansers also have been linked to health concerns ranging from allergic reactions and asthma to respiratory, neurological, fertility and autoimmune disorders to certain types of cancer.[36] Environmental scientists believe cleansers are among the household products that contribute to making indoor air pollution up to 30 times higher than outdoor pollution,[37] a particular concern given that most of us spend about 90% of our time indoors.[38]

If we want to clean our homes without placing our health or the environment at risk, there are several steps we can take.

▶ **Identify toxins.** We can start by attempting to find out what's in the cleaning products we've been using. While some companies list ingredients on product labels, there are no federal or state laws that require this disclosure. Fortunately, EWG has done much of the legwork for us. Their Guide to Healthy Cleaning database lists all of the cleaning products their scientists have reviewed, identifies any potentially harmful or allergenic ingredients and assigns each product a grade from A through F. We can use the online tool to identify the ingredients in the products we currently use and learn how those products are rated. Or we can search by category (for example, glass cleaners or laundry detergents) to find healthier product replacements.

▶ **Purchase green cleansers.** There are many eco-conscious cleaning products on the market today. But there's also plenty of greenwashing in this product category. Unfortunately, as demand for green cleansers has grown, some manufacturers have taken the shortcut of adopting product names and package designs that overstate or even completely mislead consumers about a product's green credentials. The EWG database can help us verify that a product meets our expectations for environmental health and safety. Once we've identified authentically eco-conscious choices, we can take one more sustainable step by searching for the products at local, independently owned shops rather than immediately choosing to buy them online.

▶ **Go DIY.** If the cost of eco-conscious cleaning products seems financially unsustainable, an alternative is to make our own. It was only a few generations ago that nearly all cleaning products were made at home because there were few if any alternatives. The manufactured cleansers that made their appearance in the first half of the 20th century held out the promise of less housework and a more sanitary, modern way of life. But as the environmental and health risks posed by these products have come to light, many of us have begun to replace them with our grandmother's (or great grandmother's) household cleaning recipes—or those we've found through blogs and YouTube clips. Making our own cleaning products can be a healthy choice both for us and the planet. And much like pickling and putting up jams, it can help us adopt a simpler lifestyle, reducing both consumption and expenses.

▶ **Dust and vacuum.** Many of us ignore the dust bunnies gathering in the corners of our rooms for as long as possible. But environmental health experts believe dust actually is "an important route of toxicant exposure."[39] In other words, while we may worry more about pesticide-laden food and pollution from tailpipes and industry, a large portion of our exposure to toxins comes from common household dust. In addition to inhaling that dust, we can absorb it through our skin or even ingest it in our food. Young children often are at the greatest risk since they may spend more time on floors or rugs where dust accumulates and may be more likely to transfer dust into their mouths.

Household dust consists of tiny particles (particulate matter) from a wide range of sources: personal care products, shoes and clothing, skin and hair, pets, insects, soot buildup in the air ducts of forced-hot-air heating systems, household fuels,

---

Green Cleaning Recipes

It's easy and inexpensive to make eco-friendly cleaning products from common household ingredients such as distilled white vinegar, baking soda, cornstarch, washing soda (also known as soda ash or sodium carbonate), isopropyl alcohol, eco-friendly soap (such as Dr. Bronner's organic, fair trade castile soap), beer, cream of tartar, salt, lemon, olive oil and tea tree oil. Some useful combinations include:

Glass and all-purpose surface cleaner: Distilled white vinegar + eco-friendly liquid soap + water

Oven cleaner: Baking soda + distilled white vinegar + eco-friendly liquid soap + water

Stone and marble cleaner: Isopropyl alcohol + eco-friendly liquid soap + a few drops of lavender or eucalyptus oil to mask the alcohol odor + water

Stainless steel cleaner: Cream of tartar + water

Polishes: Lemon juice + lemon oil + olive oil for wood; lemon juice + baking soda for copper, brass, bronze and aluminum; baking soda + boiling water + salt for silver

Note that vinegar also kills some germs.

soft furnishings, including rugs, draperies and upholstered furniture, the off-gassing or deterioration of building materials and household products, including both furniture and electronics, and virtually anything we bring inside. Depending on its source, dust may contain a wide range of allergens and toxins, including pollen, dust mites, mold, fungal spores, pet dander, volatile organic compounds (VOCs), lead, traces of other metals, particulates from aerosols, pesticide residues, asbestos, petrochemicals, cigarette ash, flame retardants and artificial colorants and fragrances. Such particles take longer to break down inside a home than outdoors, where they are exposed to the elements. The best way to reduce our exposure to dust is to limit how much enters our home. Placing door mats at all entrances, removing shoes[40] when we come inside and keeping anything potentially hazardous out of the house are all good measures. We can further reduce our exposure by ensuring that our homes have adequate ventilation and, yes, by dusting and vacuuming on a regular basis, ideally using a HEPA filter in the vacuum.

▶ **Clear the air.** Depending on the types of indoor air pollutants and/or allergens present in our homes, we can choose from a variety of air cleaners. A good source of information on what's available is the EPA's Guide to Air Cleaners in the Home. Air cleaners that are integrated into an HVAC system can provide benefit to an entire home. Other air cleaners are designed for local use within one room or area. Some common house plants, such as snake plants, spider plants, Boston ferns, English Ivy, ficus trees and bamboo, can help purify the air, ridding it of a variety of toxins. If we live in an area with good air quality, it also can help to simply open windows when temperatures allow and let in some fresh air.

Greenscaping

The green space outside our doors—or located nearby—can offer a peaceful oasis as well as the opportunity for exercise, reflection or even spiritual renewal. We can protect those open spaces and ensure they'll be around for years to come by managing them responsibly. Eco-conscious landscaping can help us reduce toxins in our immediate environment, reduce groundwater pollution, support biodiversity, protect native plants and wildlife, conserve electricity and water and gain affordable access to a healthier diet. Whether we're able to implement major changes all at once or need to take small, incremental steps from one growing season to the next, we can green our home's landscape by:

▶ **Considering energy efficiency.** Depending on climate and how a home is situated on a property, it may be possible to become more energy efficient by using plantings to reduce wind shear, increase shade or increase absorption of passive solar heat.

We can cool a home by:

✓ Planting deciduous trees with high-spreading crowns on the southern side to shade the roof during warmer months.

✓ Planting deciduous trees with lower crowns on the western side to provide shade from lower afternoon sun angles.

✓ Erecting a green wall or trellis for climbing vines to shade the perimeter of the house and allow for cooling breezes.

✓ Planting groundcover, trees and shrubs to shade and cool the ground and pavement around the house, patio and walkways.

We can reduce the impact of wind by:

✓ Planting evergreens and shrubs along the northern side of the home.

We can increase passive solar heat by:

✓ Eliminating or removing evergreens on the southern side of the house. The deciduous trees that keep our home cool during the summer will allow sunlight in through their bare branches in the winter months.

We can increase our home's insulation by:

✓ Planting a green roof.

▶ **Conserving water.** According to the EPA, outdoor activities such as watering lawns and gardens comprise about 30% of monthly household water usage.[41] But there are many ways to conserve water in our yards and gardens. We can check for leaks in hoses, outdoor pipes, irrigation systems and pools. We can position sprinklers where they're needed most, water plants with drip hoses, reuse greywater (e.g., the rinse water from washing machines, showers and sinks) for irrigation, water only during the coolest times of the day to reduce evaporation, water slowly to allow for absorption, water the grass only when necessary (i.e., when it doesn't spring back after being stepped on) and install in-ground

---

Installing Rain Barrels

Capturing rainwater in a barrel placed beneath a downspout can provide a convenient source of clean water for the lawn and garden, helping us reduce household water use and remain resilient during periods of drought. A water catchment system such as a rain barrel also can help prevent pollution and flooding from stormwater runoff. Rain barrels can be purchased in garden stores or made from garbage pails or other large, nonporous containers. Some homeowners attach a downspout diverter to the gutter, which sends water into the barrel until it is full, then allows excess water to flow back down the drain pipe. Water can be collected by opening the spout located near the bottom of the rain barrel or attaching a garden hose to the spout. For increased water pressure, it's helpful to elevate the rain barrel on some type of platform. Homeowners who use rain barrels save about 1,300 gallons of water a year.[42]

moisture sensors that can help us determine when it's time to water. Both native plants and organic gardening methods can help reduce our outdoor water usage. We also can harvest rainwater by capturing it in rain barrels. (More information: Installing Rain Barrels sidebar, page 112) And we can add rain gardens to the landscape to filter pollutants and reduce runoff. (More information: Managing stormwater with rain gardens and other solutions, page 114)

▶ **Losing the lawn.** In the suburbs, nothing says "respectable home" like a well-tended patch of bright green grass. But lawns, which are considered the country's largest "crop," taking up nearly three times the amount of land as corn crops, can pose a number of ecological problems.[43] Lawn mowers burn fossil fuels, increasing our carbon footprint. Chemicals used to keep lawns green and "healthy looking" can endanger pets and young children and pollute local aquifers, streams and other waterways. And the more room we allow for grass, which offers few ecological benefits, the less we leave for plants that can help keep the house temperate, absorb excess CO_2 from the atmosphere or provide us with an affordable source of healthy food.

Simply reducing the size of the lawn can be a practical option, particularly if we need areas for children to play or for dogs to get some exercise. We may want to swap some of the lawn for moss, wildflowers, heather, a groundcover such as periwinkle or pachysandra or water-efficient succulents. We also can replace lawn (even the front lawn) with an expanded edible garden. If eliminating grass isn't an option, we can reduce the impact of mowing by letting the grass grow longer between cuts to preserve soil moisture and leaving clippings in place, where they can serve as compost, enriching the soil. If our patch of green is small enough and relatively flat, we may be able to switch to a non-motorized mower. Or, if we decide to explore permaculture, we can swap the mower for a few hungry goats. (More information: page 114)

Whatever size lawn we maintain, we can make it more eco-friendly by choosing a mix of grasses suitable for the local soil, using organic lawn care products (or hiring a lawn care company that uses organic products) and following guidelines for natural or low maintenance lawns available from sources such as *You Bet Your Garden* (gardensalive.org) and sustainable lawn care books.

▶ **Choosing eco-friendly mulch.**[44] Along with green lawns, well-mulched garden beds are a mainstay of suburban yards. Mulch can reduce weed growth, maintain soil moisture and, yes, keep the garden neat and tidy. But, according to green gardening sources, the most common mulches sold at garden stores, including all types of wood mulch (triple-shredded hardwood, wood chips, root mulches) and shredded rubber mulch, may contain trace elements of arsenic, creosote, zinc and other toxins. Rubber can produce an unpleasant odor in warmer weather. Gardening experts also say that wood mulches can rob plants of the nitrogen they need to thrive and can produce a discoloring fungus capable of permanently staining house siding. Eco-friendly mulches include compost, shredded leaves, chemical-free grass clippings that have been fully dried, organic mushroom soil and pine straw. Other alternatives include mulches made from seeds (e.g., cotton seeds), nuts (e.g., pecans) and hulls (e.g., cocoa hulls). In addition to choosing eco-friendly mulch, it's important to apply it with care, keeping it a few inches away from tree trunks or the perimeter of the home.

▶ **Managing stormwater with rain gardens and other solutions.** When stormwater doesn't drain into soil adequately, it can rob aquifers of replenishing rains while increasing runoff that carries chemicals and debris from our yards into roadway drainage pipes, local streams and eventually rivers, lakes and oceans. The nonpoint source pollution resulting from runoff can make waterways unsafe for swimming and other forms of recreation. It also can cause streams to overflow during heavy storms, potentially triggering flash floods.

While stormwater issues may sound like something for our elected officials to address, homeowners not only bear some responsibility for the problem but also have the ability to address it. Some solutions, such as proper site design to ensure that water drains adequately and the use of detention basins and stormwater conveyance pipes, are the responsibility of the engineers and builders involved in our home's construction. But we can take the additional step of adding one or more rain gardens to our landscape design. Rain gardens are shallow depressions in the landscape that capture runoff and allow water to seep back into the ground filtered of pollutants. Rain gardens work because of the plants that line them. The best choices are native, noninvasive, drought-resistant plants with deep, dense roots able to break up soil and increase water absorption. The bottom of the garden should be filled with stone or sand to provide an area for water to pool. The ideal placement of a rain garden depends on the drainage situation on a particular property. Options include placing them (1) near the house to capture water from downspouts, (2) further from the house to collect runoff from the lawn or (3) along driveways and sidewalks to prevent runoff onto roads and into drainage pipes enroute to local streams. In urban areas, roof gardens can play a similar role by increasing absorption of stormwater and reducing the amount carried away in drainage pipes.

▶ **Exploring permaculture.** Permaculture (described in Chapter 3, Food) is a horticultural discipline that advocates working in harmony with nature to minimize labor, energy inputs and waste. Applying the principals of permaculture to maintaining the yard and garden can help us recycle or reuse waste efficiently and support a naturally interconnected ecosystem. Bill Mollison, considered the founder of the permaculture movement, has described the discipline as a matter of placing the right elements together so that they naturally sustain and support each other.[45] The net result should be greater self-reliance and resiliency. We can adopt permaculture practices by:

Raising chickens, which give us two types of protein, produce natural fertilizer and eat the insects that can harm our edible plants.

Reusing greywater by piping water from the washing machine or other household sources to the yard to irrigate edible gardens. This can help conserve water and increase self-sufficiency. We may be able to build a low-tech greywater irrigation system on our own. Or we may prefer to hire a knowledgeable contractor to design the most efficient system for our home.

Planting a companion garden that gives us a variety of produce while helping to combat non-beneficial insects and other garden pests.

▶ **Choosing native plants.** The native plants that comprise critical habitat for many endangered species have been rapidly disappearing for years. Environmentalists and naturalists have sounded the alarm about this loss and the impact of "invasives." Non-native (invasive) species can arrive from overseas on shipping containers, migrate from one area to the next or be introduced intentionally by landscapers or homeowners who are unaware of the problems they can cause. While non-native plants offer variety, they can push out native plants, reducing biodiversity and altering the local ecosystem in dramatic and irreversible ways. Non-native invasives pose a threat to native plants by (1) altering soil chemistry, (2) serving as intermediate hosts to plant diseases and (3) changing their DNA through cross-breeding that produces hybrids. These changes can reduce the resiliency of an ecosystem, making plants more vulnerable to disease and pests and leaving nesting birds more exposed to predators.

Non-native plants also offer few if any of the ecological benefits provided by native species. Native plants are those that have evolved for thousands of years in a particular location. Because they are well-adapted to local conditions, they can help us make our gardens and yards more sustainable in a variety of ways.

Improved water quality. Native plants have strong root systems that are adept at absorbing rainwater and filtering out pollutants. That can help reduce soil contamination and the runoff that pollutes aquifers, streams and rivers.

Drought resistance. Because native plants help rainwater infiltrate the ground, plants and soil remain moist longer and plants require less frequent watering.

Integrated pest management. Since native plants have natural defenses against local pests and diseases, they make excellent choices for gardeners using organic and integrated pest management techniques.

Natural habitat. Native plants attract native birds, bees, butterflies and animals because they provide essential food, shelter and nesting sites.

Awareness of the environmental benefits of native plants has increased demand and made them easier to find at nurseries and nature preserves. We can learn which plants are indigenous to our area at plantnative.org.

▶ **Greening the hardscaping.**[46] Our choice of materials for hardscaped areas such as patios, driveways and walkways can help make our yards as healthy and eco-friendly as possible. While the most common hardscaping materials, such as concrete, asphalt and chemically treated wood, offer durability, they also may present numerous environmental problems. Production of these materials can be energy-intensive and polluting. The materials may leach toxic chemicals into our yards and local aquifers. Asphalt may raise the local temperature by absorbing solar heat. And because these materials aren't porous, they can reduce stormwater absorption, increasing runoff, soil erosion and local flooding. Unfortunately, even seemingly natural materials, such as stone and pebbles, can be unsustainable in one or more ways. When choosing materials, it's important to consider their entire lifecycle. The mining or manufacture of materials may harm workers and the environment. The transport of materials may require the burning of fossil fuels. Materials may be nonporous and/or toxic to homeowners, pets and wildlife. Or they may be nonbiodegradable, causing pollution when they end up in landfill.

Greening our hardscaping may involve weighing the pros and cons of different materials and making tradeoffs based on our priorities. It can require us to find local, natural or salvaged materials. It can involve finding water-permeable materials that reduce stormwater runoff. Or it may mean simply reducing the amount of hardscaping, allowing moss, grasses, ground covers and other plant materials to play a larger role in our landscape design.

▶ **Creating an organic edible garden.** Rather than *consuming* ornamental plants purchased at a garden store, we can *produce* an edible garden, turning the yard into a *productive asset*. That can make us more self-reliant in the face of economic challenges and more resilient if weather emergencies or other calamities temporarily interrupt our food supply. Growing our own produce is also one of the best ways to know the source of our food. Gardening organically can be a healthy choice for us and the environment, keeping toxins out of our food, the soil and the local watershed. (More information: Chapter 3, Food)

▶ **Taking organic to another level.** Organic gardening isn't just for food. The chemical fertilizers, weed killers and herbicides used to produce greener lawns, larger plants and more abundant flowers may contribute to air pollution, soil degradation and toxic runoff. (Residential lawns and gardens actually use more pesticides per acre than farms or other types of land.[47]) As noted in Chapter 3, Food, chemicals also can weaken or eliminate the soil's ability to act as a natural carbon sink. There are many organic landscaping products available for lawns, shrubs and flowering plants. Fish emulsion and seaweed emulsion fertilizers, two staples of organic food gardening, are just as useful for nonedible plants. Soil tests can help us determine if we should also consider adding supplements to the soil.

Distilled white vinegar makes a very effective weed killer that won't harm the environment. The vinegar can be dispersed using a handheld sprayer.

▶ **Sharing the landscape.** An alternative that's increasingly popular with sharing enthusiasts is gardening across property lines. As discussed in Chapter 3, Food, where homes are relatively close together, some neighbors are collaborating to create larger, more productive food gardens that span two or more yards. Others are exchanging the bounty of one homeowner's garden for another's fruit trees… or playsets or babysitting services. Still others are forming gardening partnerships that allow an individual who doesn't have a plot of land to assist someone who does in exchange for access to some of the harvest. Composting bins and tool sheds are among the other elements that can be shared for mutual benefit. Garden sharing can help build community ties while ensuring that more of us can afford access to fresh, healthy food. In addition to working out an agreement with neighbors, it may be possible to find garden-sharing arrangements at sites such as sharedearth.com.

▶ **Becoming an apartment gardener.** We can benefit from surrounding ourselves with plants even when space is limited. In fact, plants can play a particularly important role for those living in urban areas with limited access to nature. They help improve air quality, absorbing CO_2 and other pollutants and releasing fresh oxygen. They can have a calming effect, offering a respite from the built environment. They offer us their natural beauty. And they can provide a low-cost source of food.

House plants, potted trees and succulent-adorned green walls are among the alternatives available for greenscaping an apartment. For those interested in edible gardening, a sunny windowsill or balcony can provide enough space for potted tomatoes, peppers or herbs. Many apartment complexes also have thriving community gardens located wherever space allows—on a patch of lawn next to the building, in an interior courtyard or up on the roof. In addition to enabling us to grow food on a larger scale than possible at home, a community garden can help us learn from other gardeners and forge a sense of community with our neighbors. If we own our apartment and are ready to sell, we may even find the garden to be an asset since a community garden is now widely viewed as a selling point. If our building doesn't already have a community garden—and if there is enough interest from residents— it may be possible to take the lead in establishing a new garden.

Housemates and Neighbors

Another way to make homelife more sustainable is to share space with others. Co-living is on the rise, particularly at two ends of the generational spectrum: millennials and the newly retired. Shared living arrangements can be economically sustainable, enabling us to live on less income. They may help us form or strengthen connections to community. And by reducing the need for more housing, they can lighten our environmental footsteps, helping to preserve open space and reduce the impact of sprawl and consumption. Alternatives for incorporating sharing into a sustainable homelife include:

▶ **Finding roommates.** While the initial motivation for taking on roommates may be more economic than environmental, living with others automatically reduces our environmental impact. Adding inhabitants to an existing residence is a way of using "untapped capacity," reducing the need for additional dwellings and furnishings. Living together can further help us reduce consumption if we purchase food and other household necessities with housemates or share other types of resources, such as transportation, household goods or meals. Besides renting with others, we may want to explore co-purchasing a home. While this may require special contract considerations, it can present an affordable opportunity to become a homeowner.

▶ **Buying into a cohousing development or ecovillage.** There are several hundred of these intentional communities located throughout the country, including some communities just for seniors. While their goals and bylaws vary, most allow residents to own private homes while gaining some of the benefits of communal living, including participation in collective governance and decision-making. Many cohousing communities incorporate green building and landscaping methods into their design. Most also support sharing and community resiliency. For example, communities typically have communal dining halls, recreational areas and other public spaces that allow residents to gather. Residents may decide to further explore sharing and community resiliency by creating commercial-scale community kitchens, community gardens, tool libraries or seed libraries, shared studio space or guest housing. Or they may choose to operate cooperative childcare or eldercare services or invest collectively in green initiatives such as greywater irrigation systems or community-scale renewable energy generation.

It's also possible to create our own cohousing groups. Casual cohousing can involve a small group of friends living in adjacent homes or apartments with shared communal spaces (e.g., gardens, kitchens, recreational areas, music rooms or art studios). It also may take the form of adding rental units on a property or collaboratively purchasing a single property or adjacent homes.

▶ **Moving into artist housing.** Low-income housing tax credits (LIHTCs) have been used for many years to support subsidized housing for artists, musicians, teenage moms, firefighters, teachers and other groups with shared interests or needs. In 2007, the IRS challenged the use of these tax credits for artist housing, claiming that it violated the intention of the law: to help low-income Americans obtain affordable housing. Arts groups successfully lobbied Congress to amend the tax credit law to specifically include artist housing. There is some controversy over whether using the tax credits for artists unintentionally discriminates against or harms the broader low-income community, but the artists who qualify for tax credits do earn less than the nation's median household income. Specialized housing of this type offers an opportunity for individuals who would otherwise be priced out of vibrant urban communities to pursue creative (though sometimes low-paying) careers. Housing for visual or performing artists also can be a sustainable economic choice for cities and municipalities because the arts tend to play a critical role in revitalizing local economies.

> ### Sharing Home Maintenance
>
> From collaboratively purchasing landscaping services, gutter cleaning, housekeeping or general repair services to collectively working on home, yard and neighborhood improvements, there are many opportunities to extend sharing into the area of home and yard maintenance. Forming a neighborhood home improvement group can allow neighbors to help neighbors, reducing household expenses, building community ties and enhancing both property values and quality of life for everyone on the block.

▶ **Sharing a room—or a sofa—with strangers.** This is the idea behind Airbnb, which lets individuals tap their home's unused capacity and turn one of their largest expenses into a source of extra income. Besides sharing—or renting out—a room to vacationers, it's possible to share co-working space in the form of a spare office or even a kitchen table. (More information: Chapter 7, Work, Play and Retirement) If we can engage in these types of transactions through a platform cooperative that offers true peer-to-peer sharing, we may be able to earn a bit more and maintain greater control over the terms of each "share."

Retirement Living

It's also possible to take a sustainable approach to living arrangements throughout our retirement years.

▶ **Scaling down.** Retirement typically is a time when we move from a larger home, often the place where we raised a family, to one that is smaller, less expensive and easier to maintain. As mentioned earlier in this chapter, one of the greenest decisions we can make with regard to where we live is to think small. By moving to a smaller home, we can reduce our impact on open space, reduce the environmental footprint associated with building materials, furnishings and household possessions and lower our energy use and expense. A smaller home also may make it easier to live on a reduced or fixed income, enabling greater economic self-reliance and resiliency.

▶ **Living in town.** Many retirement communities are located far from town centers. But some retirees are opting to move into less isolated settings—cities, college towns or other walkable communities. Living in town could eliminate the need for a car, helping us reduce our contribution to greenhouse gas emissions. We may have access to public transportation or opportunities to walk or bike, the latter offering the added benefit of regular exercise. (Walkscore.com can help us locate walkable communities.) In-town living also can give us easy access to educational and cultural resources. And the option of moving into an apartment or townhouse can open the door to new social connections as well as greater convenience as we age. As the next generation of retirees expresses an interest in the environmental and social benefits of in-town living, some retirement community developers are responding by choosing to build in existing population centers rather than continuing to purchase and develop farmland.

▶ **Creating a DIY retirement community.** As baby boomers reach the age at which their parents moved into communities for active seniors or into continuing care communities, they're reimagining the idea of "retirement community." Some are revisiting communal living options. While actual communes may not make a comeback, some boomers are seeking to create their own planned communities with friends or other like-minded retirees willing to provide each other with companionship, care and support for as long as possible. These arrangements can be economically sustainable, helping cohabitators save money on everything from housing and food to home-care services. They can provide individuals with support during periods of illness and encourage wellness by facilitating companionship. Like any form of shared housing, retirement cohousing also can help reduce our impact on the environment by making it easier to share resources.

Retirees can create communal living arrangements in a variety of ways, from purchasing adjacent town homes to co-purchasing houses or apartments to moving into cohousing developments or ecovillages that may have residents of all ages. In some cases, retrofitting existing premises may be helpful to accommodate needs as we age. While living with strangers is one possibility, another is moving in with extended family members in a multi-generational home.

▶ **Aging in place.** Numerous surveys have found that a majority of retirees express a strong preference for staying in their own homes and communities as late in life as possible. In fact, the prevalence of neighborhoods and apartment buildings with large concentrations of older, long-time residents has given rise to an *aging in place* movement committed to allowing individuals to live out their days in *naturally occurring retirement communities (NORCs)*. The term "NORC" also refers to programs that focus on delivering community-based social services to older individuals living independently. NORCs may coordinate nursing or social worker visits or help locate services and resources—from maintenance, housekeeping, cooking and transportation to educational, entertainment and social opportunities—that can enable retirees to continue living independently even when they are no longer able to drive or maintain their homes.

Retirees interested in aging in place also can benefit from having their homes retrofitted for safety and accessibility to accommodate their needs as health and mobility decline. Municipalities can make a difference by providing supportive resources such as increased public transportation or access to educational and cultural programs. Some municipalities are even exploring structural retrofits to buildings, streets and public spaces to make them more accessible and welcoming for individuals of all ages. By enabling older individuals to stay within the community, these and other aging-in-place efforts may begin to reverse the decades-long trend of isolating seniors from mainstream society, setting the stage for more diverse and inclusive communities.

For those requiring ongoing care, two other trends are helping to keep seniors in community settings. Medicare and Medicaid now cover more of the expense of home health care. (Medicare coverage is only available for those requiring skilled nursing care while Medicaid's Home and Community-Based Services (HCBS) represent an optional benefit for those that qualify.) And some of the newest nursing homes are taking the form of apartments or stand-alone dwellings integrated into mixed-age residential communities. There is evidence that aging-in-place services, home health care and decentralized nursing care settings can all play a role in reducing the costs associated with caring for the elderly and disabled.[48] Allowing individuals to maintain their lifestyle preferences for as long as possible also may contribute to improved health and longevity.

Doing More

We can support a more sustainable homelife for everyone by:

▶ Choosing eco-friendly furnishings, cleaning products and landscaping materials whenever possible;

▶ Pushing back against efforts to weaken environmental regulations that protect our air and water and that help ensure the safety of household consumer products; and

▶ Supporting renewable energy over fossil fuels.

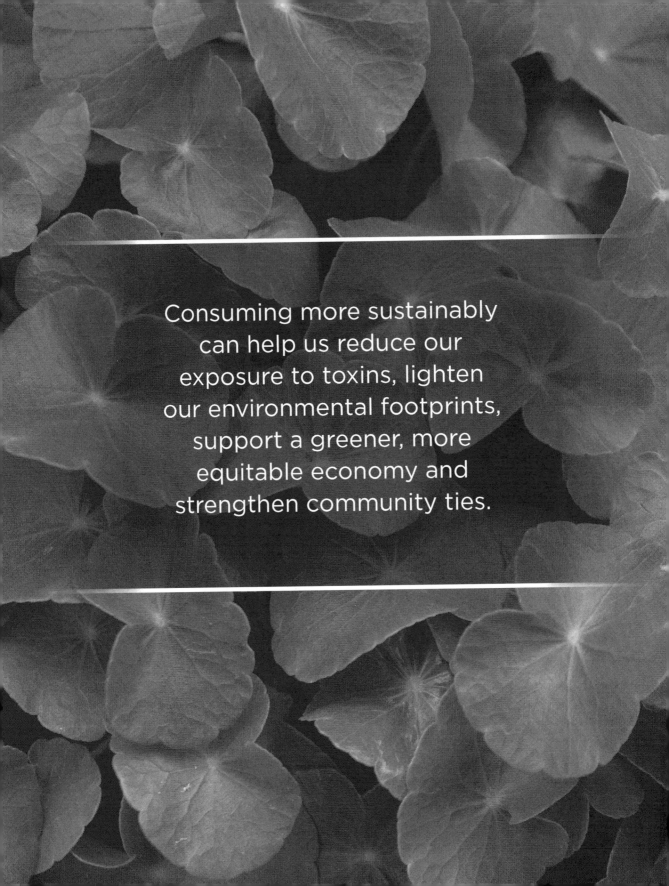

Consuming more sustainably can help us reduce our exposure to toxins, lighten our environmental footprints, support a greener, more equitable economy and strengthen community ties.

Consuming

We live in a consumer society. Consumer spending accounts for 70% of the U.S. economy.[1] Shopping is a national pastime.

We've all heard these consumer "facts." They encourage us to keep spending for the sake of the economy, even if that leaves us buried in debt. Tighter household budgets during the last major recession (the Great Recession of 2007 to 2009) led many of us to curb our shopping habit, at least for a while. During that period of low consumer confidence, some of us also began to embrace another consumer fact: We can use our purchasing power, however limited, to "vote with our dollars."

When food activists began encouraging us to view our consumer choices as a type of vote, they were making the point that we could change "the system" by preferencing organic and sustainably produced food over conventional choices. Many of us have been doing just that, buying organic, locally produced and fair trade food as much as possible. Increasingly, we're also voting with our dollars when it comes to product choices beyond food. We're seeking out green, nontoxic products to protect the environment and our health. We're preferencing local shops and producers to support the economic well-being of our communities. We're looking for the fair trade label on imported products to encourage ethical business practices overseas. And we're buying less so we can more easily live within our means while reducing our impact on pollution, climate change, natural resource depletion and waste. In short, more of us than ever before are recognizing that one of the most powerful roles we can play in the world is that of *socially conscious consumer*. We can embrace that role by:

1. **Consuming sustainably:** Shopping green, local or fair trade;

2. **Reducing consumption:** Living with less, replacing purchased goods with homemade alternatives, buying collectively and sharing as much as possible; and

3. **Managing waste:** Reducing, reusing, recycling and composting.

Consuming Sustainably

Each of our purchasing decisions can provide opportunities to live more sustainably. When we choose an eco-conscious product over a less sustainable option, our preferences are duly noted by marketers, who adjust their ideas about what to sell us next. When we shop locally, we help support independently owned local stores as well as entire downtown business districts. And when we seek out fair trade imports, we help ensure that ethical, environmentally responsible companies can continue competing in an otherwise exploitative global marketplace. Whether we're most concerned with environmental, economic or social forms of sustainability, we can wield our substantial consumer power by making choices like those that follow.

Shop Green

For many of us, consuming sustainably is synonymous with buying green or eco-friendly products. We may be motivated to shop green to protect our health, the well-being of the planet or both. But once we embrace the importance of greening our consumption, we can quickly become confounded in our attempts to identify which products are truly green. There are three challenges:

1. **Lack of transparency.** Unless federal regulatory agencies, such as the FDA (U.S. Food and Drug Administration) or USDA (U.S. Department of Agriculture), specifically require ingredient or content labeling, it can be difficult to learn exactly what a particular product contains. In the absence of transparent labeling requirements, companies interested in making their products seem eco-conscious can easily resort to greenwashing simply by using green-colored packaging and vague claims such as "natural" or "pure."

2. **Regulatory gaps.** The regulations intended to protect consumers and the environment ebb and flow with the political tides. But even when regulations exist, there is reason for concern about their adequacy. A long-time complaint of environmentalists has been the ineffectiveness of the Toxic Substances Control Act of 1976 (TSCA), the law intended to regulate chemicals used in consumer products. Critics say that only a handful of about 85,000 chemicals used in consumer products have undergone adequate safety testing prior to approval by the EPA.[2] Independent scientific studies have linked many of those chemicals to a wide range of health issues, including some that are life threatening. TSCA was revised in 2016 to require much more robust and independent research. But scientists at the EPA have expressed concern that it will take decades to catch up given the backlog of research required.

The revised law also is now under attack by anti-regulatory forces within the EPA.

Critics say inadequate regulation also has made it common for one chemical to be taken off the market only to be replaced by another that poses its own dangers. For example, BPA-free plastic often contains BPS, a nearly identical chemical;[3] and some of the newer pesticides that environmental scientists have identified as toxic are replacements for previously banned pesticides.

3. **The breadth of environmental problems.** Besides keeping track of which products could expose us to allergens, carcinogens or other toxins, we may want to know whether they are harming the environment in other ways. For example:

✓ Products may be made from nonrenewable natural resources or from resources extracted in ways that harm the environment and workers.

✓ Manufacturing processes may pollute soil, air and water.

✓ Workers involved in the manufacture of products may be exposed to toxins and/or unsafe equipment or processes.

✓ The transportation involved at every stage of the product life cycle, from the sourcing of raw materials to the distribution of finished goods, may burn fossil fuels, increasing greenhouse gas emissions.

✓ Product packaging may be excessive and/or nonrecyclable, contributing to landfill waste.

✓ The disposal of products may add to landfill waste and its impact on pollution and global warming.

Ideally, as we seek out eco-friendly products, we can choose alternatives that pass the "green test" at every stage of their lifecycle, all the way from the sourcing of raw materials to reuse or decomposition in the product afterlife. Companies committed to environmental responsibility generally make an effort to:

✓ Use only renewable or rapidly renewable resources.

✓ Reduce or eliminate manufacturing-related pollution by taking steps such as using nontoxic raw materials and installing appropriate smokestack filters and effective wastewater treatment systems.

✓ Reduce energy-related dependence on fossil fuels by increasing natural lighting in their facilities, switching to energy-saving LED lighting or powering their plants and/or vehicle fleets with renewable sources of energy.

✓ Protect the health and safety of workers on the job.

✓ Minimize waste through efficient production processes, reduced packaging and recycling. As noted in Chapter 2, a growing number of companies are even committing to a zero-waste strategy and a circular economy, producing their products and packaging from recycled materials and ensuring that old products can continue to be recycled into new goods indefinitely. (More information: Zero Waste and the Circular Economy sidebar, page 149)

✓ Ensure that products are safe and healthful for consumers.

Choosing Green Products

In the absence of full-proof regulations, consumers bear most of the responsibility for making choices that are healthy and green. Thanks to growing consumer demand and the ingenuity of sustainably minded entrepreneurs, it's becoming easier to find a wide range of eco-friendly products. We can confirm that a product is authentically green by:

✓ Checking labels for ingredients or contents, if provided.

✓ Learning how it is rated by the Environmental Working Group or the Good Guide. EWG's online consumer product rating tools (ewg.org) are excellent resources for personal care and household cleaning products, as well as for food. The free Good Guide app (goodguide.com) allows users to scan a product's bar code to learn how it is rated based on health, environmental and societal impacts. The app covers food as well as personal care, household and children's products.

✓ Researching companies to find out if they have committed to operating in an environmentally responsible manner. For example, we can learn whether a company is a B corporation by searching for the business on the site of B Lab (bcorporation.net). (More information: Chapter 1, Why It's Time for Holistic Sustainability, Chapter 7, Work, Play and Retirement, and Chapter 8, Money)

Nearly all of us have products at home that may pose risks to our health or the environment. Replacing those products all at once, before using them up, would be wasteful and costly. But when we run out of a particular product or it reaches the end of its useful life, we can take the opportunity to find an eco-friendly replacement. Some of the products we may be particularly interested in replacing with sustainable alternatives include those that follow. (Note that other types of products are covered elsewhere in the book.)

▶ **Personal care products.**[4] Along with food, personal care products can present our most significant exposure to potentially harmful chemicals since they are absorbed by our largest organ, our skin. While personal care products are regulated by the FDA under a law from 1938, the agency only requires manufacturers to list ingredients and provide warning labels. It does not require health studies or pre-market safety testing. (A law introduced in Congress in 2016 would have strengthened FDA regulations, but it failed to gain adequate support.) Regulators only have authority to intervene in taking a product off the market after an ingredient has been identified as harmful by other sources. Independent studies suggest that many shampoos, soaps, deodorants, perfumes, cosmetics, sun screens and even baby products contain ingredients that can harm our health.

Some commonly used ingredients that have been linked to health risks are: cocamide diethanolamine (DEA), triethanolamine (TEA), sodium lauryl sulfate (SLS), sodium laureth sulfate (SLES), triclosan, triclocarban, parabens, dimethyl dimethyl hydantoin, quaternium 15, talc, borax, bronopol, oxybenzone, imidazolidinyl urea, toluene and microbeads. (Microbeads, once used in toothpaste, facial scrubs, shampoos, nail polish and numerous other personal care products, have been found to end up in oceans and other waterways, where they can pose a threat to marine life that ingest them. The beads were banned by the Microbead-Free Waters Act of 2015.) Many personal care products also contain petrochemical-derived synthetic fragrances made with phthalates (discussed on page 131).

The sheer volume of ingredients in many personal care products can make it challenging to determine whether they contain known or suspected toxins. For those of us who aren't chemists, one of the easiest ways to reduce potential risks is to choose products certified as organic by the USDA. As with certified organic food, USDA-certified organic personal care products should be free of synthetic chemicals and GMOs. We also can seek out healthier alternatives using the Good Guide app or the Environmental Working Group's Skin Deep Cosmetics database. Like the organization's Guide to Healthy Cleaning Products, EWG's cosmetic guide rates products for health and environmental risks based on available scientific research. For those seeking low-cost alternatives and/or greater self-reliance, some personal care products, such as soaps and shampoos, can be made at home with ingredients found in the garden.

▶ **Canned goods.** Canned goods may contain BPA and phthalates (described on page 131), both linked to health concerns. BPA was first used in canned foods in the 1950s and 1960s, so this isn't a new problem. Nor is it a problem with all cans. But because the FDA does not require product labeling for canned goods, there's no way to know which cans contain BPA unless a company voluntarily provides that information. For most of us, it won't be easy or practical to eliminate all canned goods. Boxed packaging, which contains paper, aluminum foil and polyethylene, generally is considered safer. But the healthiest alternatives are buying fresh, unpackaged foods and producing our own homemade versions of canned goods, such as tomato sauces and soups.

▶ **Nonstick cookware.**[5] Great for frying eggs or sautéing veggies, nonstick cookware also is especially easy to clean. But as with many modern conveniences, nonstick surfaces may expose us to potentially harmful chemicals, including PTFE (polytetrafluoroethylene) and perfluorochemicals (PFCs) such as PFOA (perfluorooctanoic acid or C8). PTFE, which has been used since the 1940s, provides the nearly frictionless surface that has made nonstick cookware so popular. But exposure to fumes, both by workers involved in the manufacture of PTFE and consumers who heat cookware at high temperatures, can cause flu-like symptoms including headache, chills, fever, coughing and chest tightness. Fumes from cookware also have been known to kill pet birds. PFCs are considered toxic and they are persistent, remaining in our bodies and in the environment for many years. A large percentage of Americans are estimated to have detectable levels of PFCs such as PFOA in their blood. Scientists are still determining all of the sources of human exposure, but PFOA (along with other PFCs) has been found in drinking water and household dust. PFOA is a suspected carcinogen. Studies suggest that PFC exposure also may be linked to birth defects, endocrine system dysfunction, immune system disorders, high cholesterol, thyroid disease and harm to organs including the liver and pancreas.

PFCs also have been linked to environmental harm. The manufacture of PFOA has caused widespread pollution, including contamination of drinking water in some areas of the country. (More information: Chapter 3, Food) Pollution from PFOA and other PFCs comes not only from point sources, such as manufacturing facilities, but also from nonpoint sources, such as wastewater and landfill contamination from our use of products that contain these chemicals. Mounting evidence of harm to human health and the environment led the EPA to order the phaseout of PFOA, although regulation of the chemical has since been weakened. Similar compounds are still unregulated and widely used. We can reduce the environmental impact and health risks associated with these chemicals by living without nonstick cookware. Healthier alternatives include stainless steel, copper, ceramic and cast iron. There also are newer nonstick cookware alternatives on the market that don't contain PTFE, PFOA or cadmium. Unfortunately, it may be difficult to learn exactly what has replaced those chemicals and whether the replacements are any safer.

▶ **Takeout food containers made of polystyrene.**[6] Styrene, often referred to as Styrofoam, can dissolve in foods containing oils or butter. A known carcinogen, styrene also has been linked to liver damage and nervous system disorders. Additional sources of exposure to styrene include cigarette smoke, building materials, insulation materials and drinking water. The manufacture and disposal of styrene, which is nonbiodegradable, also contributes to greenhouse gas emissions, water pollution and landfill waste.

▶ **Anything stain- or water-resistant.**[7] It may seem desirable to have our new sofas or carpets treated for stain resistance. And we may not give much thought to how our raincoats or umbrellas manage to repel enough water to keep us relatively dry in a storm. But the modern miracles of stain resistance and waterproofing are brought to us by perfluorinated chemicals (PFCs), described previously. We can reduce our exposure by purchasing new soft furnishings that have not been treated with stain blockers and limiting our use of waterproof clothing. (More information on furnishings: Chapter 4, Home)

▶ **Nonreusable and nonrecyclable paper products.** The production of paper can contribute to deforestation, pollution and greenhouse gas emissions, while its disposal can add to toxic landfill waste.[8] We can reduce these negative impacts by choosing unbleached 100% recycled paper products and replacing nonreusable plates, napkins and tablecloths with reusable alternatives. We also can choose to go paperless, using electronic bill pay services, opting for electronic rather than paper receipts and printing less.

▶ **Electronics.** It wasn't that long ago that a typical household's electronics consisted of a few television sets, a stereo system and perhaps a ham radio. Today we're obviously inundated with electronics, which continually shrink in size while containing far more computing power than the Mission Control mainframes that guided astronauts to the moon. While some hail the digital age as inherently green, mounting evidence disputes that claim. The manufacture of electronics, including smart phones, requires mining of rare earth and other heavy metals, a process that can be harmful to workers and highly toxic to the environment. Labor activists have found unhealthy and exploitative working conditions in off-shore electronics factories.[9] E-waste accounted for about 2.14 million tons of trash sent to landfill or incinerators as of 2013. Waste from both the production and disposal of electronics releases toxic chemicals and heavy metals that contaminate soil and groundwater.[10, 11] And extensive use of electronic devices may pose health risks, including eye strain and vision deterioration from staring at computer screens,[12] orthopedic problems such as carpal tunnel syndrome, upper-back pain and cervical spine injury from poor posture at our desktops[13] and cerebral tumors, suspected by some scientists of being linked to use of cell phones.[14] Most of us won't want (or be able) to live without our electronics. But we can take steps to protect our health. And we can do our part to encourage the industry to live up to its green promise. For example, we can:

Place safety first. We can reduce the health impact of electronics by taking practical steps, such as:

✓ Ensuring that our workstation setups, including the position of our screens, keyboards and chairs, are ergonomic.

✓ Holding cell phones to our ears as little as possible, choosing instead to use the speaker setting or wear earbuds or a Bluetooth headset.

✓ Unplugging. We could probably all benefit from spending less time with our phones and other devices and more time with our friends and family members…or ourselves. Neuroimaging research has shown that addiction to online gaming and other excessive Internet use can reduce brain function in areas related to emotion, attention, decision-making and cognition. Even "ordinary" daily screen time can reduce our concentration and creativity and interfere with sleep. The dangers may be more significant for children and teens, placing them at risk of diminished academic performance and behavioral problems.[15]

Purchase Energy Star-rated electronics, which must meet energy efficiency standards set by the U.S. Department of Energy and use eco-friendly materials with minimal packaging and maximum recyclability.

Conserve and repair. We can reduce energy consumption and potentially extend the life of our electronics by choosing power-saving settings, turning off screen savers and closing programs we're not using. We also may be able to delay purchasing new devices simply by having existing equipment repaired.

Recycle responsibly. Electronics may be among the most important items to recycle given their potential environmental impact in landfill. According to the EPA, recycling of e-waste has been steadily rising, reaching 40.4% in 2013, up from 30.6% in 2012.[16] (More information: Recycling, pages 151 to 152)

Boycott or speak out to demand that electronics companies protect workers and the environment.

▶ **Plastics.** "Can't live with or without them" may sum up our relationship with the miracle materials that shape much of modern life. While it's difficult to imagine a world without plastics, environmental scientists warn that it's important to be aware of the potential risks they can pose to the environment and our health. The manufacture of plastics contributes to air pollution when chemical by-products are released into the atmosphere.[17] The durability that makes plastic such a useful material also makes it nonbiodegradable. Americans discard about 33.6 million tons of plastic each year, with only 6.5% recycled and 7.7% combusted in waste-to-energy facilties.[18] And plastics that escape the waste stream often find their way to the ocean, creating floating garbage dumps that harm and kill marine life and birds.[19] A growing body of evidence also suggests that exposure to the many chemicals in plastics can pose significant risks to human health. As with personal care products, there are countless chemicals of concern, including polyethylene terephthalate (PETE or PET), high-density polyethylene (HDPE), polyvinyl chloride (PVC), low density polyethylene (LDPE), polypropylene, poly-carbonate and polystyrene (Styrofoam).[20] Two categories of chemicals found in plastics that have received a lot of attention are BPA (bisphenol A) and phthalates.

BPA is used in the manufacture of polycarbonate plastics. It is found in plastic water bottles, baby bottles, rigid plastic dishes and many other everyday items made from plastic as well as in the epoxy resin linings of many canned foods and beverages. Industrial waste from the production of plastics containing BPA is believed to have contaminated rivers, estuaries and soils. As plastics made with BPA deteriorate, the chemical is believed to migrate to household dust particles and into the air we breathe. Studies have found that due to widespread use, significant levels of BPA are present in samples of urine, cord blood, amniotic fluid and breast milk in a wide swath of the population. BPA is known to be *estrogenic*, meaning it imitates naturally occurring estrogens, and studies have linked BPA exposure to health problems including diabetes, heart disease and certain cancers. BPA may be most dangerous at low concentrations. Exposure in utero and in infancy and childhood are believed to be the most harmful. There is evidence that in utero exposure to BPA can change genetic predisposition to diseases that may not develop until much later in life. Safety concerns led the European Union to ban BPA in baby bottles in 2011 and Japanese manufacturers to discontinue its use between 1998 and 2003. In the U.S., the FDA has acknowledged that BPA poses health risks. But the agency doesn't have authority to regulate BPA and the chemical remains in widespread use. Consumer concern has led some companies to voluntarily remove BPA from reusable plastic water bottles and other items. Unfortunately, this is a case in which a known toxin may be getting replaced with a virtually identical agent, BPS (bisphenol S).[21]

Phthalates, which comprise a very large group of chemicals, are essential to making plastics both durable and flexible. They can be found in plastic cookware, tool handles, computers, the plastic components and accessories in cars, vinyl flooring, toys and medical devices, including IV bags. Phthalates also are prevalent in a diverse range of non-plastic consumer products, such as soup can linings and other food packaging (including packaging for organic foods), cleansers, air fresheners, shampoos, nail polish, other cosmetics and personal care products, furniture and carpeting. Phthalates pose a health risk because the chemicals are unstable, especially when heated, and because they accumulate in our bodies over time. As the chemicals build up in our bloodstream, they can act as endocrine disrupters, increasing our risk of reproductive and fertility issues and certain cancers. Studies also have linked phthalates to a wide range of other health problems. The most vulnerable populations may be pregnant women and young children. As far back as 2003, the extent of our exposure to phthalates was noted by the

Centers for Disease Control and Prevention (CDC), which found the chemicals in samples taken from a cross-section of Americans. While research has led to some regulation by states and the federal government, phthalates remain ubiquitous in consumer products and are mostly unregulated.[22]

Reducing Exposure to Plastics

Since plastic is such a useful and necessary material and so widely used, it can present sustainable consumers with a conundrum. As safer plastics, such as "bio-based" plastic alternatives made from corn and other plants, become more widely available, we may be able to enjoy all the benefits of plastic with fewer risks. For now, we may want to take the precaution of limiting our net exposure. For example, we can:

Phase out plastic food containers. Up until fairly recently, plastic containers numbered 2, 4 or 5 were considered safe because they don't contain BPA or phthalates. But a study published in the scientific journal *Environmental Health Perspectives* concluded that, when it comes to food, there's no such thing as safe plastic.[23] Replacing all our plastic food containers can be a challenge, especially when we need portability, such as for school lunches or weekend picnics. But, as possible, we can opt for safer alternatives, such as stainless steel, ceramic and glass. Even when buying organic foods, it's best to choose glass packaging over plastic. For plastic containers we can't live without, we can reduce our risk exposure by keeping them out of the microwave and dishwasher and using them only for foods that don't contain oils (as discussed below).

Wrap safely. Plastic wrap, another staple in most kitchens, may present both health and environmental concerns. As with other plastic products, plastic wrap is made from by-products of petroleum, increasing the use of fossil fuels. The lightweight film also can cause problems once it enters the waste stream since it doesn't biodegrade and can easily blow away and end up clogging sewers and entering streams. Additionally, a lot of plastic wrap is now made from low-density polyethylene (LDPE), which may contain diethylhydroxylamine (DEHA), a suspected endocrine disrupter linked to breast cancer in women and low sperm count in men. DEHA may leach into our food if we use plastic wrap to cover dishes in the microwave. As with other plastics, this risk is greater with oily or fatty foods.[24] Healthier alternatives include unbleached wax paper made with soybean oil, recycled wax paper bags from cereal or cracker boxes or homemade cloth covers. We also can purchase eco-friendly wraps and bags for food storage at Whole Foods and at sites such as ecobags.com. Biodegradable plastic wrap currently is being developed.

Sustainability and Our Children

Much of the information in chapters 3 through 5 is relevant to both children and adults. But since babies and children generally are more vulnerable to toxins, many will want to focus their green buying decisions on their children. That may include choosing organic bedding, organic or eco-friendly personal care products, non-plastic toys, particularly for younger children still exploring the world with their mouths, and stainless steel beverage and food containers. When it comes to clothing, organic may be best. Environmentalists say children's clothes also should not be treated with certain fire retardants, which are suspected of off-gassing even after repeated washings and are associated with serious health concerns.

Avoid heat. As mentioned previously, we can reduce the risk of exposure to toxins in plastics by keeping them away from heat, which can destabilize molecules, increasing our risk exposure. Specifically, we should avoid microwaving food in plastic containers, washing plastic plates, utensils, cups or containers in the dishwasher or storing plastic water or soda bottles in a warm location.[25]

Avoid oils. Chemicals in plastics also can become unstable when exposed to fats and oils, such as those in salad dressings, mayonnaise and other condiments.[26] While plastic bottles are less expensive and, of course, less breakable than glass containers, they may expose us to toxins. Glass bottle packaging is more difficult to find but tends to be available in smaller-sized containers and products that are USDA-certified organic.

Drink water from reusable bottles.[27] Bottled water may be one of the best examples of greenwashing around. Influenced by the questionable health claim that we should consume about eight glasses of water a day, many of us began purchasing bottled water around a decade ago, convinced it was healthier than water from the tap. Bottlers have claimed that their "spring" water comes from pure mountain streams, free of pollutants. In fact, much of it comes from public water supplies (the same as tap water) and doesn't offer any bona fide health benefits. Worse, plastic water bottles are associated with a number of health and environmental concerns. Studies have found that the bottles often contain a large number of petroleum-based chemicals, including some that may act as endocrine disruptors. The production and distribution of the bottles requires large amounts of fossil fuel. And only about 30% of all plastic water bottles are recycled, with the rest contributing to landfill waste and ocean pollution. Bottled water also is subjected to less rigorous regulation than household tap water.

Other consumer product categories are covered elsewhere in this book:

Food: Chapter 3, Food

Furniture and cleaning products: Chapter 4, Home

Clothing: Dressing Sustainably sidebar, pages 140 to 141

Children's products: throughout

Sustainability and Our Pets

When it comes to our pets, we can take a sustainable approach by:

Adopting responsibly. Animal rights activists want us to know that, each year, millions of cats and dogs are abandoned and eventually euthanized, while many exotic and non-domesticated animals are released into the wild or otherwise removed from households. We can help alleviate these problems by adopting from rescue organizations, avoiding puppy mills, choosing common domesticated pets that have not been captured in the wild (and that are not members of endangered species), making a long-term commitment to our pets and having them spayed or neutered.

Buying sustainable pet products. From bedding to kitty litter to toys, collars and leashes, it's now possible to buy pet products made from organic, natural or recycled materials. Homemade and old-fashioned alternatives also may be worth exploring, with our veterinarian's approval. (Chapter 3, Food covers sustainable pet food.)

Boxed water is a new addition to the marketplace that offers several sustainable benefits. The cartons are made from wood pulp derived from sustainably harvested forests. The containers and caps are fully recyclable. And because the boxes are shipped flat and only filled at a filling center, the product takes up less space than bottled water and may require fewer trucks to transport. The water is from municipal sources, just like tap water. Usually, the healthiest alternative remains filling a reusable stainless steel water bottle with our own tap water. But, while the U.S. generally has very safe drinking water, there are growing concerns about local contamination from lead and other toxins. The EWG's Water Filter Guide is a useful resource for those who believe their household water may need filtration.[28] Chapter 3, Food provides more information on safe drinking water.

Replace PVC vinyl shower curtains and liners.[29] That new shower curtain smell may seem fresh and clean. But environmental scientists have attributed the odor to chemicals that can pose risks to both us and the environment. In particular, they warn that these shower curtains can off-gas, producing indoor air pollution that may increase our risk of headaches, nausea and a wide range of serious health problems. Healthier alternatives include liners made from linen, organic cotton or hemp. The latter is naturally mildew-resistant.

Shop Local

Another way to become a more sustainable consumer is to shop locally whenever possible. As discussed in Chapter 2, keeping our consumer dollars local can help reduce our carbon footprint and show support for independently owned businesses that have demonstrated environmental responsibility. Along with other localist strategies, shopping local also can help support or create strong, community-based economies.

In recent years, some communities have embraced "shop local" campaigns to help revitalize their downtown shopping districts. Downtowns were hit hard by the Great Recession. But, in many cases, the demise of local shopping districts actually began decades ago, when large, enclosed shopping malls first enticed us with an unprecedented variety of stores, other forms of entertainment (e.g., movies, restaurants, arcades) and abundant free parking. Next came the "big box" discounters, which by the 1990s seemed to be upstaging malls, offering a no-frills shopping experience in exchange for supersized discounts. Unable to compete, many small, independently owned stores closed their doors, sometimes taking entire downtowns along with them. Critics have described the success of discount chains as both a cause and symptom of the vicious cycle triggered by globalization. The steep discounts offered by these chains were made possible by inexpensive imports produced either by foreign manufacturers or American companies that offshored operations wherever they could find the lowest production costs. The theory is that as American workers lost good-paying manufacturing jobs, their buying power shrank, making discount stores not just attractive but essential.

The emergence of online retail in the early 2000s dealt another blow to downtown shopping districts. As of 2017, online shopping actually represented only about 8.9%[30] of total retail sales, with the vast majority of sales still taking place at brick-and-mortar businesses.[31] But e-commerce continues to grow rapidly, winning over even the greenest shoppers, thanks to its ability to offer unparalleled variety and convenience while keeping many purchases free of shipping fees and sales tax. Online shopping also has been adopted as green, even though it tends to support global transport of goods that is far more fossil-fuel-intensive than a mere trip into town.

While national chains seem to be succumbing to online competition, the state of independent downtown shopping districts remains mixed today, with some responding well to shop local campaigns and others continuing to slip away due to cash-strapped consumers and nonlocal competition. If we've been watching our own favorite local stores struggle to stay in business from one year to the next, our options should be clear: We can either accept the loss of our downtown shopping districts, along with all the environmental, economic and social benefits they offer, or we can make a commitment to "love our local."

Like being a *locavore* with food, becoming a local shopper can offer several sustainable benefits.

▶ **A lighter environmental footprint.** It's often said that shopping local reduces our carbon footprint. And it's true that taking a short drive, walk, or bike ride into town is less carbon-intensive than making a journey to a nonlocal mall. But, by that measure, online shopping is better yet, since it involves no driving at all (except for the delivery trucks that bring online purchases to our homes, burning fossil fuel along the way). The greater carbon impact of nonlocal shopping comes from the global transport of goods. Even as American consumers have rediscovered the benefits of buying local and American-made, we continue to purchase many consumer products that are either entirely made overseas or contain raw materials or parts from outside the U.S.

While trade has always existed, the globalization of consumer goods was accelerated by trade agreements such as NAFTA and CAFTA, which lowered or eliminated many trade tariffs on imports. Another huge factor has been the low cost and efficiency of container shipping, which has supported a global consumer product supply chain in which raw materials from one country may be shipped to another for processing or manufacture, another for packaging, then back to the country of origin to be exported around the world. Globally, about 90% of

---

When Online Is Local

While only about 28% of small businesses have an e-commerce presence,[32] it is possible to shop local—or at least small—online by:

▶ *Buying online from retailers we know to be small and independently owned, including businesses located in our communities.*

▶ *Seeking out vendors that promote themselves as members of a particular geographic community on makersites such as Etsy.*

▶ *Buying from independent sellers on online sites. Some of these sellers struggle to attract enough foot traffic at their brick-and-mortar locations.*

▶ *Checking out the shopping section of a town's visitor website to locate businesses that sell online.*

consumer goods are transported on container ships.[33] And critics say those ships run on a relatively inexpensive and dirty brand of crude oil known to emit exceptionally high levels of both greenhouse gases and other pollutants.[34] Just 15 of the largest cargo ships can produce as much sulfur and other pollutants as all the cars in the world combined.[35] Studies also have described the carbon dioxide (CO_2) emissions from container ships as the equivalent—if they constituted a nation—of the world's sixth-largest greenhouse gas emitter.[36]

While it may seem insignificant, we can help reduce the environmental impact of global consumerism by doing more of our shopping at independently owned local businesses. We can have an even greater impact by localizing our consumption from *source to household*, seeking out products made locally from locally sourced raw materials. In addition to reducing the impact of consumption on global warming and pollution, relocalizing the supply chain can help us create and sustain a strong, community-based economy founded on local natural resources.

▶ **Economic stability.** As described in Chapter 2, shopping local also triggers a multiplier effect, keeping money within a community and setting in motion a virtuous cycle that can help strengthen the local economy. According to one source, for every dollar spent at a local business, 45 cents is reinvested locally, compared with only 15 cents of a dollar spent at a national chain.[37] Another source puts the numbers at 68 cents for local spending versus 43 cents for non-local.[38] An example of the local multiplier effect would be the owner of a clothing store using the money we spent on our new fall wardrobe to purchase lunch at the sandwich shop across the street, have her car serviced at the local gas station and, of course, pay wages to her employees. Each of her local purchases and expenditures would generate others, and so on. If we came into town to shop at the clothing store but stayed to shop elsewhere or run errands, we would create what economists call a *downstream* multiplier effect. And if we bought locally made goods produced from locally sourced raw materials, we would extend the effect further by involving additional local businesses.

Most of us won't be able to localize all our purchases. But each time we opt for local over nonlocal, we can make a small but meaningful difference. We can help create the need for additional hiring at stores, restaurants, service businesses or even small manufacturing companies. We may help inspire budding entrepreneurs to take a chance on the local economy. And we can help support the municipal tax base that is so important to our schools and first responders.

▶ **Community resiliency.** Shopping local also can help us create and sustain safe, resilient, interconnected communities. When local stores are able to attract shoppers, downtowns become fertile ground for restaurants, other food businesses and cultural venues. Locally owned businesses may offer us products, foods or entertainment that reflect the distinct cultural tastes of the area (rather than bland, mass-produced offerings that could be found nearly anywhere). Busy sidewalks, parks and other common spaces can provide the backdrop for community celebrations and concerts. And a vibrant downtown street life can reduce the incidence of crime while giving us ample opportunities to enjoy being members of a cohesive community.

Choosing Local

We can become local consumers by:

▶ **Shopping downtown.** If we're fortunate enough to have access to even a small downtown shopping district, we can help support it by finding opportunities to shop there instead of someplace outside the community. In particular, we can make an effort to buy less online and more in town. For example, we might use the Internet to research a product but then find out if it's available at a local store. Many shopkeepers will be willing to order desired items if they don't have them in stock. We also can make a point of strolling through town occasionally to find out what shops are available to us. Small, independently owned stores may not always be able to compete with online retailers based on variety, price and convenience. But they can offer us other important benefits, including friendly, knowledgeable service, the ability to see and touch a product before it arrives at our door, the pleasure of discovering items not already on our "search list" and the possibility of bumping into friends and neighbors while we shop.

▶ **Shopping "local" away from home.** If our community doesn't have a downtown shopping district, we can shop local by visiting places that do. Many weekend getaway destinations and vacation areas feature revitalized downtowns full of unique shops, restaurants and entertainment venues. Communities with vibrant retail districts also may host a wide range of events and activities that attract both locals and visitors throughout the year.

▶ **Purchasing goods produced locally.** Some communities have revitalized their economies by supporting specialized local production. Whether we're home or on vacation, we can seek out locally produced products that may represent the foundation of a local economy. For example, if a town has a large population of artists and craftspeople, we may be able to purchase original artwork at galleries or artists' studios. If a rural community has farms that market directly to consumers and small businesses,

> ### Budgeting for Our Values
>
> *Green, local and fair trade goods often cost more than their less sustainable counterparts. For that higher price, we may enjoy benefits including healthier products, a cleaner environment or a stronger local economy. Even so, there's no getting around the fact that many consumers will have difficulty paying more for everyday products. One way to make sustainability more affordable is to budget for it. By keeping track of day-to-day expenses for a few weeks, we may discover that there are some items we could happily live without in exchange for a greener, more sustainable way of life.*

we may have opportunities to purchase farm-fresh food at roadside stands and farmers' markets or enjoy restaurant meals prepared with locally sourced meats, produce and dairy products. Similarly, if an area has become home to vineyards, microbreweries or small-scale distilleries, we may be able to stock up on artisanal local libations.

▶ **Purchasing goods made with locally sourced raw materials.** Depending on where we live, we may have opportunities to buy goods produced from indigenous natural resources. A local farm may be the source of flax for locally designed clothing, wool for a local weaver's shawls or plants used to make herbal remedies. Similarly, a local, sustainable forestry operation may supply wood for locally produced furniture, while a local quarry may provide masons and artisans with a source of local stone.

▶ **Supporting local culture.** Some communities are distinguished by the shared ethnicity or culture of residents. We can support that authentic heritage by enjoying its unique products, foods and celebrations.

▶ **Using local currency.** Some communities have established local currencies to encourage consumers to buy local. We can support these efforts and potentially receive discounts on our local purchases by trading in a few U.S. dollars for the complementary currency. (More information: Chapter 7, Work, Play and Retirement, and Chapter 8, Money)

▶ **Buying "made in the U.S.A."** When it's not possible to buy local, the next best thing is to choose products made regionally or at least someplace in the U.S.A. Like shopping local, buying American-made has become an increasingly popular choice in recent years. Buying American-made goods signals to manufacturers that we are willing to pay a bit more to keep jobs in our country. It may not reduce our carbon footprint as much as buying local, but it's likely to have

---

Comparing the Real Costs of Local versus Nonlocal

It's easy to argue that shopping local is too costly. Small, independent shops generally can't pass along the *economies of scale* offered by discount stores and large online retailers. But even when local purchases cost more, the externalities of our nonlocal purchases can make local ones seem far more affordable. For example, a drive to the mall is likely to require more gas, increasing the cost of our shopping trip. Buying products made offshore may contribute to job loss and income decline here in the U.S. And the environmental impact of nonlocal purchases may cost us, down the road, in the form of taxes, our health or a declining quality of life. By contrast, while we may (or may not) pay a bit more at local shops, we'll probably save gas and time, enjoy friendly, personalized service and experience all the environmental, economic and social benefits described previously.

a more positive impact than buying products imported from other parts of the world. American products also may be less harmful to us and the environment since our regulatory system, while far from perfect, establishes and enforces guidelines that may be entirely absent in developing nations.

▶ **Using shop local apps,** such as the 3/50 Project (the350project.net), to locate independently owned shops in our own community or the places we visit.

Shop Fair Trade

Even if we're committed local consumers, there are some products—bananas, coffee, chocolates—that can't be produced close to home. Of course, we also may simply fall in love with unique items made in distant lands. If we want to ensure that our foreign purchases won't contribute to environmental harm, exploitation of workers or destabilization of their communities, the most responsible choice is to look for products certified as fair trade. Some believe that by raising production standards in developing countries fair trade may even help slow the tide of American companies moving their operations overseas.

The *fair trade* concept is attributed to Edna Ruth Byler, founder of the nonprofit retailer Ten Thousand Villages. In the 1940s, Byler traveled with her missionary husband to Puerto Rico, where she became interested in helping local women sell their handcrafts. Her success at selling the goods back in the U.S. led Byler and her business partner, Ruth Lederach, to create the Overseas Needlepoint and Crafts Project, which eventually became Ten Thousand Villages. While the organization's handcraft stores have been around for many years, consumer demand for fair trade products has grown only recently, along with interest in green and ethically produced goods.

Today, there are many fair trade organizations involved in helping workers in the developing world earn a living selling their goods in more affluent markets. These organizations generally pursue their mission by offering companies or worker-producers the opportunity to have their products labeled "fair trade," a stamp of approval that lets them charge a premium price, if they adhere to certain criteria. As described in Chapter 2, fair trade organizations generally require producers to pay workers fairly, invest in workers' communities to help alleviate chronic poverty and operate in an environmentally responsible manner. As consumers, we can support fair trade by taking these steps:

▶ **Learn more about it.** Fair trade standards aren't regulated by the federal government, and they vary from one organization to the next. We can learn about a particular fair trade organization's guidelines by checking out their website or Facebook pages.

▶ **Buy products labeled "certified fair trade."** Fair trade once was limited to handcrafts and a few agricultural crops, such as coffee and bananas. It's now possible to find fair trade labels on a wide range of goods, including wines, flowers, specialty crops, jewelry and clothing.

▶ **Shop at fair trade retailers.** Ten Thousand Villages' stores continue to offer consumers the opportunity to shop fair trade. But there are now many other fair trade organizations and companies selling products online and at brick-and-mortar retail outlets. Examples include Fair Trade Federation, Fair Trade Winds, Society B, We Dash Love, Ethica, Accompany, Ames & Oates and The Little Market.

Dressing Sustainably[39]

Clothing has always been a challenging area for sustainable consumers, particularly those who also care about fashion. Unfortunately, the situation may have grown worse in recent years with the advent of "fast fashion." According to the documentary *The True Cost,* some clothing manufacturers responded to shrinking household budgets following the last major recession by offering consumers a constant stream of new "looks" at extremely low prices. The documentary suggests that the low cost and poor quality of these goods has encouraged consumers to discard clothing after only a few wears. The documentary also explores how the need to sell these inexpensive, readily disposable garments at a profit has led to a particularly aggressive approach to cost-cutting. That, in turn, has worsened two types of unsustainability in the fashion industry.

▶ **Labor practices.** Many clothing manufacturers produce garments overseas in an effort to reduce labor costs. Often, countries with low-wage workers also lack environmental and health and safety regulations. In some cases, long, complex supply chains can prevent companies from knowing exactly which factories are involved in producing their garments. That can leave even the most well-meaning companies dependent on factories with terrible working conditions. This problem was dramatized in 2012, when a fire in a Bangladesh textile factory killed more than 100 workers. Some clothing manufacturers responded to the tragedy by vowing not to work with similar factories in the future.[40]

▶ **Environmental and health issues.** The production of both fabrics and dyes can pose a range of potential environmental and health hazards. Cotton is a particularly water-intensive crop and conventional growers rely heavily on chemical inputs known to pollute waterways and threaten ecosystems.[41] Cotton clothing is not known to pose health risks to consumers. But studies have linked farmworkers' exposure to the agricultural chemicals used on cotton plantations with higher-than-average rates of certain cancers and other health problems. Workers exposed continuously to fibers from cotton and other materials also can develop respiratory illness.[42] The production of synthetic fabrics, such as polyester, rayon and nylon, which contain petroleum-derived by-products, can contribute to pollution and global warming.[43] Some clothing is coated or finished with the known carcinogen formaldehyde.[44] And chemical dyes used for clothing can pollute water supplies and expose workers and wearers to additional toxins and carcinogens.[45]

What to Wear

Some textile and clothing companies are beginning to clean up their supply chains, seeking out manufacturers that are more responsible to workers and the environment. There also is a new generation of farmers, entrepreneurs, small-scale fashion designers and retailers committed to offering sustainably made garments. (We can learn which companies are leading the way toward more sustainable clothing production at Greenpeace's Detox Catwalk, greenpeace.org.) The commitment of the former and success of the latter will depend largely on how much we, as consumers, align our clothing purchases with our values, consistently demanding choices that are green, local or fair trade. With a little extra effort, we can begin to:

▶ **Dress green.** Just as organic produce has undergone a metamorphosis over the past few decades, sustainable clothing has finally moved beyond "crunchiness" into a more fashionable and sophisticated realm.

▶ **Buy fair trade items at national chains.** The power we wield as conscious consumers is increasingly obvious at national retail chains, many of which now offer a range of sustainable product choices, including fair trade. Thanks to the significant buying power of large chains, they can help move fair trade and other sustainable choices from the economic margins to the mainstream.

▶ **Ask for it.** Shops that sell other sustainable products may be happy to add fair trade items if we ask for them.

▶ **Shop fair trade online.** If fair trade products aren't available in local stores (or wherever we travel), we can find them online at the sites of numerous fair trade organizations.

Eco-conscious clothing lines are now available everywhere from specialty boutiques to major department stores. It may still be a challenge to have an entirely green wardrobe, but adding a piece here and there can begin to make a difference. When shopping for sustainable garments, we can look for:

Organic and sustainably grown fibers and materials. This includes organic cotton, silk, rapidly renewable hemp, bamboo, flax, tencil (made from natural cellulose from wood pulp) and wool from sustainable farms. Organic cotton is grown without chemicals, protects biodiversity and allows more water to be retained by soil, reducing the need for irrigation. OEKO-TEC and GOTS labels indicate that cotton was grown sustainably. Cotton growers complying with the Better Cotton Initiative support environmental and social sustainability.

Shoes made with leather from organically raised livestock and soles from sustainable rubber plantations.

Natural, nontoxic dyes. This typically means the type of plant-based dyes and natural mordents (the minerals that make dyes color-fast) used for centuries prior to industrialization.

Recycled clothing, shoes and accessories. Buying vintage, swapping with friends or online communities, "shopping our closets" (i.e., taking a fresh look at the clothes we already own) and choosing clothing made from recycled materials can all help reduce natural resource depletion, pollution and landfill waste.

Dress, local, American-made or fair trade. As with other purchases, buying garments made locally, regionally or someplace in the U.S. can help reduce transportation-related use of fossil fuels while allowing us to support local economies and American jobs. For goods made outside the U.S., choosing fair trade lets us support environmental responsibility, workers' rights and social justice overseas.

Cleaning Our Clothes Sustainably

Even if our entire wardrobe is made from organic fair trade hemp, we still need to consider the environmental impact of cleaning our clothes.

▶ For clothes that are machine washable, the best green practices include (1) using cold water to conserve energy and reduce wear and tear and (2) choosing detergents rated as eco-friendly by an organization such as the Environmental Working Group.

▶ For clothes that require dry cleaning, the key is avoiding dry cleaners that use perchloroethylene, or "perc," which has been linked to cancer and memory loss as well as liver, kidney and central nervous system damage.[46] The EPA restricts the use of perc. Some states, including California, are in the process of phasing out its use. We can reduce our exposure by purchasing clothes that don't require dry cleaning, handwashing with eco-friendly soaps or, if we must dry clean, airing out clothes outside for a few hours before returning them to the closet. A list of green dry cleaners (such as those that use liquid CO_2 in high-pressure machines) can be found at wellbeing.com.

Reducing Consumption

Simply buying less may be one of the most sustainable steps we can take as consumers, helping us live within our means and lighten our environmental footsteps. There are three ways to accomplish this. We can:

1. Live with less;

2. Learn to make the products we need or want instead of purchasing them; and

3. Opt for access over ownership by sharing and finding other ways to consume collaboratively.

Living With Less

Our so-called consumer society encourages us to overconsume. That leads some of us to go on clothes shopping sprees to brighten our mood, only to end up with impulse purchases we rarely wear. Others buy supersized packages of goods at buyers' clubs, then end up tossing unused items in the trash. Still others stock their homes with all the accoutrements of domestic life without first considering what they'll actually use.

Even if it's not our style to wildly overconsume, we may be able to live comfortably with less. That doesn't mean we need to adopt a Spartan lifestyle or even forego every impulse purchase. But we may want to consider:

▶ **Planning.** Creating lists of items we need before we go shopping can help us become more focused consumers.

▶ **Planning financially.** The ability to use credit cards for larger purchases can convince us that it's unnecessary to delay gratification. Then, when the bills arrive, we realize we've exceeded our budget. Disciplining ourselves to save for big ticket items may help turn us into "slow consumers," taking more time to consider what we want, need and can afford.

▶ **Prioritizing quality.** It's easy to find household products—vacuum cleaners, toaster ovens, blenders—at what seem like attractive prices. But if a product isn't well made, we may end up replacing it far too soon. Buying quality products can cost us more up-front, but it's likely to save us money over the long term while also reducing waste.

Becoming Makers

Concerns about the impact of consumption on the environment and the need to survive in a "jobless economy" have inspired some of us to embrace ideas about self-reliance that were commonplace in the past. Emulating earlier generations of sub-sistence farmers and homemakers, today's DIY enthusiasts are foregoing consumption for production, making things they would otherwise need to buy. The blogosphere is full of creative ideas for adopting a DIY-maker lifestyle. Depending on our skills and interests, we can:

✓ Produce our own food, growing vegetables, berries and herbs, raising chickens and other livestock, processing harvest for storage, foraging, hunting, fishing and cooking at home. (More information: Chapter 3, Food)

✓ Make our own clothing by sewing, knitting, crocheting or weaving, or even produce our own fabric from homegrown flax or wool from a backyard flock of sheep.

✓ Create decorative items and gifts using raw materials from the garden, art sup-plies and odds and ends that we might otherwise discard.

✓ Build our own furniture or repurpose and refinish existing pieces.

✓ Make our own personal care and cleaning products using homegrown plants, essential oils and inexpensive, eco-friendly household staples, such as distilled white vinegar and baking soda. (More information on homemade cleaning products: Chapter 4, Home)

✓ Make virtually anything—or at least the prototype—using 3D printers and the resources available at makerspaces.

Sharing

Today's sharing economy actually is a social movement with roots in both the technologi-cal revolution that brought us open-source software, file sharing and social media and the back-to-the-land 1960s counterculture, with its experiments in communal living. Mod-ern-day sharing enthusiasts encourage us to adopt collaborative consumption—sharing, bartering, swapping and buying with others—to help us lighten our environmental foot-steps while reducing the need for income and forging stronger community ties.

The sharing movement's motto, "access over ownership," may sound radical to some—a challenge to our consumer economy or even capitalism itself. But sharing doesn't need to replace *all* consumption. As with other types of sustainability, even a moderate, incremental approach can make a meaningful difference. Whether we opt to make sharing our *raison d'etre* or simply view it as another tool for living more sus-tainably, it can help us:

✓ Spend less so that we can live within our means and make our financial lives more sustainable.

✓ Consume less so that we can reduce our impact on natural resources, greenhouse gas emissions, pollution and waste.

✓ Gain access to goods we might not want or need to own.

✓ Enjoy new friendships and social connections within our sharing community.

✓ Increase economic security by enhancing our self-sufficiency and our community's resiliency.

Sharing can involve casual agreements between friends and neighbors or formal contracts that establish how we will share with strangers. We may decide to increase our use of existing sharing institutions, such as libraries, or create new sharing enterprises that address evolving community needs, such as car-sharing groups or seed libraries. Some sharing alternatives are discussed elsewhere in this book. Chapter 3: Food discusses food and garden sharing. Chapter 4: Home covers shared living arrangements. And Chapter 6: Transportation offers information on bike and ridesharing as well as carpooling. Following are some ways we can share consumer goods.

▶ **Share casually with friends and neighbors.** If we have friends or acquaintances that are willing to forgo ownership for access, we may be able to casually share a variety of items on an ad hoc basis. For example, we might borrow our neighbor's grill or lend out our snow blower. Or we might borrow or lend an outfit for a special occasion or an extra bicycle for a play date.

▶ **Make formal sharing agreements.** When sharing extends to a community beyond our friends and family members—or when we're sharing the types of resources that could present legal or insurance issues—we may want to put things in writing, possibly even drawing up formal contracts. For example, it's advisable to have a written agreement for sharing a car, a house or the services of a childcare provider. *The Sharing Solution: How to Save Money, Simplify Your Life & Build Community*, by attorneys Janelle Orsi and Emily Doskow, is an excellent source of information on the legal aspects of sharing.

▶ **Swap or trade.** From clothing that doesn't quite flatter us anymore to books we've read and electronics we've decided to replace, the stuff of life tends to pile up over time, reminding us how much we consume. On the flip side, we never stop needing new household goods, larger clothes for growing children or supplies for our new favorite hobbies or sports. The idea of swapping gently used goods has gained popularity along with other forms of sharing, and there are many ways to go about it. Car trunk swaps in a school parking lot can be great for trading children's clothing, toys and sports equipment. A clothes-swapping party at a friend's apartment can be an entertaining and affordable alternative to buying new clothes. And, of course, we can swap nearly anything online at sites such as swap.com, Listia, Yerdle and ThredUp. Peerby can help us borrow an item from someone in or near our community. Trashnothing lets us give or receive used items. We can even create our own online sharing community using the innovative platform Near-Me.com.

▶ **Revisit libraries.** Seemingly old-fashioned and mundane, libraries are among the country's oldest and most enduring sharing institutions. Our first libraries were founded in the 1600s and, along with public schools, they came to be viewed as essential institutions for our young democracy. In recent years, technology has made libraries seem irrelevant, while budget cuts have threatened their very existence. Yet for anyone seeking to reduce consumption, become more self-reliant and reconnect with community, the public library can be a terrific resource. In fact, threatened with extinction, some libraries have begun to reinvent themselves in ways that dovetail amazingly well with today's sharing and resiliency movements. For example, when we borrow books and other media from a library, we automatically reduce spending and our impact on natural resources, pollution and waste. Now we also may be able to borrow larger or more unusual items, including electronics and household tools. (More information: Join or start a tool library, page 146) Similarly, educational programs offered by libraries have always brought together people with shared needs and interests. Today, in addition to hosting the book clubs, literacy groups and how-to classes that have been public library staples for many years, some libraries are helping members of the community learn about and experiment with the latest technology by providing access to music and video recording rooms or even makerspaces with 3D printers and other related equipment. Libraries also are helping to support the local economy and the creation of jobs by providing co-work and business incubator space. In addition to the modernization of actual libraries, *little free libraries* are appearing in public spaces in many towns and cities. Often comprising nothing more than temporary shelving units stocked with donated books, these pop-ups offer even greater accessibility than traditional public libraries by doing away with library cards and allowing anyone to linger, read, borrow, donate or swap whenever the kiosk or storage unit is open.

▶ **Consume collectively.** Another form of sharing, collective consuming or purchasing is about pooling resources with others to buy goods that everyone needs. It can give us access without *full* ownership, helping to reduce household expenses, lower our environmental impact and eliminate the need for extra storage space, all while strengthening social ties in a way that makes everyone more resilient. Co-purchasing supersized packages of goods from buyers' clubs along with our friends, neighbors or family members is one way to consume collectively. We also may want to co-purchase durable goods that aren't used every day, such as lawnmowers, power tools, skis or kayaks.

▶ **Join or start a tool library.** Consuming collectively also can be scaled up to allow the wider community to share certain items. The most common example of this is a tool library, a storehouse of garden or household tools that can be organized through an existing public library or a newly formed nonprofit organization. In either case, tool libraries generally are run by volunteers, stocked with donated tools and funded through annual dues, grants or donations.

   The most obvious benefit tool libraries offer is the ability to borrow the tools we need, just when we need them. Tool libraries also may appeal to those who can't afford all the tools they need, have no place to store them or simply don't use certain tools enough to warrant owning them. Tool libraries also can provide access to a much wider range of tools than any one individual is likely to own. *The Sharing Solution* offers information that can help us start a tool library in our own community.

▶ **Start or participate in a "library of things."** Similar to a tool library, this usually takes the form of a store or warehouse where a wide range of donated items can be accumulated, displayed and offered to "shoppers." Members can borrow and return items as needed. The MyTurn.com platform can be used to set up and manage a library of things.

Managing Waste

We can reduce the amount of trash we produce—and the environmental impact of that trash—by (1) eliminating our use of packaging and other "instant waste," (2) transforming would-be garbage into something useful or (3) discarding trash in a way that lets others manage that transformation.

Reduce Instant Waste

Buying less is one way to reduce the amount of trash we produce. But we also can make a difference by eliminating instant waste, the wide range of materials produced for one-time use or transient purposes. For example, we can:

▶ **Reduce product packaging.** Consumer product packaging and containers represent about 30% of solid municipal waste according to the EPA.[47] Eco-conscious companies are redesigning their packaging, reducing it substantially or making it from recycled or recyclable materials. Choosing products with green or minimal packaging, such as package-free food items (e.g., rice, oats, cereal) sold loose in bins, can be just as important as reducing overall consumption. We can also reduce instant waste by buying refills for cleaning products or purchasing supersized packages of staple items (e.g., toilet paper, canned goods), instead of repeatedly buying smaller packages, provided we expect to use the products and not discard them. The latter may be more practical when we co-purchase goods with others.

▶ **Shop with reusable cloth bags.** Large quantities of plastic bags add to landfill each year. The many that blow away and find their way into storm drains and waterways end up polluting streams, rivers and, eventually, our oceans According to a recent study of coastal nations around the globe, approximately eight million tons of plastic debris is discarded into oceans each year.[48] In addition to causing dead zones, such as the "Great Pacific Garbage Patch," plastics can break down into tiny, nonbiodegradable particles that may attract chemical pollutants in the water.[49] A wide range of marine life is poisoned or contaminated by eating these particles,[50] and the contamination can work its way up the food chain and into our diets.[51] One of the easiest ways to help reduce plastic garbage is to refuse plastic bags when we make a purchase. Alternatives include bringing our own reusable cloth bags to the supermarket or, for smaller purchases, doing without bags altogether. Paper bags aren't a good substitute because paper can contribute to pollution at every stage of its lifecycle.[52]

▶ **Repair instead of replacing.** It's tempting to simply throw away household items that have broken or stopped working. Some of us are handy enough to fix them ourselves. But others may benefit from visiting repair cafés, a relatively new phenomena inspired by the sharing movement. A repair café generally consists of a workshop or classroom setting where individuals with the skills needed to repair common household products help others learn the tricks of the trade.

▶ **Stop junk mail.** With a bit of leg work, it's possible to stop most of the unwanted solicitations that arrive in our mailbox. Individual catalog companies and direct mail organizations offer opt-out information on their websites. Other alternatives include contacting the Direct Marketing Association's Mail Preference service at DMAchoice.org, contacting our state's consumer protection division or downloading the free junk-mail-deterring app PaperKarma.

Don't be a litter bug

Decades ago, a national public service campaign successfully admonished Americans not to litter. While most of us have gotten the message, there's clearly still plenty of trash in our midst. Besides managing our own waste responsibly, we may want to participate in organized cleanup days to rid our local communities of unwanted litter.

Rethinking Straws

Millions of plastic straws end up in the waste stream each day, often making their way to oceans and other waterways where they can harm marine life. Better options include using a stainless steel or glass straw or simply going strawless.

Reuse and Upcycle

Finding new purposes for our trash can help us save money, significantly reduce waste and even explore our creativity. It all starts with taking one last look at the objects we're about to discard and considering the alternatives.

Reuse

Reusing an item until its useful life is spent reduces waste and prevents the need to extract additional natural resources for the manufacture of new products. Here are a few common reuse ideas:

✓ Stainless steel water bottles and straws, stainless or glass food containers, ceramic coffee mugs and thermoses all help reduce the trash associated with the drinks and meals we enjoy away from home. Reuseit.com is one of many sites that sell these and other reusable products.

✓ Glass jars from store-bought condiments make perfect containers for home-grown herbs, homemade pickles and our own made-from-scratch condiments.

✓ Old newspapers can be used to clean windows or to protect surfaces when we're tackling a painting or staining project.

✓ Some of our food scraps—eggshells, tea leaves, coffee grinds, fruit and vegetable scraps—can be turned into the compost that is so important to a productive garden. (More information: Compost, page 155, and Chapter 3, Food)

✓ Old t-shirts make great dustrags and furniture refinishing cloths.

✓ Tuna cans filled with beer can be placed in garden beds to attract slugs before they nibble away at our lettuce.

✓ Bubble Wrap, packing peanuts, wrapping paper and ribbon can all be used more than once to wrap gifts and prepare packages for shipping.

✓ Fabric scraps can be used for gift wrapping, á la the Japanese art of furoshiki.

✓ Old maps, posters, artwork and magazine pages all make unique gift wrapping.

Upcycle

The range of recyclable items and materials continues to grow. But there may always be items that can't be recycled easily or cost-effectively. We can keep them out of landfill through both reuse and upcycling. There are endless possibilities for creative upcycling, either for practical purposes or artistic endeavors. Many of us have seen colorful handbags made from plastic bags and wallets made from gum wrappers. Other examples of upcycling include patchwork quilts made from men's suits, felted hats and scarves made from old sweaters and candleholders and torches for the garden made from old glass jars. Fair trade artisans are even transforming the remains of weapons and land mines into jewelry and other decorative gift items. Upcycling ideas are abundant online and in books and magazines. Sites for selling our upcycled creations also are in no short supply. Etsy may be the most well-known. A few others are Zibbet, aftcra, ArtYah and Big Cartel.

Recycle

According to the EPA, about 34.3% of household waste was recycled as of 2013.[53] Recycling offers significant environmental benefits while also having a positive impact on local economies and our household finances. For example, recycling can:

▶ **Reduce the need to deplete natural resources,** including trees for paper, flooring and furniture, petroleum for plastics, precious metals for computers and stone for countertops. Extraction of natural resources can pollute air and water, harm wildlife and sicken workers. Recycled materials are now routinely used in the manufacture of new goods, often reducing production costs. (More information: Zero Waste and the Circular Economy sidebar, below)

While the U.S. has been increasing its recycling for many years, China's recent decision to stop taking our single-stream waste for sorting and resale threatens to undermine decades of progress. But some sorting is done in the U.S. and new recycling enterprises may eventually enter the marketplace. In the meantime, it's important to keep recycling.

Zero Waste and the Circular Economy

Crafty DIY enthusiasts aren't the only ones transforming used goods and materials into new creations. Some companies are committing to a *zero waste strategy* and a *circular economy* by producing products and packaging that have a green lifecycle. That generally means manufacturing goods from recycled materials ad infinitum to reduce the use of natural resources and energy and keep waste out of landfill. Common examples include lumber and roofing shingles made from reconstituted sawdust or plastic, filler for pillows and sleeping bags made from plastic fiber, plastic bottles and aluminum cans made from recycled bottles and cans, paper made from recycled paper and Patagonia jackets made from old Patagonia jackets. Many decorative and wearable items also are being produced from recyclables. Most of these products indicate their recycled content with one of several recycling labels. Another aspect of the circular economy is using compostable packaging made from natural materials such as hemp, bamboo, potato starch and corn. Even cities and smaller municipalities are embracing a zero-waste strategy. Touting the "five Rs"—Refuse, Reduce, Recycle, Reuse and Rot—they are not only assuring residents have access to recycling services but also offering citywide composting of food and other organic waste.

▶ **Reduce energy use.** Since recycled materials have already been processed and refined, using them to manufacture new products requires less energy and produces less pollution than making items from scratch. For example, recycling aluminum cans saves 95% of the energy needed to manufacture new cans. One ton of recycled aluminum saves 14,000 kilowatt hours (Kwhs) of energy, 40 barrels of oil, 238 million Btus of energy and 10 cubic yards of landfill space.[54]

▶ **Preserve open space** by slowing the growth of landfill.

▶ **Reduce greenhouse gases emissions** from fossil fuels used in the production of new goods and from methane, which is released into the atmosphere as trash in landfill decays.

▶ **Reduce water pollution** caused by leachate, decaying liquids in landfill that can contaminate surface and groundwater and eventually make their way into our drinking water.

▶ **Help mitigate the impact of climate change** by reducing demand for lumber from carbon-sequestering old-growth forests.

▶ **Create local business opportunities and jobs** related to recycling and reclamation.

▶ **Lower taxes for municipal waste management** by reducing the amount of waste that needs to be collected.

▶ **Lower the cost of household trash collection.** Finding ways to recycle more of our trash may allow us to rent a smaller, less-expensive garbage can from our waste management service.

Even if we recognize the many benefits of recycling, we may sometimes end up throwing items in the trash if we aren't sure whether or how they can be recycled. Knowing our recycling options ahead of time can help take the effort out of this daily activity. Those options may include:

▶ **Recycling through our waste management service.** Many of our recycling solutions are as close at hand as the end of the driveway. Recycling typically is handled by the same waste management company that picks up our trash. Generally, the most comprehensive source of information on what we can recycle curbside or at recycling depots will be either our private waste management service or our county's solid waste and recycling department. Even if we're familiar with the list of allowable recyclables, it's worth checking periodically, as items may be added or eliminated from time to time. This is particularly important now, since some waste haulers are taking fewer items because they can no longer ship them to China. Local waste management professionals also will be the best source of information on details such as which number plastics can be recycled, whether to flatten bottles and cans, whether bottle tops and labels must be removed, how thoroughly bottles and cans must be cleaned and whether recycling is single-stream (i.e., everything can be recycled in one container) or requires sorting of different types of items into separate containers. The app IRecycle can help users locate nearby recycling facilities, including those for out-of-the-ordinary items.

According to a study by the Sustainable Packaging Coalition, about 94% of Americans have access to some type of recycling program. About 73% have curbside recycling or drop-off recycling.[55] Allowable recyclables may include:

Bottles and jars. Plastic and glass bottles typically can be recycled curbside. A few states also have "bottle bills" that require stores to buy back empty glass bottles from consumers and reuse them.

Aluminum cans and clean foil.

Paper, including newspapers, magazines, catalogs, paperback books, phone-books, junk mail, inserts, envelopes, office and school paper and paper bags.

Cardboard, such as toilet paper rolls and egg cartons, and clean boxboard from pizza, cereal, cake and cracker boxes.

Milk cartons and other coated cardboards.

Tin cans such as tuna fish and cat food cans.

▶ **Finding Options for Other Recyclable Materials.** Waste management companies have expanded the scope of what can be recycled curbside. But there are still countless items that require us to track down recycling options on our own. Following is a lengthy, but by no means comprehensive, list of recyclable items.

Hazardous waste. Many counties have scheduled hazardous waste cleanup days, usually requiring drop-off at designated centers. Hazardous waste may include batteries, engine oil and filters, antifreeze, old tires, weed killers, aerosol cans and oil-based paints. Sometimes hazardous waste and electronics recycling are combined.

Electronics. Everything from laptops to televisions to peripherals and electrical cords can and should be recycled. In most states, it's required by law. Since, as noted previously, electronics contribute about 2.14 million tons to landfill annually,[56] recycling them can help reduce the overall volume of landfill significantly. Because electronics can leach heavy metals such as mercury and lead into soils and nearby streams—or, if incinerated, release dioxins into the air—recycling also helps prevent water and air pollution from toxic waste.[57] When those heavy metals are kept out of landfill, they can be reclaimed and reused in the manufacture of new electronics, reducing costs as well as the need to deplete more nonrenewable resources. Many counties hold electronics recycling days. Other options for recycling these items responsibly include manufacturer take-back programs and on-site drop-off programs at office supply chains. It also may be possible to donate computers to schools, libraries or thrift shops.

Cell phones. Rainforest Connection (rfcx.org), a nonprofit focused on curtailing deforestation, transforms donated cell phones into "autonomous solar-powered listening devices" that can "monitor and pinpoint chainsaw activity at a distance" as it occurs.[58]

Printer ink cartridges. Some national office supply chains offer on-site drop-off for recycling.

Batteries may be among the hazardous waste items that can be recycled on county cleanup days. Some national home construction supply retailers and office supply stores offer battery collection for recycling. A mail-in option is available from Battery Solutions (batteryrecycling.com). Of course, using rechargeable batteries can eliminate this item from the trash altogether.

CDs, DVDs and video games often can be sold or swapped at game retailers.

Gently used furniture, household appliances, fixtures (toilets, sinks), housewares and building supplies. Many of these items can be donated to Salvation Army stores or local religious and community donation centers. Habitat for Humanity's ReStore centers sell donated household goods at reasonable prices to individuals setting up homes, often following periods of homelessness. The ReStore website, restore.org, lists center locations and identifies the types of items each location accepts. In states that require recycling of large appliances, with recovery of refrigerants and other chemicals, municipal or private waste management companies may offer curbside recycling.

Organizing Our Recycling

Finding practical and convenient ways to store the various items we're going to recycle can make the process much easier. (Note that if our waste management company offers single-stream recycling, there is no need to sort items by type.) Newer kitchen cabinets often have enclosed, pull-out bins for both garbage and recycling. Depending on how much room we have at home, in the garage or a shed, we may be able to set up an organized system of plastic buckets for various types of recyclables. Labeling the buckets can help encourage household members to comply, so that it doesn't become the job of one person to sort the recycling each week. We can help young children become responsible recyclers by incorporating pictures into those labels. If we're limited on space, we may choose to simply stuff all types of recyclables into spare bags and then sort them out directly into their curbside containers each week.

Plastic bags can be discarded in the plastic bag recycling bins found at many supermarkets and chain stores. We also may be able to use these bins to recycle other types of "plastic film" (i.e., plastic that we can stretch and poke holes in), such as clean plastic wrap and baggies. A plastic film recycling locator tool is available at plasticfilmrecycling.org.

Towels. Old towels, washcloths and bath mats that are in reasonably good condition may be donated to thrift shops and charitable collection centers for resale or donation to those in need. Animal shelters often take used towels even if they are not in perfect condition.

Clothes. We can keep our clothes out of landfill by selling them to vintage and second-hand shops, swapping online or with a group of friends or donating to the Salvation Army, veterans' organizations, religious congregation clothing drives, programs that help low-income individuals transition to work or any other organization or group gathering clothing for those in need. As mentioned previously, Patagonia runs a unique recycling program: They recycle used Patagonia garments dropped off by customers, breaking the clothing down into fiber that is then reused to make new garments. The process substantially reduces the use of energy and release of CO_2 associated with making new garments from non-recycled raw materials. Information on the program is available at patagonia.com. As described in Chapter 4, Home, some clothing retailers now recycle used denim jeans.

Compact florescent lightbulbs (CFLs) can be recycled at some national home construction supply stores.

Packing peanuts and Bubble Wrap. Besides reusing these items when we need to ship something fragile, we may be able to donate them to a local shipping business.

Styrofoam. UPS stores may accept block Styrofoam. We can search for Styrofoam drop-off centers in our area at Earth911 (earth911.com) or the Alliance of Foam Packaging Recyclers (epspackaging.org).

Plastic planters. Gardeners often end up with lots of lightweight plastic containers from the plants they've purchased. Some garden stores will take our empties and reuse them the following planting season.

Recycling Facts[59]

▶ In 2013, Americans generated about 254 million tons of trash, of which 87 million tons (34.3%) were recycled or composted.

▶ On average, each of us generates about 4.4 pounds of trash a day, of which about 1.51 pounds are recycled or composted.

▶ In 2013, recycling and composting diverted about 87.2 million tons of material from landfill, up from just 15 million tons in 1980. Keeping that amount of trash out of landfill prevented the release of about 186 million metric tons of CO_2, the equivalent of taking more than 39 million cars off the road for a year.

▶ According to a 2016 Pew Research survey, 46% of U.S. adults said they recycle or reduce waste whenever possible, 30% said they do this "most of the time" and 19% said they do so "occasionally."[60]

Scrap metal. Some waste management companies recycle lids from tin or aluminum cans, aluminum foil and other lightweight scraps. Private scrap metal recycling companies may pay us by the pound for scrap metal and copper wire.

Medicines. Prescription and over-the-counter medications are a significant non-point source of water pollution. Many police departments and pharmacies have drop-off programs that assure the drugs will be disposed of responsibly.

Arts and crafts supplies and odds and ends. Creative reuse centers are a relatively new option for recycling these items. The centers may accept two types of donations: (1) items that can be repurposed creatively and (2) materials that can be used for creative repurposing. For example, they may take old furniture that can be brought back to life with refinishing or decorative painting, or odds and ends that can be turned into entirely new items, either useful or whimsical. They also may accept arts and crafts or decorating supplies, including partially used tubes of paint, half-empty crayon boxes, leftover wool skeins, extra floor tiles or wallpaper samples. Sometimes a reuse center will weigh the materials it accepts and track the tonnage kept out of landfill. Some of these centers hold workshops on upcycling and invite the public to experiment with various techniques. Public schools, art centers and after-school programs also may accept donations.

Books. In addition to recycling paperbacks curbside, we may be able to donate them and our hardcover books to the local library, booksforafrica.org or booksforsoldiers.com. Selling through Amazon or other online booksellers is another option that can keep books out of landfill, at least for a while longer.

Tennis balls. Recycling and refurbishing of tennis balls is offered by rebounces.com, which also sells eco-conscious tennis equipment.

Everything else. Recycling possibilities extend well beyond the information covered here. Sources of information about recycling out-of-the-ordinary items include county waste management guides and earth911.org. Another option is giving away unwanted items through countywide freecycling programs. Some municipalities provide storage for hard-to-recycle items (e.g., paints, tools, computers) that others in the community can take as needed. Peer-to-peer recycling services include Freecycle and Freegle.

Compost

The fifth R refers to removing organic matter, such as food, from the solid waste stream by composting it. Food scraps represent about 15% of the solid waste sent to landfill each year.[61] Since lack of oxygen in landfill can prevent organic waste from fully decomposing, that waste can become a significant source of methane, a potent greenhouse gas and air pollutant. Fortunately, composting is on the rise, with about 1.84 million tons of food composted in the U.S. in 2013 versus 1.74 million tons in 2012.[62] Chapter 3, Food includes information about how to compost at home. It also describes the growth of municipal composting services. Some states are phasing in bans on the burial of organic waste, making composting a requirement.

Doing More

We can work toward a world in which individual consumers won't need to make complex decisions each time they buy a product by:

▸ Staying abreast of environmental issues related to consumer products through organizations such as the Natural Resources Defense Council and the Environmental Working Group;

▸ Urging our elected representatives to take action to improve regulation of consumer products and the chemicals they contain. This is particularly critical as the EPA begins to undo long-standing regulations;

▸ Supporting fair trade, not only by purchasing fair trade products but also by donating to or volunteering for a fair trade organization, participating in organized boycotts of companies that harm the environment or exploit workers or encouraging elected representatives to support a fair trade approach to global trade;

▸ Supporting companies that adopt zero waste strategies; and

▸ Urging representatives to support efforts to build recycling sorting operations in the U.S. and to develop markets for recycled materials.

Making sustainable choices about transportation can help us reduce our environmental impact and household expenses, lead healthier, more active lifestyles and reconnect with our communities.

Transportation

"You're either part of the problem or part of the solution" was a popular refrain among 1960s activists. Unfortunately, when it comes to transportation, most of us are still part of the problem. And we make matters worse each time we get behind the wheel. Second only to electricity production, transportation produces 27% of the nation's greenhouse gas emissions.[1] With a population of just over 322 million and about 210 million licensed drivers, the U.S. has an estimated 253 million registered vehicles on the road, obviously more than one vehicle per driver. As of 2011, only about 11 million of those vehicles ran on alternative fuels.[2] That helps account for why the U.S. remains the world's second-largest contributor to global warming despite having lowered its annual greenhouse gas emissions significantly over the past decade.[3, 4]

Besides contributing to our use of fossil fuels and our impact on greenhouse gas emissions, our transportation habits also are unsustainable in a variety of other ways. Despite the positive impact of the Clean Air Act, our tailpipes still spew a number of known air pollutants, including particulate matter, sulfur dioxide, carbon monoxide, hydrocarbons and nitrogen oxides—unless we drive alternative fuel vehicles. Owning and fueling a car can be financially unsustainable, taking a large bite out of the household budget. Driving can be dangerous, although fatal collisions are on the decline. Driving rather than walking or biking can reinforce a lifestyle that is sedentary, unhealthy and even socially isolated. And at the end of our vehicle's lifecycle, it's likely to contribute to the growth of unrecycled scrap and waste in landfill sites.

Transitioning to sustainable transportation will take time and effort. But we *are* headed in the right direction. Alternative fuel vehicles are now a mainstream consumer choice. Commercial airlines and the U.S. military have been exploring ways to reduce the impact of their fuel usage on greenhouse gas emissions. And a growing number of Americans are choosing not to own cars, opting instead to walk, take the bus, bike or rideshare to lower both their expenses and their impact on the environment.

In fact, thanks to technological advances and greater environmental awareness among at least some public officials, businesses and consumers, it's becoming easier and more affordable to choose sustainable transportation. Whether we want to reduce our carbon footprint and dependence on fossil fuels, spend less at the pump, spend less time in traffic or adopt a healthier, more active and community-focused lifestyle, greening our transportation can be part of the solution. Generally, that will involve increasing fuel efficiency, choosing renewable sources of fuel and/or choosing alternative types of transportation. Put another way, it will mean making decisions not only about *what* and *how* we drive…but *whether* we drive at all.

Greening Our Rides

Few lifestyle decisions are likely to have as direct an impact on the environment as choosing a greener vehicle. While still evolving, today's automotive technologies already offer significant opportunities to reduce emissions of both greenhouse gases and other air pollutants. Even if rushing out to replace the vehicle we now own isn't practical, we can make a meaningful difference the next time we're in the market for a new car or truck. Depending on our budget and comfort with new technology, we can opt for:

▶ **A fuel-efficient vehicle.** For many of us, this is the most affordable and practical alternative. Prioritizing fuel efficiency can lower our contribution to greenhouse gas emissions and reduce the country's consumption of oil. Fuel-efficient vehicles also can save us money on gas while often costing no more to

A Brief History of Fuel Efficiency

Ironically, finding a fuel-efficient car was easier 35 years ago than it has been in the decades that followed. In the 1970s, it was trendy to drive small European or Japanese vehicles. Their fuel efficiency made them even more popular when tensions in the Middle East led to skyrocketing gas prices, shortages and, ultimately, the 1973 oil embargo. The embargo awakened many Americans to the realization that our way of life, dependent on foreign oil, could be disrupted by outside forces. In 1975, Congress passed the Corporate Average Fuel Economy (CAFE) law, which set annual goals for increasing fuel efficiency in American-made vehicles. Confronted with the new regulations, as well as consumer demand for better gas mileage and competition from foreign car manufacturers, the American automotive industry began producing cars that got in excess of 40 miles per gallon.

Unfortunately, in the 1980s, many consumers began preferencing size, safety and status over good gas mileage. Carmakers responded by producing large, fuel-*inefficient* vehicles while Congress placed CAFE standards on hold, keeping them unchanged from 1990 to 2012, when they were increased significantly. Today, consumers are once again prioritizing fuel-efficiency. But the EPA is now seeking to reverse the latest tailpipe emission and CAFE standards, undoing years of progress.

purchase than their less fuel-efficient counterparts. And it's no longer difficult to find cars or even light trucks that offer good gas mileage. In recent years, car manufacturers have improved fuel efficiency in many of their vehicles in response to both consumer demand and regulatory reforms. After letting fuel efficiency guidelines languish for two decades, Congress passed updated CAFE (Corporate Average Fuel Economy) standards in 2012 that call for vehicles to get up to 54.5 miles per gallon (mpg) by 2025. According to the Union of Concerned Scientists (UCS), the new standards have the potential to decrease U.S. oil consumption by more than three million barrels a day by 2030.[5] Car companies have been working to comply with those guidelines by making vehicles lighter and more aerodynamic, improving engine and transmission technologies and using tires with reduced rolling resistance.

CAFE standards have never guaranteed universally higher fuel efficiency. They only require that the average fuel economy of a car company's fleet reach the target goal. Companies have leeway to respond to changing consumer demand, which tends to fluctuate with the price of gas. Even so, the standards provide a powerful incentive for carmakers to develop more fuel-efficient gas-combustion vehicles while also making improvements to vehicles that run on alternative fuels.

We can do our part to support fuel-efficiency standards by placing "good gas mileage" at the top of our checklist when shopping for a new vehicle—even if gas prices happen to be low at that particular moment. That may mean foregoing an SUV or truck for a smaller, lighter vehicle, since weight has a direct bearing on fuel efficiency. Lighter vehicles have smaller engines and power trains and therefore use less gas. In fact, it was the added weight of the SUVs and trucks that became popular in the past few decades that undid the fuel efficiency gains of the 1970s. (More information: A Brief History of Fuel Efficiency sidebar) Comparisons of vehicle fuel efficiency by weight are available from the Automobile Association of America (AAA) and at fueleconomy. gov. If our household has more than one vehicle, we can make a difference by maximizing use of the car that gets the best gas mileage.

► **An alternative-fuel vehicle.** Alternative fuels can play a critical role in helping us slow climate change. According to the UCS, the alternative fuel vehicles currently available can help us significantly reduce greenhouse gas emissions. The UCS estimates

---

Greenhouse Gas Emissions from a Typical Passenger Vehicle (Source: EPA):[6]

Burning one gallon of gas produces about 8,887 grams of CO_2. Fuels contain varying amounts of carbon. After combustion, emissions contain hydrocarbons and carbon monoxide as well as CO_2. Most emissions are in the form of CO_2.

One mile = 423 grams of CO_2 emissions.

The typical passenger vehicle emits 5.1 metric tons of CO_2 annually.

that switching to vehicles fueled by alternative energy sources could cut U.S. oil consumption in half over the next 20 years.[7] Alternative-fuel vehicles also could help reduce air pollution and lower the cost of driving a car. The alternative-fuel vehicle industry is rapidly evolving. At this time, our choices include:

Electric vehicles (EVs). As of 2014, the U.S. had just over 450,000 electric vehicles on the road.[8] The first ads for these vehicles conveyed the image of an entirely new, 21st-century technology. But electric vehicles (EVs) actually have a long and winding history. The Scottish inventor Robert Anderson is credited with creating the first electric "carriage" in the 1830s. The first electric car was produced in 1891 by William Morrison, a Des Moines, Iowa, automaker. By 1900, electric cars represented roughly *one-third* of the vehicles driven in America's major metropolitan areas. But by the 1920s, inexpensive gasoline and advancements in gas-powered cars, including electric starters that replaced hand cranks, had pushed electric vehicles to the sidelines.

From the 1960s through the 1980s, concerns about pollution and dependence on foreign oil led to legislation encouraging development of alternative fuel vehicles *and* to the actual invention of both hybrids and EVs. In the late 1990s, the first modern electric car, the EV1, was briefly available under a lease arrangement.[9] But the next chapter in EV history really didn't begin until 2008, when Elon Musk shook up the auto industry with his state-of-the-art electric Tesla Roadster. In 2010, General Motors introduced the Chevrolet Volt (described as a blend between an EV and a hybrid) and Nissan began selling the all-electric LEAF. Around the same time, electric vehicles from various other automakers also entered the marketplace. This time around, a number of factors—high oil prices, concerns about dependence on foreign oil in the age of terrorism, extreme weather linked to climate change, the availability of new technologies and renewed consumer eco-consciousness—came together to support a *sustainable* reintroduction of electricity-powered vehicles.

So what do EVs offer? Well-reviewed by automotive critics for their high performance and comfort, today's EVs are among the cleanest vehicles on the road, producing *no* tailpipe emissions (i.e., no greenhouse gases or other forms of pollution). They do rely on electricity that may come from nonrenewable energy sources. But the UCS reports that almost 50% of Americans live in areas where the energy used to recharge EVs produces a lower level of greenhouse gas emissions than even the most fuel-efficient hybrid and gas-combustion vehicles.[10] EVs also are more energy efficient than gas-combustion vehicles because they are lighter and use regenerative braking systems, the latter allowing stored energy from breaking to help power the car's electric motors and accessories.

A Threat on the Horizon

EV sales have been very strong in recent years, spurring optimism that, this time, these vehicles are here to stay. But just as EVs have become more common, some states have decided to stop offering tax incentives to purchase these vehicles and charge EV owners higher-than-average registration fees.

The EVs currently available run on lithium ion batteries that travel between about 80 miles and 300 miles on a full charge. The variation in range depends on the model (with the newest Teslas at the top of the heap) and factors including driving speed, road conditions and passenger load. These ranges are continually changing as technology advances. But, to date, gas-combustion engines still offer by far the highest range, typically about 460 miles between filling stations.

Charging an EV can take a considerable amount of time, depending on the type of vehicle and charging station and the amount of charge required. But just as we don't typically wait until our gas tanks are on empty to fill up, EV drivers generally aren't recharging from zero. Most EV owners recharge at home overnight, often "filling up" enough to drive about 40 miles during the course of the next day. Some utilities offer special rates for EV charging. When away from home, EV drivers can use apps such as PlugShare, ChargeHub and Charge-Point to locate charging stations at locations including highway rest stops and shopping mall parking lots. Privately owned charging stations belong to various networks and require a driver to open an account and pay a charging fee. Government-funded stations offer free charging. So do some eco-conscious employers interested in encouraging employees to switch to EVs.

At this time, there are four levels of EV charging, ranging from about 4.5 miles an hour up to about 170 miles in one-half hour.[11] Charging levels 1 and 2 supply alternate current (AC) electricity to a vehicle's onboard charger. Level 1, sometimes called "trickle charging," is the slowest and requires only a 120-VAC (volts of alternating current) outlet, the type typically found throughout our homes. Level 2 charging utilizes a 240-VAC line, the type used for electric dryers and stoves. Many EV owners obtain level 2 charging from electric vehicle service equipment (EVSE) devices, which can be installed at home. Significantly faster is DC fast charging, which bypasses the EV's onboard charger and provides direct current electricity to the battery through a special charging port. Fast charging is not available for all EVs. Tesla supercharging remains by far the fastest option.

As battery storage and charging technology improve and the nationwide network of charging stations expands, EV owners should be able to travel widely without concern about running out of juice. Developments in storage of residential solar also are likely to make EV charging easier and more convenient. Up until recently, relatively high prices, limited range and lengthy charging times have kept most consumers on the sidelines, with EVs garnering just 1% of annual auto sales to date.[12] That could change soon with the introduction of a new generation of vehicles offering significantly higher ranges and more moderate sticker prices.[13]

Hybrids. Initially viewed as the future of green vehicles, hybrids achieved notoriety when Hollywood celebrities began buying Toyota Priuses back in the early 2000s. Hybrids combine two engine technologies: smaller-than-average gas-combustion engines and electric motors powered by advanced batteries that absorb energy from breaking and downhill travel (like electric car batteries) as well as from the gas engine. The vehicles switch back and forth between the two engine types depending on speed. This reduces the amount of gasoline required, increasing fuel efficiency, reducing gas expense and lessening tailpipe emissions. While critics say hybrids aren't green enough because they still rely on gasoline, others believe they offer a good transitional technology between gas-combustion and all-electric vehicles.

Plug-in hybrids. Developed in the early 1970s by Andrew Frank, a professor of engineering at the University of California, Davis, plug-ins are hybrids with electric motors that can be plugged into an outlet to recharge, just like an EV. Recharging allows the motors to run on electricity longer (and the cars to sustain higher speeds, over longer distances) so that the gas-combustion engine doesn't need to take over as frequently as with traditional hybrids.

Advanced biofuel vehicles. A variety of plant and animal-based sources of biomass are being developed as possible replacements for (or additives to) gasoline. These liquid fuels are known collectively as "biofuels." U.S. taxpayers have subsidized one particular biofuel, corn ethanol, since the late 1970s. More recently, soybeans, sugar cane and other food crops have been developed as alternative sources of ethanol. Biofuels have been billed as environmentally sustainable because of their ability to reduce tailpipe emissions. Some envision them replacing gasoline entirely. Others believe they'll find their purpose as alternative fuels for larger vehicles (e.g., jet planes, trucks) that are not well suited to electric vehicle technology. But critics, such as Princeton University research scholar Timothy Searchinger (author of a 2015 study on biofuels and the global food supply), believe that it's never a good idea to "grow" fuel given that land is desperately needed for food and carbon sequestration.[14] Our history with corn ethanol illustrates other potential problems with food-based fuels. Critics believe that growing corn for ethanol has raised the price of corn produced for food, disproportionately impacting populations in poorer areas of the world. Sustainable farming advocates note that corn is grown in an environmentally unsustainable manner, employing GMO seed and synthetic chemical inputs. And environmentalists point out that production and transportation of corn ethanol involves large amounts of fossil fuel, increasing, rather than decreasing, net greenhouse gas emissions.

More environmentally sustainable sources of biofuel may include wood and paper waste, prairie grasses (e.g., switch grass, willow, poplar), fast-growing trees, algae, organic municipal waste, sewage and industrial or agricultural waste. There also are some enterprising drivers who create "grease cars" by converting their diesel engines to run on biofuels made from leftover vegetable oil and grease.

Adopting Sustainable Driving Habits

Whatever type of vehicles we choose, there are several ways to drive more sustainably.

▶ **Lightening our footsteps on the pedal.** Simply driving a bit slower can enable us to use less gas, save money, improve fuel efficiency,[15] reduce greenhouse gas emissions and increase our safety. For about 20 years, one federal law encouraged us to do all of that. In response to the 1973 oil embargo, President Nixon signed the National Maximum Speed Law (a provision of the Emergency Highway Conservation Act), which established a national maximum speed limit of 55 miles per hour for interstate roads. The national speed limit, which went into effect in 1974, never gained the support of those who spent a lot of time on the road or lived in wide-open areas of the country with minimal traffic (or who simply disliked any mandate from the federal government). The law was modified in the 1980s. Then, in 1995, the law was rescinded and states resumed setting their own speed limits. Today, highway speed limits range from 55 mph to 85 mph, with higher limits more common on interstate highways and in less-populated areas of the country. According to numerous sources, the higher speed limits reversed two decades of progress. Average fuel efficiency declined because cars generally are designed to reach optimal efficiency at about 55 mph to 60 mph.[16] Because driving faster burns more fuel, higher speed limits increased fuel consumption and expense as well as greenhouse gas emissions. And faster speeds also may have made us less safe. Road fatalities declined 16.49% in the year after the National Maximum Speed Law was passed. According to a report from the Insurance Institute for Highway Safety, between 1995 and 2013, there were 33,000 more traffic fatalities than would have been expected had the maximum speed limit of 55 mph remained in force.[17]

▶ **Hypermiling.** Besides slowing down, we can make a difference by adopting some or all of the driving techniques known as "hypermiling." This includes:

Using cruise control on flat terrain, which cuts down on speed fluctuations that require more gas and helps reduce the tendency to drive faster the longer we're on the road. Cruise control is not considered fuel efficient in hilly conditions.

Accelerating slowly from stops rather than "gunning it."

Breaking gradually, taking our foot off the gas earlier and coasting to a stop rather than stopping short.

▶ **Idling less.** Each time we keep the motor running while we hop out of the car to check the mail or wait for the kids to finish ballet classes, we contribute to global warming and air pollution while also wasting gas and money. We may not be able to avoid idling altogether. For example, even if we work a flex-time schedule, we're bound to experience the occasional traffic jam, a common cause of unintentional idling. We also may use a remote starter to cool or heat up the car in the morning, or we may "warm up the engine," a practice that is no longer considered either necessary or desirable. According to the Environmental Defense Fund, even adjusting such habits a bit can make a meaningful difference.

▶ **Keeping up with maintenance.** Regular vehicle maintenance, including oil changes and proper tire inflation, are among the simple things we can do to make our driving habits more fuel efficient.

▶ **Modifying the work commute.** Changing when or how far we drive on a regular basis is another way to reduce our environmental impact. Many Americans now work flex-time schedules that allow them to commute at off-peak hours. That can help lower greenhouse gas emissions by reducing rush-hour traffic and the idling it tends to cause. Shortening the commute, if possible, is another good option. We may be able to accomplish this by requesting a transfer to a branch office closer to home or, conversely, moving closer to our place of work.

▶ **Giving up the commute.** A growing number of Americans are working from home offices, either part- or full-time, for employers or themselves. Enabled by technology, telecommuting has become increasingly attractive both to employers seeking to reduce the costs of office space and employees interested in a better work-life balance and fewer work-related expenses. According to one study, working from home can reduce our travel time significantly and cut as much as 98% of our work-related carbon footprint.[18]

▶ **Trip chaining.** Even if we need a car for virtually all our daily activities, we can reduce the impact of driving by consolidating into a single trip a chain of errands or activities that take us in one particular direction.

Giving Up Our Cars

Finding an alternative to driving our own vehicle can be the most sustainable choice of all. Fortunately, that choice is becoming a popular one, particularly with some of the nation's youngest drivers. A survey conducted by rideshare company Zipcar found that millennials widely preferred access to a vehicle over ownership. And they weren't alone. The same survey found that nearly 50% of individuals between ages 35 and 44 were interested in foregoing car ownership for alternative modes of transportation.[19]

Even so, a 2013 report from the U.S. Census Bureau noted that 86% of Americans still travel to work by car—and about 76% drive alone.[20] Driving less may not be practical or desirable for everyone. In fact, Americans have long been known for their love affair with cars and the open road. But the UCS notes that lowering our VMT (vehicle miles traveled) by driving less is a critical step to reducing global warming and climate change. Choosing alternative modes of transportation also may help us save money, increase our daily exercise and reengage with our local community. Those alternatives include:

▶ **Public transportation.** Riding the train, bus, subway or trolley, if available, can reduce our contribution to pollution and greenhouse gas emissions while potentially adding a social element to routine transportation. Historically, the U.S. has focused more attention on interstate highways than on public transportation. But the growing preference for living without a car is making this forlorn infrastructure much more popular. Use of public transportation has risen steadily over the past decade. In 2014, Americans took 10.8 billion trips using some form of public transportation; that represented the highest ridership in 58 years.[21]

In addition to offering environmental and social benefits, public transportation can help support local economic development and community resiliency. Cities of all sizes have been incorporating light rail and other public transportation systems into downtown revitalization projects. Besides encouraging a car-free lifestyle, the best of these projects have resulted in stronger local economies and more vibrant communities as people come into "town" to work, shop, eat and enjoy local culture and entertainment.

▶ **Walking.** Many of us don't have the option of walking to work, school or other activities. But if we're able to live in a walkable community, we can enjoy a wide range of benefits. As with other alternatives to driving, walking can help us reduce our impact on the environment. As an aerobic and weight-bearing form of exercise, walking can help improve both our cardiovascular and musculoskeletal health. Of course, walking costs absolutely nothing (unless we need to invest in good walking shoes) and may help us reduce transportation expenses. It also offers opportunities to enjoy both our surroundings and some spontaneous socializing as we travel to and from our destination.

Like public transportation, walking also is now recognized as a powerful tool

Shared Mobility

Encouraging more of us to get around without owning our own cars is the goal of the "shared mobility movement." Shared mobility alternatives tend to reinforce each other. For example:

▶ Public transportation may help bring people into walkable areas of a town or city.

▶ Ridesharing can support use of public transportation by helping people get from home to the bus or train without owning their own car.

▶ Bike lanes can support walkability by adding distance between sidewalks and thoroughfares.

Shared mobility opportunities are still relatively limited outside of major cities. But even the Federal Highway Administration has recognized their potential environmental and economic benefits. In 2016, the agency published a report detailing how all levels of government can help support this growing movement. The apps Citymapper and Transit can help us coordinate various forms of shared mobility, including trains, buses, bike shares, ride shares and cabs.

for building stronger local economies and more resilient communities—something that hasn't been lost on municipal governments and city planners. Forward-thinking cities, towns and even suburbs have been taking steps to become more walkable. They've converted "rails to trails," added sidewalks and built pedestrian bridges across highways. They've lowered speed limits and reduced the number of lanes on less-traveled roads. They've redesigned intersections to increase pedestrian safety, improving signage, shortening walking distances (by adding medians and extending walkways into intersections) and adding "walk/don't walk" modes to traffic lights. As noted previously, many municipalities also have expanded public transportation, which tends to encourage walking.

Some municipalities also now consider the pedestrian impact of any proposed development or roadway project. That may lead to zoning ordinances that require ground-level shops in new buildings, additional walking paths and sidewalks or more mixed-use or transit-oriented development. Some municipalities that have taken these and other steps toward walkability have reported significant benefits. Residents have described feeling a greater sense of community and safety in public spaces. And local, independently owned downtown businesses have found it easier to grow and thrive.

▶ **Biking.** Like public transportation and walking, bike riding offers opportunities to achieve several types of sustainability. It can reduce or eliminate our need for a car, helping us save money, decrease the number of cars on the road and reduce our carbon footprint. It offers a healthy form of exercise. And because we can easily stop and get off a bike to chat with friends or check out something of interest, bike riding, like walking, can transform our transportation experience from an isolated, goal-driven activity into a social and enjoyable one.

In recent years, many cities have introduced bike lanes, public bike racks and bike-sharing programs to make this mode of transportation safer, easier and more affordable. Among the largest bike-sharing programs in the U.S. are New York City's Citi Bike, Chicago's Divvy and the San Francisco Bay Area's Ford GoBike, all of which have expanded to meet growing demand. Typically, bike-sharing programs allow a member-rider to unlock a bike using a key or passcode. When a bike is no longer needed, it can be dropped off at the nearest depot, ready for the next rider to come along. While bike-sharing programs have been criticized for neglecting the needs of lower-income residents, some programs are in the process of addressing this issue by expanding their reach into a wider range of neighborhoods. Bike-sharing programs also may offer adaptive bikes to provide accessibility to individuals with disabilities. Advocates of bike sharing as a green, community-oriented form of transportation are urging local governments to view the programs as public transportation and fund them accordingly.

▶ **Ridesharing.** Arguably the "hottest" alternative to owning a car, the idea of ridesharing emerged from the broader sharing movement. The initial concept was to foster a direct, peer-to-peer approach that connected car owners with those in need of a ride. A car owner could either "rent" out a car on a short-term basis or drive a passenger to a destination for an agreed-upon fee.

Sharing advocates view ridesharing as sustainable environmentally, economically and socially. Since the average car sits idle about 95% of the time,[22] maximizing the use of existing cars—tapping their unused capacity—can reduce the environmental impacts of manufacturing more new cars, fueling them and eventually discarding them. A study concluded that ridesharing helps us reduce our impact on traffic, along with oil consumption and global warming. The study, which focused on the car-share service car2go in five North American cities, found that each car2go kept up to 11 privately owned vehicles off the road and prevented 10 to 14 metric tons of CO_2 emissions a year.[23] Ridesharing also has been viewed as a way to support public transportation because it offers first- and last-mile coverage (i.e., it can help us get from home to public transportation and back without using our own car).

On the economic side, ridesharing lets unemployed or underemployed car owners turn what is often their second-biggest expense (after a home) into an income-producing asset. Conversely, it can help cash-strapped riders get around without having the expense—about 10% to 19% of annual income, on average[24]—of buying/leasing, maintaining, licensing, registering and fueling their own vehicles. Finally, peer-to-peer ridesharing can offer social benefits by bringing people together for the duration of a ride and helping to address the transportation needs of an entire community.

Typical of many new industries, the ridesharing landscape is evolving rapidly. While alternatives will continue to come and go, the types of ridesharing available are likely to include the following:

Alternative rentals. Zipcar is referred to as the pioneer of ridesharing, though it has more in common with a car rental company. Focused on consumers who need cars for short periods of time or to travel short distances, Zipcar and similar companies, such as car2go, allow member-drivers to pick up cars at locations throughout a city or town and rent by the hour. For example, drivers who join Zipcar can book a rental period via app and then access a car using their Zipcard. Cars can later be dropped off at any of Zipcar's designated parking spots. In addition to simplifying the car-rental process and providing an alternative to car ownership, Zipcar and car2go are doing their part to reduce carbon emissions and increase exposure to alternative vehicles by including EVs and hybrids in their fleets.

It's also possible to explore ridesharing by signing up for peer-to-peer companies that allow individuals who own vehicles to earn extra income renting them out. Companies such as Getaround (getaround.com), Turo (turo.com) and JustShareIt (justshareit.com) maintain web and mobile platforms to facilitate these transactions, provide car owners with insurance and allow both owners and renters to rate their experiences. While rates are set by the companies, owners and renters can judge in advance whether a rental transaction will be worth their while. Alternatively, we can form our own peer-to-peer rideshare groups. This can involve one car owner sharing a vehicle with a friend, two neighbors co-purchasing a vehicle to share, a small group of friends or neighbors forming an agreement to share one or more vehicles or a wider group of drivers forming a rideshare club. Of course, all of these arrangements require vehicle owners to obtain the necessary insurance coverage ahead of time. A good source of information on starting a car-share group is *The Sharing Solution: How to Save Money, Simplify Your Life & Build Community* by Janelle Orsi and Emily Doskow.

Peer-to-peer ridesharing. This term can apply to the type of rental alternatives just described. But it also encompasses arrangements in which a vehicle owner provides a ride to someone else for a fee. While there are successful businesses offering this type of service, sharing movement advocates would prefer to see a non-corporate, worker-cooperative model. At this time, the closest examples are several carpooling platforms (discussed below).

Carpooling. Long before peer-to-peer ridesharing, people shared rides via carpooling, the act of traveling to and from work or school each day with at least one passenger. Carpooling first came into vogue during the recession of 1914, when enterprising car owners began offering rides to strangers, touting the option as a comfortable alternative to street cars. Over the years, interest in carpooling has fluctuated in response to changing conditions. Americans carpooled to conserve fuel during World War II and to reduce the nation's dependence on foreign oil during the 1970s. By the end of that decade, about 23.5% of Americans were carpooling, according to the U.S. Census Bureau. Prosperity, peace and low oil prices pushed carpooling to the sidelines from the 1980s through the early 2000s. Then in the past decade, economic challenges and concerns about global warming and climate change helped inspire a new generation of carpoolers. According to the U.S. Census, as of 2011, about 11% of Americans were carpooling to and from work.[25]

Like other transportation alternatives, carpooling can offer environmental, economic and even social benefits. By decreasing the number of cars on the road during rush hour, carpooling helps reduce emissions of CO_2 and other pollutants. Carpoolers typically share the costs of fuel or even maintenance, allowing everyone to lower household expenses. And the regularity of carpooling arrangements can open the door to new friendships or at least friendly acquaintanceships. Some employers help connect employees interested in sharing the daily commute. While conflicting schedules can make work carpooling arrangements challenging, some municipalities and regions offer help through Guaranteed Ride Home Programs that cover the cost of the occasional need for a cab or rental car.

Carpooling often is arranged directly between co-workers. But, a growing number of carpoolers are connecting through social networking apps and websites such as Zimride (zimride.com), 511.org and TwoGo (twogo.com), which match individuals that have compatible commutes. Another peer-to-peer ridesharing company, Carma (gocarma.com), offers automated car passenger counting to make it easier for drivers who carpool to obtain HOV (high occupancy vehicle) toll discounts. Some municipalities are creating pickup locations to encourage "slugging," carpooling arrangements made on the fly by strangers traveling in the same direction. Other municipal and state government incentives include designating carpool car spaces in public parking lots and on the street, adding park-and-ride lots and increasing the number of carpool lanes on highways. Those HOV lanes can even help speed our journey since they're typically far less traveled than non-HOV lanes.

Doing More

We can increase the opportunities available to us and others to travel more sustainably by taking a stand on a variety of issues. For example, we can:

▶ Vote for candidates who support strong CAFE standards and the development of alternative fuels;

▶ Learn when it's time to sign petitions or participate in public comment periods related to green transportation issues by signing up for alerts from the Union of Concerned Scientists, Natural Resources Defense Council or other environmental organizations;

▶ Urge elected representatives to increase funding for public transportation;

▶ Ask local municipalities to support green transportation infrastructure, including walking and biking paths, carpool hubs and designated rideshare parking; and

▶ Continue to vote with our dollars by choosing alternative-fuel vehicles, riding public transportation or engaging in peer-to-peer ridesharing.

Making sustainable choices
about how we earn a living and
spend our free time may lead
us to work for a better world,
adopt a more creative or self-
reliant lifestyle or reconnect
with Mother Earth.

Work, Play and Retirement

The last four chapters explored how our consumer choices can help us live more sustainably. Just as important are the choices we make about how to spend our time. We may be able to embrace sustainable approaches to our work (paid or unpaid), our leisure time and even our eventual retirement.

Changing our jobs or careers—or rethinking our idea of work—may involve a more complex set of decisions than adopting an organic diet or a greener homelife. This won't be possible or even desirable for everyone. But some of us may be able to choose a job in a green or otherwise sustainable field, adopt a sustainable mission where we already work or explore sustainable alternatives to traditional employment. We may find opportunities to support sustainability through volunteer work. Depending on our interests, we also may be able to trade in unsustainable pastimes for eco-friendly alternatives. And when we're ready for some form of retirement, we may want to consider the sustainability of the various choices that will define that brand-new stage of life.

Work

There are two distinct ways to embrace sustainability in our work lives. If we're just starting out or have decided to change direction mid-career, we can seek work in a field that supports environmental, economic or social sustainability. If we've found ourselves outside the traditional workforce, intentionally or not, we can explore a variety of work alternatives that have the potential to make our lifestyles greener, more self-reliant and resilient.

Sustainable Work

The average American manages to log approximately 90,000 hours at work over a lifetime.[1] That's a lot of time and energy that could go into making the world a better place. But, to state the obvious, most of us don't have the opportunity to earn a paycheck for saving humankind. We certainly shouldn't feel guilty about that, particularly in a challenging job market. On the other hand, if skills and circumstances allow, it may be possible to align our career path with sustainable values by considering a variety of alternatives.

▶ **Choosing a green career.** The growth of green-collar jobs in recent years has opened the door to a wide range of sustainable career options. Some of the more obvious choices include jobs in environmental advocacy, environmental science, renewable energy, green building, recycling and conservation. But many other fields, including engineering, municipal or regional planning, education, the arts, social services and communications, also may provide opportunities to work toward environmental, economic or social sustainability. Some of those opportunities lie with mission-oriented employers, such as nonprofits, social enterprises and B corporations. (More information below) Others are with mainstream employers, such as corporations, municipal governments or universities that have launched sustainable initiatives requiring a diversity of talent. There are numerous books on the ins and outs of choosing a sustainable career. There also are many sustainable job sites, including jobs.greenbiz.com, greenjobsearch.org and sustainablebusiness.com.

▶ **Working for a mission-oriented nonprofit organization or foundation** that is dedicated to promoting environmental, economic and/or social sustainability. According to AARP (the American Association of Retired Persons), there are more than 1.5 million nonprofits in the U.S., employing more than 13 million people.[2] Job listings and employment information can be found at idealist.org, opportunityknocks.org, commongoodcareers.org, the Foundation Center's philanthropynewsdigest.org and the Philanthropy & Nonprofit Employment Resources page of the John D. and Catherine T. MacArthur Foundation website.

▶ **Creating or working for a social enterprise.** Some nonprofits employ a *social entrepreneurial* approach to development efforts, for example, by raising money from the sale of products. But the term "social enterprise" usually refers to a for-profit business engaged in addressing environmental, economic or social challenges. Some social entrepreneurs view a for-profit model as a more direct, effective way to achieve social goals than the nonprofit approach. For example, while nonprofits must allocate substantial time and resources to the pursuit of grant funding and donations, socially responsible for-profits can derive income directly from the sale of the goods or services they produce, just like traditional businesses. In some cases, that income is used to support sustainable solutions. For example, Newman's Own donates profits from the sale of its packaged foods to a variety of philanthropies. With other social enterprises, the goods and services produced *are* the solution. For example, social enterprises may build their businesses around development and distribution of affordable health care products, water purification equipment or school supplies for communities in developing areas of the world.

▶ **Working for a B corporation.** As described in Chapter 1, a growing number of for-profit companies today are embracing the idea of making traditional businesses a force for good. While it is possible for a social enterprise to be a B corporation, many B corps (and other companies that measure their profits and losses as well as their impact on people and the environment) are in business to sell ordinary products or services not directly related to sustainability. What sets these companies apart is a management philosophy that embraces environmental, economic and social sustainability as tangible business goals. B corporations are legally required by their corporate charters to produce benefits for society as well as for shareholders. Toward that end, they may support economic and social sustainability by paying workers competitively, offering robust employee benefits, ensuring health and safety on the job and investing in the local communities where they do business. They also may strive for environmental responsibility by sourcing raw materials locally or using rapidly renewable rather than nonrenewable natural resources, reducing the pollution and greenhouse gas emissions associated with their manufacturing processes and eliminating unnecessary waste. Many states allow companies to register as B corporations. Companies also can receive certification from the nonprofit organization B Lab. Among the more well-known B corporations are Patagonia, Seventh Generation and Ben & Jerry's. A list of certified B corporations can be found at bcorporation. net. (More information on B corporations: Chapter 8, Money)

▶ **Launching or working for a local, sustainable business.** As communities embrace the ideals of sustainability and resiliency, opportunities are emerging for sustainably minded entrepreneurs. Business possibilities include biomass pellet manufacture, solar panel installation, greywater system design and installation, mushroom farming, permaculture-based landscape services, urban farming and green-home consulting.[3]

▶ **Launching or working for a local, small-scale manufacturing business.** Beyond food producers and retailers, local economies need a diverse range of businesses—and employers—to achieve true resiliency. Manufacturing remains one of the best ways to create sustainable middle-class jobs. Small-scale manufacturing is becoming more competitive thanks to advancements in 3D printers and other maker technologies that allow for relatively inexpensive proto-typing and even production of new products.

▶ **Creating or finding employment with a worker cooperative.**

Worker cooperatives (co-ops) are for-profit companies owned and democrat-ically managed by employees. While they vary widely, worker co-ops typically place a high value on labor rights, environmental responsibility, product quality and community. Workers generally buy into a co-op either with a small up-front investment or ongoing payroll deductions. They also may be eligible to receive a share of any annual profits or surpluses, a benefit that can offer a strong incentive to work toward the company's continued success. Accumulated equity is returned to employees when they leave the company.

Worker co-ops have been around for many years, though their popularity has ebbed and waned. Co-ops helped alleviate widespread poverty in the midst of the Great Depression, fell out of favor during the postwar economic boom and were rediscovered in the 1960s by individuals attempting to build a more democratic society. While most of the roughly 300 worker co-ops in the U.S. today are quite small, a handful are large, highly successful companies that generate millions in annual revenue.[4] One of the world's best-known worker co-ops, Spain's Mondragon Corporation, was founded in the Basque region in 1956. Today, Mondragon is among Spain's largest companies, employing nearly 75,000 workers across the financial, industrial, retail and knowledge sectors of their economy.[5]

Encouraging sustainability at our current place of work

Wherever we work, we may have opportunities to demonstrate a personal commitment to sustain-ability and encourage others to do the same. We can change our own behavior by:

▶ Joining an employer-assisted rideshare or carpooling program.

▶ Conducting virtual rather than in-person meetings.

▶ Printing less and using fewer office supplies.

▶ Becoming vigilant about recycling paper and other office waste.

▶ Reducing energy use, turning off lights when there is adequate natural light, powering down or unplugging computers at the end of the work day, turning off power strips and turning down the thermostat.

We may encourage co-workers to become more sustainable simply by setting an example. If our boss seems receptive (or if we are a boss), we might suggest that our department initiate strate-gies for motivating daily workplace sustainability, such as giving out awards for meeting recycling or energy-saving targets. At larger organizations, there may be opportunities to participate in exist-ing efforts, for example, community service proj-ects focused on cleaning up litter or raising funds for a worthy cause, or to suggest new compa-ny-wide initiatives, such as farm-to-table procure-ment for the cafeteria, programs to reduce food waste, an electronics recycling day for workers and their families or creation of sharing networks that encourage workers to find ways to save money and go green by sharing goods, services and resources.

The health food groceries that emerged in the 1960s remain part of the co-op landscape. But worker co-ops now span a wide range of industries, including manufacturing, retail, utilities, insurance, education, media, the arts, house-keeping and health care. Variations on the worker co-op model include community-owned enterprises, platform cooperatives and staff-controlled nonprofits. There also are companies that enable workers to obtain partial ownership by participating in employee stock ownership plans (ESOPs), which offer the opportunity to purchase company stock, often at attractive share prices.

Until recently, it has been relatively complicated to create a new worker co-op in the U.S. But that's beginning to change in response to renewed interest in the ability of co-ops to offer secure, fulfilling and democratic employment alternatives. Among the newest American worker co-ops are several created through a partnership between Mondragon and the United Steelworkers union.

Sustainable Work Alternatives

Most of us need at least one member of the family to hold down "a real job." But in recent years, systemic changes to the economy have made that goal increasingly elusive. Globalization, rapidly changing technology and laws that preference corporations over employees may all have played a role. But, whatever the causes, numerous sources have consistently tracked a decline both in the number of middle class jobs and the average salary of the jobs available. As a consequence, despite a low official unemployment rate, many Americans are facing economic instability and downward mobility. Middle class workers are drifting into the working class. Recent college grads are struggling to find jobs that are commensurate with their education and that enable them to balance student loan payments with living expenses. And older workers are being pushed out of the workforce prematurely.

All of this begs the question: Would it be possible to earn a living without a job? Perhaps not. But more than a few of us are attempting to find out by experimenting with work alternatives that also may offer the promise of a more environmentally, economically and socially sustainable way of life. Some of these work alternatives are intended to replace full-time employment. Others may enable us to live on a smaller income by meeting some of our needs without money.

Alternatives to 'Traditional' Employment

For some expenses, such as the mortgage or rent, car payments and tuition, there's generally no substitute for money. Ideally, one member of a household can meet those expenses with income from a traditional job or business. But if that's not possible, or if the goal is to supplement income, there are several alternatives, including some touted by advocates of a sharing economy.

Become self-employed. Starting a business has always been an alternative for those who are entrepreneurial or simply too independent and self-directed to be satisfied as employees. While self-employment actually has declined in recent years, representing about 12.2% of the workforce in 1994 but only 10% in 2014, that still adds up to about 14.6 million Americans, who in turn employ another 29.4 million workers.[6] Additionally, a number of recent studies have found that about one in three U.S. workers now participates in the "gig economy," working on contract or as freelancers.[7]

Back in the 1990s, writers, graphic designers and software developers were among the first to leverage laptops and the Internet to launch independent contractor careers. Today, the menu of self-employed occupations is incredibly diverse, encompassing everything from marketing consultants and Etsy shop purveyors to artisanal food producers and technology start-ups. Many millennials have kicked off their work lives with self-employment, believing it offers more opportunity for fulfillment, flexibility and success than the traditional labor market. Some of the long-term unemployed view self-employment as the last option available to them. And retiring baby boomers are forging self-employed "second acts" as small business owners and social entrepreneurs.

While self-employment can be empowering, there are many potential pitfalls. It can be difficult to obtain the necessary capital. It can take months or even years to earn an adequate living, afford health benefits and enjoy the luxury of vacation time. And technology and global competition have made it more difficult for self-employed workers to control rates of pay or maintain enduring customer relationships. The latter trend began with online job sites that forced independent contractors to compete based on price with workers from areas of the country (or the world) where the cost of living was entirely different from their own. Gig economy apps that broker one-off assignments (ranging from driving to house painting to gardening) between workers and customers have further undercut the ability of independent workers to control the terms of their employment.

Whether our work consists of one-off gigs or something more closely resembling a traditional business, the key to making self-employment a sustainable option is to work for ourselves on our own terms. That may mean registering our business as a sole proprietorship, LLC or S corporation and/or working only for clients or customers that recognize us as a business, rather than viewing us as a "freelancer." Another alternative is to join a peer-to-peer gig-economy group, such as the platform cooperative Loconomics, which enables service providers and customers to connect without any for-profit intermediaries. Platform cooperatives, which may be owned and operated by user-members or even by municipalities, can enable self-employed workers to negotiate directly with potential clients and earn customer loyalty based on the quality of their work. True self-employment can increase our negotiating power, potentially boosting our income, while also enabling a more sustainable balance between work and family or other pursuits. It also can place us in the driver's seat when it comes to making key sustainability decisions, such as whether we will pay our employees fairly, power our offices with renewable energy or give something back to our communities.

Start or join a co-working space. The growth of the gig economy has given rise to co-working, the practice of sharing office space with other contractors, freelancers and entrepreneurs in order to reduce expenses, enjoy the company of colleagues and increase opportunities for networking. Some co-workers are particularly interested in the exchange of social capital that these arrangements can help foster. For example, workers may see opportunities to exchange information about their various fields, direct each other to resources, hire each other or provide referrals to attractive prospects. In addition to office space for independent contractors who offer professional business services, co-work space may take the form of a shared kitchen for chefs and artisanal food producers, studios for artists or musicians or makerspaces for technology entrepreneurs. Co-work spaces can be located in warehouses, traditional office buildings, public libraries or residential settings. They even can consist of little more than a spare office or kitchen table. Desksnearme (desksnear.me) is one of many apps that help connect hosts interested in earning extra income with renters in need of work space. Some platforms help individuals find co-work space virtually anywhere in the world.

Worker Collectives Are Empowering Freelancers
As the gig economy continues to replace formal employment, many contractors and freelancers are finding economic security, fair pay and benefits beyond their reach. Some are banding together in guilds, cooperatives and unions to fight for better pay and portable benefits.

Create income streams. In the mainstream economy, this can refer to interest from a portfolio of bonds, an annuity (annual payment) from an insurance policy or monthly income from leased or rented properties. In the sharing economy, the source of an income stream can be virtually anything we own that holds untapped value or capacity. The most common ways to create income streams are renting out all or part of a home to a traveler, turning a household car into a part-time taxi or rental car or, as noted above, renting out extra space to co-workers. These options can help us derive income from assets (i.e., our home or car) that otherwise simply represent monthly expenses. But with the rise of for-profit corporations acting as intermediaries in such transactions, the benefits can be minimized or even lost. As with self-employment, in order for *individuals* to benefit from turning their possessions into income-producing assets, they need to have as much control over transactions as possible. In many cases, that will mean tracking down peer-to-peer apps such as Getaround (getaround.com) for cars and rides or Desksnearme for co-work rentals, rather than signing up with for-profit platforms that may use "sharing economy" lingo simply for marketing purposes.

In addition to leasing or renting out assets, we may have opportunities to generate income by selling some of the food we produce at home. If we generate our own solar or wind power, we may be able to send excess electricity back to the grid and earn income in the form of a credit on the utility bill. We also may be able to transform a variety of at-home activities—handcrafts, sewing, herbalism, carpentry—into sources of part-time income.

Share the workload. Some employers offer opportunities for two or more employees to share a job. The success of such arrangements depends on the ability and willingness of all parties to communicate and coordinate well. But when job sharing runs smoothly, it can provide an alternative for those interested in working part time to accommodate family responsibilities or creative pursuits. A prospective employer may view the arrangement as an affordable way to maintain an adequate workforce.

Alternatives for Living on Less

Whether we attempt to rely on unconventional sources of income in place of, or in addition to, actual employment, our success may hinge on simultaneously committing to spend less, consume less and find ways to obtain what we want or need without traditional forms of money. Alternatives such as those that follow may help us become more economically resilient while further lightening our environmental footsteps.

Relocate. If we're out of the traditional workforce either by choice or due to economic circumstances, moving to a lower-cost area of the country could make a difference in our ability to reduce household expenses. The cost of housing, food and other consumer goods varies widely from one region of the country to the next, while climate obviously can impact how much of our budget goes toward utilities. A bit of comparative research on a site such as Livability (livability.com) could help us find just the right location for our household budget.

Scaling down the size of our dwelling is another alternative, one embodied by such trends as shared living arrangements and tiny homes. We also may want to search for places known for their commitment to sustainable values, including eco-consciousness, localism, sharing and community resiliency. For example, numerous towns and cities across the country have become sharing economy hubs, offering a wide range of alternatives for creating a viable lifestyle without a traditional job. Possibilities may be found through shareable.net.

Start or join co-op organizations. Virtually any type of organization can be run as a co-op, with members pooling resources and sharing the work load to achieve commonly held goals. Belonging to a co-op can help us lower living expenses while also adopting a greener, more local and community-focused lifestyle. Co-op groceries can help members obtain healthy organic and local food at a discount and participate in decision-making with a like-minded community. Cooperatively run community gardens, urban farms, CSAs (community-supported agriculture co-ops—or similar arrangements for ranches or fisheries) and seed libraries can all help individuals and their communities reduce food insecurity and support sustainable food production. Nursery school co-ops can enable parents to afford quality preschool for their children and get to know families with similar needs and values. And tool libraries can provide affordable access to a wide range of equipment while reducing our net consumption and strengthening community ties.

Use local currency, if available. Some communities encourage support for downtown business districts by creating their own complementary currencies. Those currencies often entitle users to a small discount on the goods and services they purchase from local merchants. That makes local currency another useful tool for anyone attempting to live on a limited income. The economic activity produced by our local purchases may even help create new local jobs. (More information on local currencies: LETS, page 182, as well as Chapter 5, Consuming, and Chapter 8, Money)

Adopt a DIY/radical homemaker lifestyle. There's been an explosion of interest in "going DIY," particularly since the last major recession. Some DIYers are motivated by a desire to reduce the environmental impact of their consumption. Others are more interested in exploring their creativity or replacing mass-produced goods with those that are handmade and one of a kind. Often, DIYers also want to reduce the need for income so that they can work less, "live more" and enjoy greater economic self-reliance.

With those goals in mind, many of us are acquiring skills once taken for granted by our ancestors. Forays into the DIY lifestyle often begin with food: We learn to grow an edible garden, harvest and process what we grow, raise chickens or even forage in the woods. (More information: Chapter 3, Food) But as Shannon Hayes reports in her book *Radical Homemakers*, some are taking DIYism far beyond the kitchen, learning to produce many of the goods that make up a typical household, from clothing, bedding and dishware to cleaning products, utensils and tools. DIY enthusiasts may even become their own carpenters, electricians, plumbers and mechanics, all in the interest of affording a simpler, greener, lower-cost way of life.[8]

Share. Sharing goods, services and other resources with friends, neighbors, co-workers or members of a local or online community can help us reduce expenses and consume less. We may be able to share:

> ▷ *Childcare* by forming a network of parents who take turns watching each other's children or by retaining a paid childcare provider for several families. Over time, the sharing arrangement may evolve into a cooperatively run nursery school, an after-school carpool or shared tutoring services or music lessons.

> ▷ *Gently used goods* by swapping with friends, neighbors or an online community. (More information: Chapter 4, Consuming)

> ▷ *Transportation* by carpooling, co-purchasing a car with a friend, lending our car to a friend or neighbor or using it as a part-time taxi or rental vehicle. (More information: Chapter 6, Transportation)

> ▷ *Food* by gardening, farming, fishing or hunting collectively, holding potluck dinners, participating in crop swaps or co-purchasing bulk food items with others. (More information: Chapter 3, Food)

> ▷ *Larger items* that are expensive, difficult to store or infrequently used (e.g., snow blowers, power tools, blow-up mattresses, kayaks) by co-purchasing them with friends or neighbors or creating a local tool library or a library of things. (More information: Chapter 5, Consuming)

> ▷ *Housing* by renting with roommates or living in a semi-communal setting, such as artist housing. Or we may choose private housing that offers some elements of sharing by buying into a cohousing development or an ecovillage. (More information: Chapter 4, Home)

> ▷ *Office, studio, production or makerspace* by co-renting a designated work space or using peer-to-peer apps to host or be hosted in an at-home setting.

> ▷ *Books, magazines, movies and more* by joining the local library or an online exchange.

Barter. We can further reduce daily living expenses by finding opportunities to exchange goods or services for something other than traditional currency. Bartering can involve trading goods of similar value, reciprocally providing services to others or using alternative currencies as a means of payment. Time banks and Local Exchange Trading Systems (LETS) are two organized ways to barter for services, from dental care to electrical work to tutoring.

▷ **Time Banks.** Typically run as nonprofit organizations that provide members with a systematic way to barter services, time banks promote the idea that the capital that matters in life is our social capital. According to Edgar S. Cahn, founder of the modern time bank movement and Time Banks USA, these arrangements "link untapped social capacity to unmet social needs" [to build] "caring community economies."[9]

Each time bank member, regardless of the individual's type or level of skill, agrees to offer services to other members in exchange for a unit of pay called a "time hour." For example, one hour of professional engineering services earns the same time hour as an hour of housekeeping. A member

The Benefits of Time Banks

Time banks generally offer these sustainable benefits:

A lower-carbon, greener lifestyle. Like shopping local, obtaining necessary services from local providers may help us reduce our carbon footprint by driving less.

Economic self-reliance. Time banks offer a do-it-yourself approach to achieving self-reliance and economic stability for a variety of populations, including:

▶ *Low-income communities.* The earliest time banks sought to create self-sustaining economic activity in communities where little to none existed previously. Time banks have provided low-income members with access to otherwise unaffordable services while helping them gain the skills, experience and confidence necessary to transition into the mainstream economy. In some cases, time bank transactions may connect members with their first customers or employers.

▶ *Retirees.* Time banks can help retirees remain active and socially engaged while accessing services in a way that doesn't strain their fixed incomes. Belonging to a time bank also can provide opportunities to pass along a lifetime of accumulated skills and knowledge to younger members of the community.

▶ *The unemployed and underemployed.* Time banks offer a no-cost way to obtain services

that may otherwise get postponed during periods of joblessness. They also can help individuals regain a sense of control over their lives, providing a DIY complement to unemployment benefits and other government-funded resources. Time banks may even serve as a bridge to future employment by offering opportunities to keep skills sharp and up to date, uncover previously untapped abilities or discover new professional connections within the community.

▶ *Those in search of work-life balance and/or a low-consumption lifestyle.* For those who opt out of the traditional workforce to care for loved ones or pursue creative endeavors, time banks can offer both flexible "work" schedules and a way to reduce household expenses. For those seeking a low-consumption, low-carbon, *radical homemaking* lifestyle, time banks can help facilitate the transition to an economy based on social forms of capital.

▶ *Communities seeking greater resiliency.* Time banks can help foster the old-fashioned ethic of neighbor helping neighbor. By creating an organized framework for providing mutual aid and assistance, a time bank can bring people together even in places that otherwise lack any sense of community. By removing money from the equation, the focus shifts to social capital built on relationships.

can use accumulated time hours to purchase services from other members. But it's not necessary to accrue hours before spending them; a time hour deficit can be repaid once the debtor provides services to another time bank member. Members' hours, accrued and spent, may be tracked by a designated time bank administrator or with software designed specifically for time banks. Either way, the goal is to continually return each member's balance to zero.

The practice of trading services and goods obviously is as old as civilization itself. While there are examples of "time-based currencies" in the 19th century and during periods of economic crisis such as the Great Depression, the modern time bank only emerged in the 1980s, the brainchild of Cahn, an activist and law professor. Since the Great Recession of 2007 to 2009, time banks have become increasingly popular as a tool for addressing economic insecurity. Today there are about 300 registered time banks in the U.S., with a total of about 30,000 members.[10]

▷ **LETS (Local Exchange Trading Systems),** like time banks, enable members to barter services. But with LETS, members pay each other with local, complementary currency. Some LETS treat that currency as the equivalent of time hours, with payment representing an IOU to provide a service to another LETS member at a future date. Other LETS link their local currency to actual market value. For example, a member might be paid the equivalent of $10 an hour for babysitting or $50 an hour for electrical work. This option can make it easier for small businesses to become LETS members. It also enables members to use LETS currency to obtain goods as well as services.

Volunteer Work and Activism

Whether or not we're able to align our career goals with sustainable values, we can make a difference through volunteer work or activism. Involvement with issues of importance to us can offer such benefits as:

▶ **Personal fulfillment.** Becoming "part of the solution," adding our voice to the struggle and seeing the impact of our efforts may provide a deeper sense of satisfaction than what we derive from our primary source of employment.

▶ **Knowledge.** Our involvement in an organization or cause can help us stay abreast of relevant issues and developments. We may gain a more in-depth understanding of an issue, such as the challenges of creating urban farms or protecting open space. Or we may get an early glimpse of a new solution, such as an effective way to sequester carbon or grow local food year-round in any climate.

▶ **A career boost.** Volunteering is an excellent way to develop skills, gain experience and make valuable connections, all of which may help us find a paying job in a related field.

Depending on our interests, we may decide to focus our volunteer efforts in one or more of these areas:

▶ **Environmental sustainability:** We may volunteer for environmental advocacy groups working on such issues as climate change, fracking, clean air and water, soil conservation, sustainable agriculture, nontoxic consumer products, waste reduction and recycling, open space and land preservation, renewable energy or protection of endangered species.

▶ **Economic sustainability:** We may support organizations focused on downtown development and shop local campaigns, local currency programs, farm-to-institution initiatives, other efforts to create local food-based economies, microlending or banking for the unbanked.

▶ **Social sustainability:** We may join organizations that support social justice initiatives, formal or informal sharing arrangements, community-scale renewable energy production, community gardening, urban farming, programs to reduce food insecurity and waste, seed libraries, tool libraries, little free libraries or repair cafés.

Recreation

Finding more sustainable ways to spend our free time may seem like a stretch. But we actually can align our sustainable values with recreational activities in two important ways: (1) avoiding activities that may be harmful to the environment and (2) choosing alternatives that reconnect us with the source of inspiration for living sustainably: Mother Nature.

▶ **Rethinking our toys.** Whether we spend most of our leisure time involved with sports, the arts, cultural pursuits, hobbies or simply television and video games, we may want to consider how our activities impact the environment and our health.

Recreational vehicles. Many watercrafts, including gas-powered motorboats and jet skis, can produce greenhouse gas emissions as well as air, water and noise pollution. Many boats now run on solar-powered motors. Other sustainable alternatives include boats that either don't use motors (e.g., canoes, kayaks, rafts) or use them only occasionally (e.g., rowboats, sailboats). Back on land, we may want to trade in gas-powered ATVs and dune buggies for bikes, skateboards or running gear.

Arts and crafts.[11] Depending on their medium of choice, artists may face a variety of risks as well as opportunities to protect their health and the environment.

- ✓ *Paints and inks.* Oil-based paints and inks can pose both health and environmental risks. For example, some oil paints contain heavy metals, such as lead, cobalt and cadmium, known to be toxic or even carcinogenic. Synthetic oil paint substitutes, often labeled as "hues," may be safer than those containing heavy metals, but the substituted ingredients generally have not been fully studied. Like paints, oil-based printmaking inks can contain numerous toxins. Water-based alternatives are far less toxic. But for the many artists who rely on oil-based products, it's important to manage the risks. Recommended safety steps include maintaining proper ventilation in oil painting and printmaking studios and wearing nitrile gloves to prevent absorption of toxins through our skin.

- ✓ *Airborne toxins.* Turpentine, mineral spirts, fixatives and numerous other mediums and sprays can release toxins into the air. Proper ventilation is always important. A fume hood may be desirable if fumes are excessive. Oil painters can use walnut, poppy or safflower oils in place of both traditional mediums and solvents. Printmakers can reduce exposure to toxic solvents by wrapping pallets in wax paper and cleaning up with corn oil or vegetable oil.

- ✓ *Waste.* Since oil paints, inks and solvents are toxic waste, it's important to discard them properly. Waste can be accumulated in a special trash container and taken to a community hazardous waste cleanup site. We also can reduce the production of waste by using paints and solvents as sparingly as possible.

- ✓ *Studio sustainability.* Artists also can protect the environment by choosing energy-efficient LED lighting in their studios and seeking out recycled or eco-conscious materials (e.g., paper, pencils, studio furnishings, storage systems) that reduce both pollution and landfill waste.

- ✓ *Textiles and mixed media.* If our creative interests involve knitting, crocheting, sewing, quilting or other textile-oriented crafts, we can reduce our environmental impact by using organic or natural raw materials. Eco-conscious crafters also are incorporating a wide range of discarded materials into upcycled works of art.

Digital devices. As discussed in Chapter 5, Consuming, electronics can pose health and environmental risks all the way from the sourcing of their raw materials to their eventual disposal in landfill. Increasing security threats and privacy concerns, coupled with burnout from never-ending technology upgrades, is triggering a low-tech revolt among some sustainably minded users. Manual typewriters, phonographs, letterpress printers and print magazines all are making a comeback, though often with some digital retrofit, such as digital recording for record players or computer monitors connected to typewriters. Even if we're not willing to abandon our 21st-century state of connectedness, we can minimize the negative impact of electronics by adopting ergonomic habits and ensuring that our devices are recycled in an environmentally responsible manner. (More information: Chapter 5, Consuming) We also may want to consider the contradiction between adopting a green, low-consumption lifestyle and continually rushing out to purchase the latest version of our phones and other electronic devices.

▶ **Traveling.** Sustainable travel is entering the mainstream, with surveys showing a growing number of travelers interested in limiting the greenhouse gas emissions and other potentially negative impacts of their vacation excursions. Ideas for traveling sustainably include:

Reducing waste and pollution by reusing hotel sheets and towels instead of having them replaced every day, packing reusable containers for personal care products and bringing along only nontoxic products, such as shampoos, conditioners, moisturizers and suntan lotions. The latter is particularly important when visiting environmentally sensitive areas, such as those with coral reefs, or developing countries with limited environmental infrastructure.

Reducing our impact on greenhouse gas emissions by turning off lights when we leave hotel rooms, adjusting the thermostat, seeking out airlines that use biofuels, choosing tour operators that only run fully booked flights, walking, biking, taking public transportation or using apps such as Green Travel Choice (greentravelchoice.com) to select lower-carbon travel options and Carbon Fund (carbonfund.org) to offset any emissions with donations to sustainable causes.

Supporting the local economy and community by interacting with locals, learning about their culture and environment, staying at locally owned hotels and preferencing locally owned shops and restaurants over those that are not owned by locals.

Choosing hotels that have met the environmental standards of the Green Seal label (greenseal.org) or that have been certified by the Global Sustainable Tourism Council (gstcouncil.org), an independent nonprofit that establishes sustainability standards for the travel industry. Hotels are considered sustainable if they pay workers a living wage, protect the environment, reduce waste, including food waste, support the local economy and possibly even invest in or donate to conservation programs.

Booking an ecotourism trip, a vacation designed to reconnect us with the natural world, support conservation efforts and/or increase our awareness of environmental challenges. The Global Sustainable Tourism Council (GSTC) says it can help travelers locate authentic and affordable ecotourism alternatives while avoiding high-priced travel options that are nothing more than green-washing. More information on traveling sustainably is available from Sustainable Travel International's Travel Better Club (sustainabletravel.org). The app Adventure Junky (adventurejunky.com) lets travelers earn points for traveling sustainably.

▶ **Celebrating.** When entertaining or celebrating birthdays and other holidays, we can remain reasonably sustainable by using nondisposable tableware (e.g., plates, cups, napkins, cutlery), decorating with natural or eco-friendly materials (e.g., native flowers, soy candles, reusable streamers, signs and ornaments) and replacing gifts of consumer goods with those that offer experiences (e.g., concert tickets, dinners at local restaurants) or support values (e.g., donations to worthy institutions or causes).

▶ **Playing outside...and communing with nature.** Much has been said about how kids growing up in the digital age don't spend enough time outdoors. But the same is true for adults. As the percentage of workers engaged in agriculture has continued to shrink, fewer of us are required to be outdoors to earn a living. We're also spending little of our free time outside. According to a survey conducted for the National Recreation and Park Association, only about 12% of adults report spending some time outside on a daily basis, with about half outside for less than 30 minutes at a time.[12] It's difficult to say whether this is due to insufficient time or lack of interest. But limited physical exercise and outdoor activity have been linked to both the obesity epidemic and deficiencies in vitamin D.[13]

Besides improving our physical health, spending more time outdoors can help us feel a renewed connection with the natural world. It was a passion for hiking and hunting that led two of the nation's earliest recognized environmentalists, Sierra Club Founder John Muir and President Theodore Roosevelt, to fight for the preservation and conservation of our majestic wilderness. (More information: Chapter 2) Any outdoor activity—team sports or a 5K race—can enhance our appreciation of clear skies and fresh air. If we're inclined toward walking, biking, hiking, kayaking or other activities that focus attention on our surroundings, the benefits can be greater still. Taking time to experience the transcendence of a mountaintop view or a still moment on a secluded pond can strengthen our spiritual bond with nature and transform us into lifelong protectors of the Earth.

▶ **Lightening our outdoor footprints.** Maintaining sustainable habits when we venture into the wilderness can help us get the most from the experience without disrupting the local ecosystem. This may involve:

Reading informational signs about hours of operation, trail closings, potential threats from wildlife or fire hazards.

Obeying posted rules, staying on marked trails, off dunes and away from known wildlife habitats, such as the nests of breeding eagles. We also may be asked not to light fires outside of marked campground areas and not to pick any wild fruit or flowers.

Bringing along a garbage bag so we can "carry in, carry out." We also may decide to pick up trash left behind by others.

Keeping our dogs leashed to prevent them from doing unintentional harm to preserved lands.

Using only allowed vehicles and recreational equipment—bikes, boats, skis, snowboards, skateboards—and only in designated areas.

Being courteous to others we meet along the way, limiting noise, turning off cell phones and maintaining a distance that allows everyone to enjoy his or her own "slice of heaven."

Retirement

As we approach retirement, we may face a wide range of choices about our future lifestyle. That makes retirement a particularly good time to consider sustainable alternatives. Our decisions about how and where to live in retirement may help us become more sustainable environmentally as well as economically and socially. It also may be possible to become more sustainable with regard to:

▶ **Post-retirement work.** Some of the ideas discussed in Sustainable Work and Sustainable Work Alternatives may be well-suited to retirees who want to continue working "on their own terms." According to a 2015 Career-Builder retirement survey, about 78% of individuals age 60 and older are continuing to work due to financial necessity. About one in six are transitioning from their pre-retirement jobs to careers that allow them to pursue a strong interest or passion they set aside earlier in life. And many view retirement as the right time to find meaningful work that lets them give something back and make a difference.[14]

Other Retirement Considerations

▶ **Where we live.** Alternatives include scaling down to a smaller home, moving to a walkable community, sharing living space or building or moving into a sustainably designed and furnished dwelling. Even arrangements for those with deteriorating health and mobility are gradually benefitting from the sustainability movement. Aging in place programs increasingly support the desire of most retirees to continue living in their homes for as long as possible. And a new breed of nursing home developers is integrating small-scale, residential facilities into vibrant, mixed-used communities. (More information: Chapter 4, Home)

▶ **Money.** Retirees living on a reduced or fixed income may want to explore some of the strategies described in Alternatives for Living on Less, as well as those for managing money sustainably, described in Chapter 8, Money.

▶ **Health.** Eating well, exercising, staying active and involved and avoiding common toxins are increasingly important as we age. It also can be important to live near a high-quality hospital, choose physicians that respect our sustainable mindset and continue to take responsibility for our own daily wellness.

▶ **Community involvement.** Retirees have long played a vital role as volunteers for nonprofit organizations and grassroots social movements. The emergence of community-based initiatives outside the traditional nonprofit world—community gardens, time banks, LETS, tool libraries—has only increased the number and variety of opportunities for retiree volunteers. Many of those opportunities involve some aspect of sustainability, from the environmental (fighting a local source of pollution) to the economic (providing gardening or business mentoring to participants of an urban farm) to the social (helping homeless individuals build their own homes through groups such as Habitat for Humanity).

Doing More

In addition to reevaluating our view of work, leisure and retirement, we may want to support or advocate for:

▶ Portability of health and retirement benefits;

▶ Union representation for gig-economy workers;

▶ Employment equality for all workers; and

▶ An end to age discrimination.

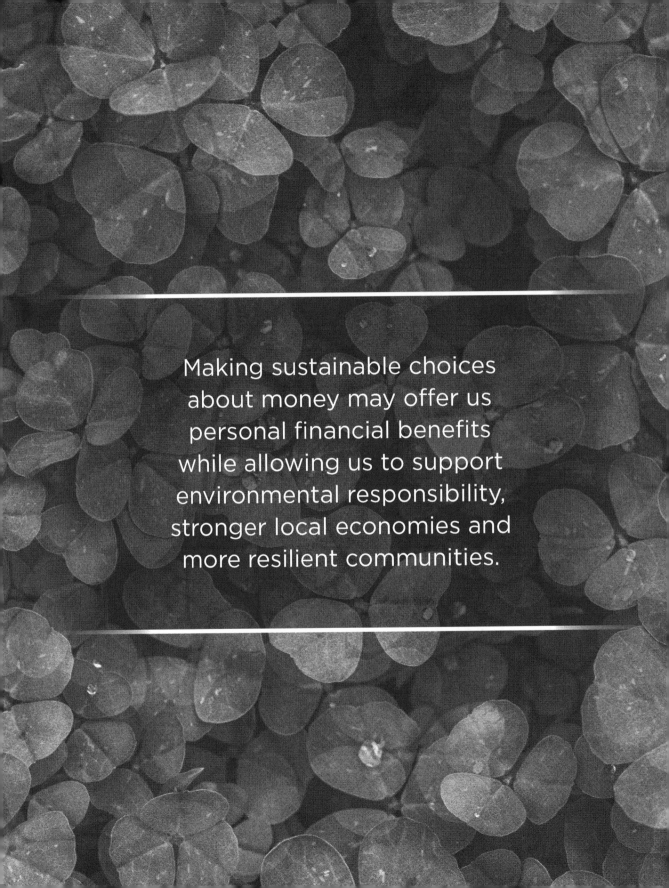

Making sustainable choices
about money may offer us
personal financial benefits
while allowing us to support
environmental responsibility,
stronger local economies and
more resilient communities.

Money

The adage "Don't leave money on the table" takes on new meaning when it comes to living sustainably. At first glance, finances may seem entirely unrelated to this subject. But how we manage money can make a significant difference in our ability to forge a greener, more economically stable and resilient lifestyle.

We may become more financially resilient by living within our means, investing in ourselves[1] or choosing financial institutions committed to serving our needs. We can green our finances by investing in environmentally responsible companies or donating to organizations that work to protect the environment. And we may have opportunities to support strong, community-based local economies by choosing saving, borrowing and investing alternatives that put our money to work close to home.

One word of caution: Whatever goals we hope to achieve by living more sustainably may be undone by uninformed financial decisions. In other words, becoming sustainable with money starts with financial literacy. So before exploring the ideas covered in this chapter, it's important to have the financial basics covered. Those in need of guidance will find no shortage of books, courses and professional services offering a wide range of financial information. Trustworthy sources will encourage us to start with such building blocks as (1) budgeting realistically, (2) saving regularly, (3) planning for long-term financial goals (e.g., college, retirement), (4) understanding the impact of interest rates and (5) learning the basics of investing. Once we are reasonably well-organized, we can decide if we want to consider ways to fine-tune our financial decision-making with an eye toward sustainability.

Decisions about saving, borrowing, investing and making charitable contributions all may hold possibilities for becoming more sustainable environmentally, economically and socially.

Saving and Borrowing

Choosing a local, independently owned financial institution for our saving and borrowing needs may be the easiest and single most effective step we can take to incorporate sustainable values into our financial decision-making. Banking local isn't for everyone. For example, individuals who live or work in more than one country or who own certain types of businesses may require the services of larger banking institutions. But those interested in greater financial sustainability may find what they're seeking in a community bank or credit union.

Community Banks

Community banks are relatively small depository financial institutions[2] focused on serving individuals and businesses (and, in some communities, farmers) in particular geographic areas. These institutions come in a variety of forms—savings banks, mutual savings banks, commercial banks and savings and loan associations, also known as "thrifts"—but they share a number of important qualities. For example, they're usually chartered as community banks, headquartered in the communities they serve, staffed by individuals who live in or near those communities and committed to keeping responsibility for business decisions, such as loan approvals, vested in local management. Community banks also have in common a commitment to support the local economy by focusing primarily on (1) accepting deposits in savings and checking accounts, money market accounts and certificates of deposit (CDs) and (2) originating mortgages, personal loans, business loans and lines of credit. Community banks also may offer credit cards and debit cards, tax-advantaged individual retirement accounts (IRAs) and some insurance and investing products.

Community banks have long comprised the majority of the nation's banking institutions. But while they still account for more than 90%[3] of all U.S. banks, their share of total bank assets has declined as the nation's largest financial institutions have captured more of the market.[4] The trend away from community banking began in the 1970s, when Congress first weakened long-standing regulations that had banned banks from operating across state lines. That allowed national financial institutions to begin buying up their smaller, regional competitors. Further deregulation in the 1990s[5] triggered a wave of mergers and acquisitions, leaving many of us banking with large institutions that were publicly traded and nonlocal. Since the financial crisis of 2007 to 2009, few new community banks have been chartered[6] and many small community banks have closed or been acquired by larger banks.

Many of us have community banks nearby. Perhaps our parents or grandparents once held accounts at these small institutions. Or perhaps we banked local until our small bank was purchased by a much larger, nonlocal institution. Taking another look at community banks could yield personal financial benefits while also helping to strengthen our local economy and community.

With only about 6,000 community banks remaining today,[7] many of us no longer have convenient access to these institutions. To learn whether we have a community bank nearby, we can:

✓ Review the websites of our local financial institutions to learn whether they are chartered as community banks.

✓ Search findabetterbank.com.

✓ Peruse banklocal.info, which provides a snapshot of all the banks in a geographic area, including their size, headquarters location, ownership type, branch concentration, small business lending activity, farm lending activity and participation in speculative trading.

Credit Unions

Credit unions are nonprofit, cooperative financial institutions owned by depositors and operated for their benefit. Like community banks, credit unions serve the saving and borrowing needs of their customers with savings and checking accounts, mortgages, personal and business loans, credit and debit cards and IRAs. Depositor-owners may receive a share of annual profits in the form of free services, higher-than-average interest rates on savings and checking accounts or competitive rates on loans.

According to the National Credit Union Administration, the first American credit union opened its doors in 1909. By the mid-20th century, thousands of credit unions throughout the country were providing banking services to specific communities of customers, such as employees of particular companies or members of certain unions or trade associations. Laws passed in the late 1990s enabled a wider range of customers to join credit unions. But membership actually was on the decline until about 10 years ago. Today, there are just over 7,200 credit unions in the U.S.,[8] searchable at creditunionsdirectory.com.

Community banks and credit unions can offer several sustainable benefits to individual customers and their communities.

▶ **Stability.** We may benefit financially from choosing an institution that is likely to be around when we need its services. Two distinct qualities—loyalty to a specific market and financial strength—can make community banks and credit unions stable, reliable choices.

Local loyalty. Many community banks advertise that they have "proudly served the community for more than 100 years." Since their business focus is local, these banks are unlikely to pick up and move out of the neighborhood to pursue higher profits someplace else. Community banks haven't been immune to the banking industry's rapid consolidation over the past few decades. But the majority of mergers have involved small community banks being acquired by larger ones that are committed to providing banking services to the same local communities.[9]

Fiscal discipline. Community banks and credit unions also are known for fiscal discipline. They typically avoid the speculative trading common at larger financial institutions, investing bank assets conservatively. Additionally, while they strive to provide access to loans, their careful evaluation of potential borrowers is intended to reduce the likelihood of defaults and foreclosures.[10]

> *The "values banking" movement encourages consumers to choose banks that focus on them and their communities, using capital to support the local economy and avoiding speculative investments that may place funds at risk.*

▶ **Customer focus.** While publicly traded institutions, which are obligated to produce value for shareholders, tend to focus on quarterly returns, community banks and credit unions are committed to serving the long-term needs of local customers. That commitment may translate into helpful, quality service and personalized attention.

▶ **Lower-cost services.** Access to affordable banking services is critical to the financial well-being of individual customers and their communities. While community banks and credit unions offer many of the same services as larger banks, they often charge lower fees, offer lower rates on loans and provide higher interest rates on customer accounts. As noted above, with credit unions, these benefits are considered a form of profit sharing in a cooperatively owned institution.

▶ **Commitment to the community.** Our communities can benefit in a variety of ways from the charitable inclinations of community banks and credit unions. These banks and their employees may have a strong track record of community service, supporting local nonprofits as generous donors, board members and volunteers.

▶ **A local stimulus.** Like independently owned local businesses, banks committed to a geographic region or community can help stimulate the local economy by increasing the local multiplier effect. When we make purchases with a credit card issued by a local bank, merchant card fees stay in the community, helping to fund other economic activity. The greatest benefits occur when we choose our local bank as a lender, whether for our home mortgage, business loan or other forms of credit. With a steadfast commitment to turn deposits into productive loans for local residents and businesses, community banks and credit unions play a critical role in the success of local economies.[11] This is the primary reason that banking local can be such a powerful way to support both personal financial resiliency and the economic well-being of the community.

Even as their share of bank assets has declined, community banks and credit unions have continued to underwrite about two-thirds of all small business loans.[12] While larger banks generally rely on algorithms to make loan determinations and require substantial collateral for business loans, smaller banks practice "relationship banking," meeting with potential borrowers in person and making lending decisions based on in-depth knowledge of customers and the local business climate. That may lead to a more nuanced evaluation of the creditworthiness of a small business (although some banks complain that relationship banking has been undermined by banking regulations passed since the financial crisis). Of course, when local businesses have access to capital, they can grow, hire, create local wealth and increase the tax revenue available for municipal services.

Community banks and credit unions also support personal and community-wide financial resiliency when they leverage our deposits to originate mortgages and increase home ownership. Owning a home can enhance personal financial resiliency in two ways: (1) Since our home is usually our most valuable asset, home ownership generally increases our net worth (i.e., our personal bottom line, equal to the sum of all our assets less all our debts) and (2) since proceeds from the sale of our home may help support us in retirement, home ownership can help protect our financial future. Home ownership and upkeep also can help the entire neighborhood by stabilizing or increasing home values. The relatively low loan-default rate at many community banks and credit unions can help communities maintain their housing stock and avoid the economic devastation triggered by widespread foreclosures.

Access

The Community Reinvestment Act (CRA) of 1977 was intended to increase the availability of banking services in low-income communities by requiring banks to lend to local customers wherever they maintained branches. Unfortunately, despite the CRA, many low-income communities, both urban and rural, have remained among the "unbanked." In these "financial institution deserts," it can be difficult to save, plan for emergencies or access credit at affordable rates. Costly alternatives such as pay-day lenders and check-cashing services can worsen the situation, leading borrowers to accumulate nearly insurmountable levels of debt. Some credit unions are beginning to fill the void in these neighborhoods. Working in partnership with local social service agencies, credit unions are providing communities with traditional banking services along with support services such as financial literacy education.[13]

▶ **Social lending.** Some community banks and credit unions enable customers to have their deposits put to use to support the community through targeted lending programs. A common example is the issuance of specialized certificates of deposit (CDs) to be used as collateral for certain types of low-interest loans. In some cases, the CDs are issued at the request of local nonprofit organizations involved in economic development, social services or sustainability initiatives. CDs may back loans to borrowers who would otherwise lack access to credit. For example, the loans may provide capital to sustainable small businesses, such as organic farms or solar panel installers, or help an individual meet such basic financial needs as making a down payment on a car or providing the security deposit for an apartment. While interest rates may be the same as or even lower than rates available on other CDs (and there is always the risk that borrowers could default), investors can gain the *social return* of helping members of the community.

▶ **Environmental responsibility.** Community banks and credit unions may demonstrate environmental responsibility in several ways. As part of their commitment to serve the community through volunteer and charitable endeavors, they may support environmentally focused local organizations, such as land trusts or nature preserves. They may provide loans for green home improvements or sustainable businesses. And by helping to meet business lending needs, they may increase the number of business owners in the community who, as locals, should have a vested interest in running their companies in an environmentally responsible manner.

Investing

Those of us with the ability to invest some of our income typically purchase shares of publicly traded companies (those that sell shares to investors on exchanges such as the New York Stock Exchange) without knowing whether they are committed to any form of sustainability. This tends to be true whether we own individual stocks or mutual funds and whether our investments are in taxable brokerage accounts or tax-advantaged accounts (e.g., IRAs, 401(k) retirement plan accounts or 529 college savings plan accounts). Financial professionals will tell us that our investment goals, return expectations and tolerance for risk must be our most important criteria when selecting investments. But it's also increasingly possible to factor in the sustainability of the companies in which we invest. That may mean purchasing the stock of companies (directly or through mutual funds) committed to environmental, economic or social sustainability. Or it may involve rethinking our idea of investing to encompass innovative alternatives that are environmentally, economically or socially sustainable.

Some sustainable investments are accessible only to affluent investors who meet income and net worth criteria set by the Securities and Exchange Commission (SEC). Other alternatives are available to all investors, though sometimes with certain limits on the amounts that can be invested. We may be able to choose some of the sustainable investment alternatives described in the next few pages through our employer's retirement plan account or through an investment company or a professional financial advisor. For other alternatives, it may be necessary to seek out or create opportunities, working together with members of our communities. As with any financial or investing decision, it's important to seek professional advice and guidance before making any decision and to understand that all investments pose risks. The following simply describes some possibilities.

▶ **Socially responsible mutual funds.** Among the earliest sustainable investments, socially responsible mutual funds were introduced in the early 1980s. Originally defined by what they *excluded*, such as tobacco and oil companies, socially responsible mutual funds, index funds and exchange traded funds (ETFs) now tend to focus on what's *included*, the stock of companies committed to environmental and social sustainability, such as B corporations and social enterprises. It's possible to purchase shares of socially responsible mutual funds through full-service, online or discount investment firms. Such funds also may be among the menu of choices in our employer-sponsored retirement plans (e.g., 401(k) plans, 403(b) plans) or 529 college savings plans. Choosing these mutual funds may enable us to support companies that meet high standards for environmental and/or social sustainability. But mutual funds marketed as "socially responsible" are no more or less likely than other mutual funds to produce desirable investment returns, reduce investment risks or charge reasonable fees. (Socially responsible index funds and ETFs may charge relatively lower fees than mutual funds that are "actively managed," i.e., funds that buy and sell their underlying investments on a frequent basis.) It's also possible that we won't always agree with a fund manager's definition of "socially responsible" or "sustainable." As with other mutual funds, it's important to review prospectuses and identify a fund's major investment holdings before making a decision to invest.

▶ **Impact investments.** This can refer to any type of security (e.g., stocks, mutual funds, bonds) that offers *social returns* in addition to—or instead of—traditional investment returns. An investment can make an impact, producing social returns, by supporting environmental, economic or social sustainability or promoting good corporate governance. In some cases, impact investing also fits the description of *slow* or *patient capital.* For example, investments in start-up renewable energy producers or locally owned clean tech firms may not produce investment returns—or may take years to do so. (Of course, there is no guarantee that *any* investment will yield returns.) Investors need to be comfortable knowing that their capital is enabling a sustainable business to become established and grow, perhaps helping to repair the environment or produce local jobs. Other impact investments may include:

B corporations. In addition to purchasing socially responsible mutual funds that invest in these types of companies, it may be possible to purchase their stock directly if they are publicly traded. As described in Chapter 1, these companies are committed to turning a profit while also having a positive impact on the world. B corporations are monitored by independent entities such as B Lab,

True Cost and HIP. The companies evaluate their own success by measuring "the three P's":

✓ *Profit.* Traditional accounting determines the financial bottom line of a company or organization.

✓ *People.* Companies also measure their social impact on (1) employees (e.g., compensation, health care, retirement benefits, job safety, opportunity for growth), (2) the community (e.g., local reinvestment) and (3) consumers (e.g., safe, healthy, reliable products, ethical business practices, good customer service).

✓ *Planet.* Companies measure their impact on the environment, evaluating their success at conserving natural resources and energy, reducing waste, employing eco-conscious production methods and remediating any environmental damage or harm they have caused.

Social enterprises. As described in Chapter 7, Work, Play and Retirement, these are companies focused on addressing environmental, economic or social challenges. For example, a company that manufactures affordable water-filtration systems for communities without access to clean water would be considered a social enterprise because its products address a social need. If we are able to invest in these companies, we may benefit from the social return of supporting their endeavors.

Social impact bonds. Bonds represent debt on the part of an issuer and a loan on the part of the investor. Technically, social impact bonds aren't bonds because the issuer does not guarantee return of principal and interest when the investment is held to maturity. That said, these debt securities are intended to offer municipal and state governments an alternative way to pay for social programs. Government agencies issue the bonds to nonprofits to fund high-impact social programs designed to address specific challenges, such as homelessness or high rates of youth incarceration. Investors who purchase the bonds provide the working capital necessary for a nonprofit to achieve the designated goal. If the goal is achieved (e.g., if homelessness is reduced by 10% or if 15% fewer teens serve jail sentences), the government agency provides funds to the nonprofit, which in turn repays the investor with a small amount of interest. If the goal is not achieved, the investor stands to lose 100% of the investment.

▶ **Local investments.** Like shopping and banking locally, investing in local companies and nonprofit organizations can help strengthen our local economy. Affluent, *accredited investors* are free to invest in privately owned businesses in or outside of their communities. In the past, the rest of us—nonaccredited investors—also could invest in local businesses, usually through local stock exchanges. But Depression-era securities laws passed with the intention of protecting ordinary investors led to the demise of most local stock exchanges. Local economy advocates believe this has greatly limited the amount of capital available to the small and midsize companies that historically have produced the majority of American jobs. It's also left most of us without an alternative to investing in nonlocal, publicly traded corporations.

  As interest in creating strong local economies has grown, so have efforts on the part of economists, financial professionals, lawyers, community activists, mission-oriented businesses, nonprofits and others to help ordinary investors find ways to invest locally. For proponents of local investing, the ideal would be having the ability to invest in the organic farms or solar panel manufacturers in our own communities. But "locavesting" advocates express optimism about developments that are moving us toward that goal. For example, recent federal and state regulatory changes allow nonaccredited investors to invest in small and midsize companies that may or may not be local to them or even in-state. At the same time, local investing advocates are raising the profile of a range of alternatives that allow nonaccredited investors to invest in their communities without running afoul of the SEC. Some of these alternatives fit the definition of impact investments because they offer social returns in addition to, or instead of, financial returns. Possibilities include:

An accredited investor is an individual with income of at least $200,000 a year ($300,000 with a spouse) and net worth of at least $1 million, excluding a primary residence.

Equity crowdfunding. Crowdfunding refers to raising small amounts of money from many people rather than large amounts from a handful of investors. Title III of the JOBS (Jumpstart Our Business Startups) Act, which went into effect in May 2016, allows both nonaccredited and accredited investors to invest in small and midsize start-up companies via equity crowdfunding platforms. The investments represent the type of early-stage financing that larger start-ups typically seek from venture capital firms or angel investors. Under the law, start-ups cannot advertise offerings and the crowdfunding platforms must act as intermediaries, vetting companies in accordance with SEC rules and managing investment transactions. Investors are responsible for carefully reviewing information the exchanges provide about companies before investing or sending money. Early-stage investing presents risks to investors since many new businesses don't succeed. And unlike investments in publicly traded stocks or mutual funds, these deals may require investors to hold shares for a significant period of time before selling them to other investors. (Potentially, it may never be possible to sell the shares.)

  Equity crowdfunding limits the amount a company can raise to $1 million in a 12-month period. The amount that nonaccredited investors can invest depends on their income and net worth. Those with annual income or net worth of less than $100,000 can make annual investments totaling the greater of $2,000 or 5% of the lesser of their annual income or net worth. For those with $100,000 or more in earnings and net worth, the limit is 10% of the lesser of their annual income or net worth.[14] These limits are designed to prevent average, nonaccredited investors from taking extraordinary investing risks. They also enable companies to obtain small investments from many investors, which may allow them to retain more control over their companies than possible when receiving large amounts of capital from a small number of investors.

Since very few start-ups receive conventional venture capital, equity crowdfunding may represent a substantial boon to new business development. That was the primary motivation for passing the JOBS Act. But while equity crowdfunding may make it easier for ordinary investors to invest in mission-oriented and local businesses, deals available on equity crowdfunding platforms will not necessarily fall into either category. Investors who want to keep their money more local may be able to utilize state-run crowdfunding platforms. At this time, 35 states operate their own platforms, allowing investors to focus on local or in-state companies. Like earlier local stock exchanges, these platforms allow investments in both start-ups and existing businesses.

Direct Public Offerings (DPOs). DPOs can enable both nonaccredited and accredited investors to invest directly in companies or nonprofits located in their communities or networks without the involvement of brokers or other intermediaries. Some DPOs are available exclusively in one state, while others extend to multiple states. Many DPOs are exempt from federal SEC registration, making the offering process easier and less expensive for start-ups than many other types of offerings. DPOs can be advertised publicly through online and print ads and social media and at events and meetings. The direct (and often local) nature of DPOs can enable all parties to become familiar with each other and make face-to-face decisions about investing.

Intrastate public offerings. Both nonaccredited and accredited investors may purchase the stock of companies located in their state of residence through intrastate public offerings. Investment minimums may be as low as $100, but there generally is no ceiling on the total amount that a company can raise through this type of offering. Since intrastate offerings require only state-level registration, rather than federal registration, filing requirements tend to be less extensive and expensive than those for many other types of public offerings. After the initial offering period, investors may buy and sell shares, provided that all investors reside in-state. This is the type of offering used by residents of Saranac Lake, New York, to fund the start-up of a much-needed local department store.

Investments based on preexisting relationships. It's possible for a nonaccredited investor to invest locally by purchasing the stock of a company whose owner he or she already knows. This is sometimes referred to as a "friends and family investment round" since entrepreneurs often seek their first investment dollars from friends, relatives or members of their communities. Communities may facilitate these local investment opportunities by forming groups for the purpose of introducing would-be investors to entrepreneurs. Over time, these investments may help a community strengthen its local economy while supporting the creation of a diverse range of businesses that meet local needs. On the other hand, companies may be limited to a relatively small number of "known" investors and may face various registration hurdles that require them to obtain knowledgeable accounting and legal advisors.

Investments made through an investment club. Provided members of an investment club make all investing decisions as a group and pool their resources, they (nonaccredited and accredited investors) can invest relatively large amounts in local and/or sustainable businesses. Some investment clubs also make small, unsecured loans to local businesses. Members share in any profits or losses. Investment clubs tend to remain small so that it does not become too difficult for them to evaluate choices and reach consensus.

Local Investing Opportunities Networks (LIONs). These are investing networks comprising members of a community who wish to invest in or lend to local companies to support a strong local economy. LIONs generally are open to nonaccredited as well as accredited investors. Unlike members of investing clubs, who invest as a group, LIONs members make their own investing decisions. LIONs can avoid triggering federal securities laws by investing only in companies run by individuals with whom members have strong preexisting relationships.

Slow money. Inspired by the national nonprofit organization Slow Money (slowmoney.org), local investment networks throughout the country are providing financial support to local food systems through peer-to-peer lending and other types of lending or investing strategies. Investing in local organic farms, urban farms, artisanal food producers and other entities involved in sustainable food production and distribution can help us support environmental, economic and social sustainability close to home. Information about forming or joining a Slow Money investment network is available at the Slow Money website.

Co-op investments. There are more than 30,000 cooperative businesses in the U.S., including co-ops for consumers (e.g., groceries, sporting goods retailers, various services), producers (e.g., farms, electric utilities), purchasers (e.g., individuals or businesses) and workers (e.g., various types of worker co-ops).[15]

Belonging to a co-op and/or investing in one can help fund and support the local economy since most co-ops either are locally owned or, if national, tend to focus on local or regional markets.

Since most states don't regulate co-op memberships as securities, cooperative businesses can offer a variety of local investing opportunities. These generally consist of (1) memberships, (2) loans and (3) private-equity investments. The most basic type of co-op investment is a *membership* in a consumer co-op, such as a grocery store, which generally pays "returns" in the form of store discounts. Some well-established co-ops raise additional funds from members and local businesses to finance endeavors such as the expansion of a store, the addition of new cooperative services or the support of a start-up co-op in another community. Some of these investments have produced returns for member-investors in the form of dividends.

There also are co-ops—and nonprofit co-op loan funds—that establish *revolving loan funds* to support local businesses. Co-op members and others in the community can lend money to these funds, which then use the capital to extend local loans. Loan recipients may be start-up businesses in underserved communities or businesses that comprise a food co-op's supply chain, such as organic farms and artisanal cheese producers. Alternatively, cooperatives may sell equity shares to members and use the capital to invest in local businesses. One successful example described in economist Michael Schuman's book *Local Dollars, Local Sense* involves a renewable energy cooperative that invests member capital in a wide range of local energy businesses and initiatives, including solar, geothermal, biodiesel and solar heating companies, household energy auditors and community-owned/community-scale solar gardens. These investments are helping co-op members take an active role in strengthening their local economies while enabling their communities to transition to renewable energy.[16]

Investment in our employers. As described in Chapter 7, Work, Play and Retirement, worker cooperatives allow employees to buy into (invest in) their employer's company and potentially receive a share of profits. Those profits may be distributed to employees each year or reinvested as part of their equity stake in the company. Assuming an employee works for the company until retirement, the accumulated equity may become a source of retirement income. In this way, joining a worker co-op may provide one of the only opportunities available to combine investing for retirement with supporting a local business, in this case, our employer. Some businesses allow employees to become part owners through employee stock ownership plans (ESOPs). If we work for a local or sustainable company that offers an ESOP, we may be able to align our investing and sustainability goals by purchasing shares of company stock.

Targeted certificates of deposit (CDs) tied to local currency programs.
As described in Saving and Borrowing, some community banks and credit unions
(and nonprofit loan funds) issue CDs to collateralize loans made to members of
the community. A similar approach has been used in communities that have local
currency programs. In this case, the U.S. dollars traded in at participating banks
in exchange for local currency provide collateral for the loans. (More information
on local currencies: The Role of Local Currency, page 210)

Community Development Financial Institutions (CDFIs). Some community
banks, credit unions, venture capital funds and community development loan
funds are designated as Community Development Finance Institutions. These
entities seek the social return of providing financial assistance to members of
underserved and low-income communities. Because CDFIs generally focus on a
specific geographic region, they can provide nonaccredited (as well as accredited)
investors with local investing opportunities. For example, investing in a community development loan fund, which is a revolving loan fund set up for entrepreneurs and small businesses that lack access to other sources of credit, can help us
finance local business development while potentially earning a modest return,
similar to that offered by a CD. We can find CDFIs in our geographic area by
using the locator tool of opportunityfinance.net (ofn.org/cdfi-locator).

Prepurchase of goods or services. We may be able to provide capital to
(invest in) a start-up or existing company by prepurchasing goods or services. For
example, members of a community might prepurchase a certain number of meals
at a new restaurant or hours of housekeeping from a start-up cleaning service.
This investment approach enables us to support the types of businesses we want
or need in our communities and obtain desired goods or services, often at a discount. Prepurchasing arrangements are not regarded as securities by the SEC or
by most states, though some states do treat prepurchases in start-ups as securities.
Prepurchase arrangements can help companies raise relatively modest amounts
early on while cultivating relationships with individuals who may be willing and
able to make more substantial investments down the road.

Investments in community-supported enterprises (CSEs). Joining a community-supported agriculture (CSA) program is a way of investing locally. But
most CSA memberships simply represent subscriptions in a farm's future harvest,
rather than ownership shares of a farm. Shareholder CSAs, by contrast, constitute
an investment in a community-supported enterprise. With a shareholder CSA,
owner-members purchase or lease farmland and either farm the land collectively
or hire a farmer. A similar arrangement may be employed for other types of community-owned businesses. For example, a group of residents may come together

to fund a business, such as a grocery store, solar garden or childcare service, that meets a community-wide need. Or a community may pool resources to purchase a plot of land or a building and convert it into a makerspace, community kitchen, co-work space, low-income housing unit or anything else that meets local needs. Community members may purchase shares of a community-owned venture with cash, volunteer hours or a commitment of future purchases. Or they may raise money by issuing community bonds. Whether or not these investments yield financial returns, they can offer another way to support the local economy and assist members of the community.

Rewards investing through crowdfunding sites. Pioneering crowdfunding sites such as Kickstarter and Indiegogo enable us to make relatively modest investments in exchange for in-kind, noncash rewards. While these platforms do not allow us to purchase a company's stock and receive investment returns, they can provide a way to support a small, local or sustainable business by helping to fund a "project," such as expanding the warehouse of a microbrewery or designing a new line of organic clothing. Crowdfunding also lets us support non-business initiatives, such as public art projects or initiatives designed to address specific social challenges. With some sites, investors are only on the hook to provide capital if a project attracts a requested minimum amount of funding. Some crowdfunding platforms, such as Lucky Ant and Small Knot, allow us to focus on helping members of our own communities.

Investing in Ourselves[17]

In his book *Local Dollars, Local Sense,* economist Michael Schuman suggests that we may be able to earn attractive "returns" with limited exposure to risk by "investing in ourselves." Some examples of this approach to making our financial lives more sustainable include:

Increasing the amount we are able to set aside in savings each month by budgeting for household expenses, spending less and living within our means.

Strengthening our balance sheet by reducing debt. For example, paying off high-interest credit card debt, rather than carrying a balance, can help reduce our credit expense and move us into "the black."

Potentially boosting our income by investing in additional education or job training.

Increasing the equity in our home by refinancing the mortgage at a lower interest rate, if possible.

Potentially saving hundreds of dollars a year or more by making our home and vehicle more energy efficient.

Because a community is only as economically resilient as the individuals who reside there, some of these investments can benefit both us and our communities. For example, anything we do to improve our homes or our finances, preventing the risk of foreclosure, will boost our bottom line while also supporting real estate values throughout the community. Other ways of investing in ourselves can benefit both us and the environment. For example, investing time and money in starting an organic edible garden can reduce our food budget while protecting the local ecosystem. Similarly, investing in energy efficiency or renewable energy can prove beneficial to both our wallet and the planet.

Peer-to-peer lending. There are numerous peer-to-peer online lending platforms that allow us to "invest" by lending money to other individuals and small businesses (our peers). Examples include Lending Club (lendingclub.com), Prosper (prosper.com), Upstart (upstart.com) and Funding Circle (fundingcircle. com). Community Sourced Capital (communitysourcedcapital.com) lets us focus lending within our own communities. On some sites, borrowers are charged interest, providing us (the lenders) with the opportunity to earn a financial return when a loan is repaid. Other sites, such as Kiva (kiva.org) offer interest-free loans, placing the emphasis on social returns, such as supporting a mission-oriented business. Some platforms require investors to be accredited. While peer-to-peer lending platforms remove intermediaries from lending transactions, the platforms dictate the terms of the loans. Some sites receive funding not only from peers like us but also from major financial institutions.

Investments in renewable energy. As discussed in Chapter 4, Home, anyone who lives in a state with deregulated utility markets can choose an electricity supplier that generates solar, wind, small-scale hydroelectric or other types of renewable energy. By making this choice, we can essentially transform our electric bill payment into an investment in green energy. This doesn't guarantee that the power distributed to our home will come from renewable sources. But our investment will fund increased production of renewables, helping to make them an ever-larger percentage of the nation's energy supply.

> **Self-directed IRAs.** If we're able to invest some of our money, a large portion of our investments may be earmarked for retirement. If we want to invest retirement savings using sustainable criteria, we can consider opening a self-directed IRA. Tax-advantaged traditional and Roth IRAs, available through a wide range of financial institutions, are designed to potentially help us accumulate assets more quickly than may be possible with accounts that tax earnings each year. Unlike employer-sponsored 401(k) plans, which offer a limited range of investments chosen by plan sponsors, IRAs can contain many different types of investments. A self-directed IRA, which is an IRA for which we choose the custodian or trustee, may extend that flexibility to include nontraditional local and sustainable investments. Self-directed IRAs and the necessary trustee services are available from some community banks and credit unions, as well as from

Insurance

Purchasing insurance from a local, independently owned or mutually owned insurance company may provide additional opportunities to relocalize our financial lives, benefitting us and our communities. Such companies may focus specifically on our geographic region, providing the insurance necessary to protect the value of local homes and business properties. They may hire locally and invest some of their business assets within the community or state. And if they are mutually owned, treating customers as owners, they may pay us dividends in profitable years. All of these benefits have the potential to help make us a bit more financially resilient while also keeping money circulating throughout the community.

larger financial institutions. Account owners must work with trustees to identify attractive sustainable investments. These could include shares of socially responsible mutual funds, B corporations and social enterprises as well as targeted CDs or loans to cooperative loan funds.

▶ **Divestiture.** Of course, the flip side of choosing sustainable investment alternatives is pulling our investment capital out of companies that are unsustainable according to environmental, economic or social criteria. We also can have an impact by asking pension fund managers and retirement plan sponsors to consider divestiture.

Charitable Giving

Whether our "philanthropy" consists of donating spare change, employing complex planned-giving strategies or something in between, it's possible to align our charitable activities with sustainable values. This will involve deciding (1) which sustainable issues or causes to support, (2) when and how often to donate, (3) whether we can benefit from various charitable approaches or vehicles and (4) how much we wish—and can afford—to give.

▶ **Sustainable causes.** We may decide to direct our charitable giving to one or more of the following:

Environmental organizations. There are many environmental organizations and causes that accept charitable contributions. We may wish to support national environmental advocacy or conservation organizations, concentrate on specific issues, such as sustainable agriculture or consumer product safety, or focus on local organizations, such as wildflower preserves or land trusts.

Our local economy. Focusing charitable giving within our community can help boost the local economy and address challenges such as food insecurity or homelessness. In addition to donating directly to specific organizations or causes, it may be possible to contribute to nonprofit development funds that pool donations to address local needs.

Community resiliency. We can support stronger communities by focusing our philanthropic dollars on community gardens, community kitchens, urban farms, tool libraries, after-school programs or other innovative, grassroots initiatives.

▶ **Timing and frequency.** We can contribute to our chosen causes either occasionally or on a regular basis, and either during our lifetime or through our estate, after we are gone.

Occasional donations. We're likely to come across many opportunities to make occasional small donations—in the checkout line at the grocery store, at a local fundraising event or through a social media campaign we've learned about from friends. Such donations may not seem consequential. But they can get us thinking about the power of giving while providing much-needed funding to a worthy organization or cause.

Annual gifts. Many of us make donations to charities in response to their annual fundraising campaigns. Donating annually can demonstrate our commitment to a particular cause while potentially providing us with charitable tax deductions. Donations made during the course of our lives are referred to by the IRS as "gifts." Individuals who expect their estates to be subject to estate taxes may make annual gifts to reduce the tax liability of future heirs while ensuring that donations go to the charities of their choice. But gifts over a certain dollar amount may trigger additional taxes, so it's important to speak with a tax advisor about our gifting intentions.

Bequests and planned gifts. Charitable gifts that transfer to beneficiaries after our death are referred to as "bequests." Generally, bequests are made via wills or charitable trusts. This type of planned giving can help us balance personal financial goals with philanthropic objectives.

Impact Philanthropy

This relatively new approach to philanthropy isn't about the size of a donation, but rather its ability to have a measurable, sustainable impact and to make a meaningful difference in the lives of intended beneficiaries. We can become impact philanthropists by accessing the best available evidence on how to solve a problem, identifying programs or strategies with proven track records of success and the greatest "bang for their buck," actively supporting an organization's success by volunteering or joining the board or linking future gifts to measurable progress toward a goal.

The choice of where to make impact donations may not be obvious according to Kat Rosqueta, founder of the Center for High Impact Philanthropy at the University of Pennsylvania. For example, in a Tedx Philadelphia talk, Rosqueta pointed out that as a strategy for keeping teens away from crime, "Scared Straight" programs in high schools (which attempt to address a problem after the fact) have been far less effective than visiting nurse programs for new moms (which help prevent a problem from developing).[18] Similarly, those concerned that an exploding global population will trigger widespread food insecurity believe that producing more food isn't the only answer. Since educated women typically have fewer children, sending girls to school in one of the few remaining areas of the world with high birth rates, Sub-Saharan Africa, may have a greater impact in addressing this mammoth problem.

Impact philanthropy offers exciting possibilities for uncovering and supporting solutions that are effective and sustainable. Rosqueta's organization is one of many that provide data to help individuals choose philanthropic targets with the greatest likely impact, monitor whether contributions are making a difference and continually investigate how to improve their efforts.

▶ **Charitable approaches/vehicles.** Depending on the size and timing of our donations, we may wish to (1) retain professional advisors to execute specialized wealth-transfer strategies or (2) explore nontraditional philanthropic approaches.

Traditional Wealth-Transfer Strategies

Wills. Everyone needs a will, even if it's only an off-the-shelf form and our possessions consist of little more than an old coin collection and the clothes on our back. Wills allow us to identify what we wish to leave to whom, such as money or other assets to family, friends or charitable organizations.

Charitable trusts. Depending on our philanthropic and personal financial goals, we may be able to choose from many types of trusts to make larger bequests of cash, securities, real estate or other property. Trusts can offer tax benefits to donors and beneficiaries. They allow donors to execute complex financial strategies and put in place irrevocable instructions that will govern how trust assets may be used. After the donor's death, assets in a charitable trust transfer to the charitable entity named as beneficiary.

Gift annuities. A gift annuity is a contractual arrangement that lets a donor gift cash, securities or other property to a charitable organization or other entity (such as a university) in exchange for a partial charitable tax deduction and a lifetime income stream referred to as an annuity. After the donor's death, the gifted assets transfer to the intended beneficiary.

Family foundations. These are endowments established by individuals or families with very large estates and focused philanthropic goals, such as supporting sustainable agriculture or funding cancer research. A foundation's board, usually made up of family members, manages the endowment, investing assets and distributing grants to charitable organizations as directed by the donor. After the donor's death, the foundation's mission is carried on by current or future generations for as long as the endowment lasts.

Donor-advised funds (DAFs). A smaller-scale version of a family foundation, a DAF has fewer administrative responsibilities and much lower initial donation requirements (usually a few thousand dollars). A donor can establish a qualified DAF at a financial institution or through a charitable organization, such as a community foundation. The donor makes irrevocable, tax-deductible gifts to the DAF but retains authority over grant decisions. The fund's managers invest donated assets, vet potential grant recipients and distribute approved grants.

College scholarships. Another alternative for those with substantial financial resources is to endow a scholarship fund. Endowments of this type enable donors to invest in future generations in a way that has personal meaning for them. For example, a donor may wish to fund undergraduate studies in environmental science or business school for budding social entrepreneurs from underserved communities.

Nontraditional Philanthropic Approaches

Giving circles. These are small groups with common philanthropic interests that pool their donations for greater impact. A group may raise funds for a single cause or continually seek out new opportunities to make a difference. Some groups collect donations at potluck dinners or other social gatherings. Others incorporate volunteer work into their collective giving.

Microfinance. The innovation of Dr. Muhammad Yunus, who founded the Grameen Bank for microfinance in 1983, this involves lending very small amounts to entrepreneurs who would otherwise lack access to credit, enabling them to work their way out of poverty. The first microfinance loans focused on developing areas of the world, but it's also possible to use this approach to address poverty here in the U.S. Microfinance programs personalize philanthropy by allowing us to lend to particular individuals and learn exactly how they use our funds. Once loans are repaid, we can make new loans to the same individuals or others in need. Experts say that, on average, repayment rates on microfinance loans actually are higher than those on more conventional types of loans. Thanks to sites such as kiva.org, microfinance is now accessible to anyone interested in this philanthropic approach.

Crowd donation sites. Through sites such as DonorsChoose.org and CrowdRise (crowdrise.com), we can give small amounts (as little as $1) to support individuals, groups, events or small-scale fundraising campaigns. For example, DonorsChoose.org lets us support a school with a donation just large enough to pay for much-needed desks or books. Through CrowdRise, we can raise money or make our own donations to a wide range of charities and causes. Like kiva.org, crowd donation sites let us personalize our charitable giving, pro-viding a small but impactful amount and seeing exactly how our gift is put to use.

Donation of goods. Food pantries, homeless shelters and veterans' groups are among the many organizations with an ongoing need for donations of food, clothing, household goods…even cars. Donations of both cash and goods may provide a current-year tax deduction.

▶ **How much to give.** While the word "philanthropy" implies a vast endowment, meaningful donations come in all sizes. If we have limited funds, we may be able to make a greater impact with noncash donations or volunteer work. Once we're ready to make larger or more frequent gifts, we'll need to keep track of allowable tax deductions and gift-tax limits. When much larger sums are involved, it usually will be necessary to retain professional financial, tax and legal advisors who can help us choose the best philanthropic strategies for our needs and goals.

The Role of Local Currency

We can take another step toward making sustainable financial decisions by utilizing local currency. There are many local currencies in use today, along with arrangements such as time banks and LETS, which substitute national currency with time hours or local dollars. Local currencies often are introduced as a way to support "shop local" campaigns, but they can offer much broader benefits, helping to create community-based economies that are green, equitable and resilient. While local currency may not be necessary to create a more sustainable local economy, it can serve as (1) a tangible symbol of that goal, (2) a tool for achieving greater localization and (3) a lubricant, providing the incentives necessary to speed along the process of localization. A local currency program may offer the following benefits:

✓ Increased consumer loyalty to local shops, restaurants and service providers.

✓ Increased support for—and production of—locally produced goods that would otherwise be imported from other locations. For example, if restaurant owners receive local currency from customers and would have to pay a fee to redeem it for U.S. dollars, they gain an incentive to use the currency to source food, wine and other necessities from local suppliers, thereby increasing demand for those local goods. A community that produces much of what it needs can become more resilient in the face of such disruptions as severe weather events or trade wars while also reducing its carbon footprint and building a strong local economy.

✓ A stronger local multiplier effect, keeping money circulating longer within the community through both retail and wholesale transactions.

✓ A greater sense of community and place as people congregate at local shops and restaurants and enjoy foods, goods or cultural experiences that reflect unique local tastes.

✓ Additional economic supports, such as (1) time banks and LETs to help the unemployed obtain services and develop skills (more information: Chapter 7, Work, Play and Retirement) or (2) targeted CDs for business loans collateralized with dollars exchanged for local currency.

✓ An economy to fall back on in the event of national or global economic turmoil.

✓ A tool that empowers us to build the economy we need.

Creating a local currency program requires a substantial investment of time and effort on the part of dedicated members of the community. For a complementary currency to be legal it must (1) look different from the national currency, (2) be intended as complementary, rather than as a replacement for the national currency and (3) be exchangeable for national currency. The most successful efforts seem to be those that keep currency in circulation longest and among the largest circle of users. An excellent source of information for anyone interested in helping to create a local currency program is *Local Money: How to Make It Happen in Your Community* by Peter North.

Doing More

In the area of money and finance, we can do more by:

▶ Supporting legislation that specifically eases some regulations on community banks and credit unions;

▶ Supporting the expansion of local investing opportunities for nonaccredited investors; and

▶ Divesting from companies that operate in an unsustainable manner and asking our employee retirement plan sponsor to divest.

NOTE: None of the information in this chapter is intended as investment, legal or tax advice or an offer of any security. Descriptions of investment alternatives are based on the author's understanding only. To learn exactly how a particular investment alternative works, what investment risks it may present and what federal and/or state laws or regulations govern the investment, readers should consult with professional financial, legal and tax advisors, just as they would before making any other financial or investment decision.

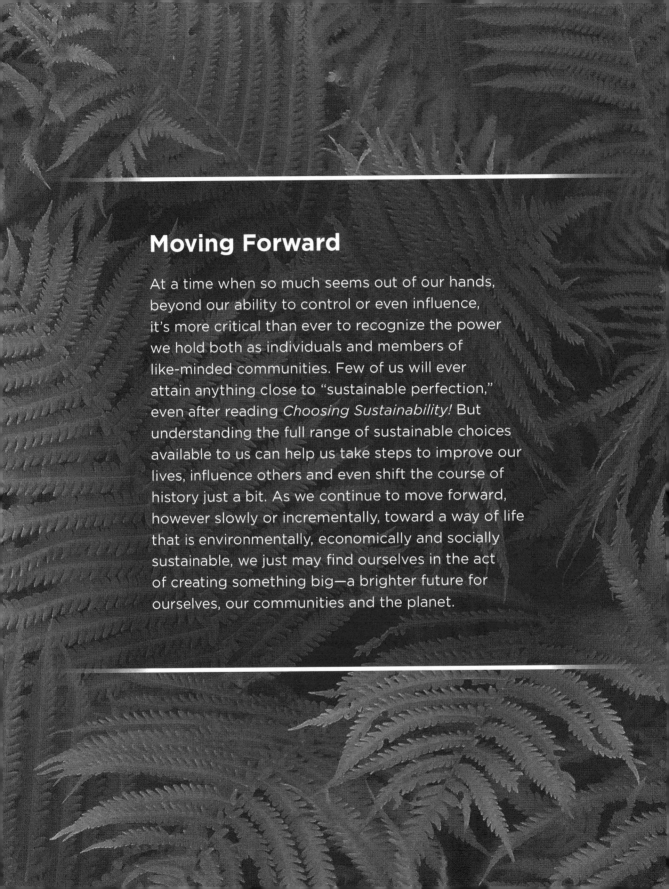

Moving Forward

At a time when so much seems out of our hands, beyond our ability to control or even influence, it's more critical than ever to recognize the power we hold both as individuals and members of like-minded communities. Few of us will ever attain anything close to "sustainable perfection," even after reading *Choosing Sustainability!* But understanding the full range of sustainable choices available to us can help us take steps to improve our lives, influence others and even shift the course of history just a bit. As we continue to move forward, however slowly or incrementally, toward a way of life that is environmentally, economically and socially sustainable, we just may find ourselves in the act of creating something big—a brighter future for ourselves, our communities and the planet.

Epilogue: A Green Afterlife

Sustainable choices can reduce the ecological impact of our departure.

After a lifetime of sustainable choices, there is one final consideration: how to leave this world sustainably. It's only natural to ignore the subject for as long as possible. But when the time comes, we may find it reassuring to know we can preserve our sustainable values even beyond our lifetime. Thanks to the Green Burial Council (GBC) and a growing number of eco-conscious funeral home and cemetery owners, sustainable alternatives gradually are becoming more widely available. The GBC is a nonprofit organization that encourages green practices, certifies the sustainability of funeral homes and cemeteries and supports "conservation burial" on land preserved as open space in perpetuity.

Like other sustainable alternatives, green death care and burial revive and update some of our oldest practices. While history is full of elaborate burial rituals (mummification of Egyptian pharaohs, for example), most of our ancestors relied on simple, low-tech methods. Shrouds and pine boxes were the norm before concrete vaults and metal-lined caskets became available. Embalming wasn't widely used until the Civil War, when it offered families the ability to retrieve the bodies of fallen loved ones from faraway battlefields. And both home funerals and burial grounds that doubled as public parks were common well into the 20th century.

Eventually, laws were enacted that banned some traditional practices on the grounds that they presented a threat to public health. Unfortunately, as with other forms of modernization, many "improvements" to death care and burial may have ended up harming us and the environment. Problems can range from pollution, greenhouse gas emissions and health hazards for funeral industry workers to depletion of nonrenewable natural resources, loss of open space, unaffordability and the institutionalization of a natural part of life.

Making a Holistically Sustainable Exit

Sustainable death care and burial offer environmental as well as economic and social benefits. They can help reduce the exposure of funeral industry workers to potential toxins while also reducing pollution, emission of greenhouse gases and loss of open space, farmland, native habit and nonrenewable natural resources. They can provide the deceased with a natural mode of internment while giving mourners a serene setting for visiting with loved ones. They can be far more affordable than traditional options. And when cemeteries are situated on preserved public land that offers recreational space, their integration into the community may bring people together to support land conservation while familiarizing them with the benefits of green burial. The ability of these cemeteries to help protect the environment has even led some municipalities to begin viewing them as part of their green infrastructure.

At this time, sustainable alternatives include:

▶ **Nontoxic death care.** Though not required by law, embalming has been common since the late 19th century, except among those whose religions expressly prohibit the practice, such as Muslims and Jews. Despite designation as a known carcinogen by the National Cancer Institute, formaldehyde continues to be used for embalming throughout the funeral industry, potentially exposing workers to significant health risks[1] and contaminating groundwater near burial sites.[2] Sustainable alternatives include using nontoxic, plant-based essential oils or forgoing embalming altogether.

▶ **Natural burial vessels.** Green burial advocates say they ban traditional caskets and concrete vaults because they (1) are made from nonrenewable natural resources, (2) may contain materials that are harvested in ways that destroy habitat, (3) are nonbiodegradable, (4) can leach toxic substances into the ground, including embalming fluids and materials used in their production (e.g., metals, plastics, polymers, varnishes) and (5) require a substantial amount of fossil fuel to manufacture and transport, increasing greenhouse gas emissions.[3] Combined with natural embalming (or no embalming), eco-friendly burial vessels allow us to return to the earth quickly, naturally and with minimal impact on the environment. Alternatives include shrouds as well as unlined caskets made of pine, wicker or sustainably grown and harvested raw materials, such as bamboo or willow. Finishes must be nontoxic and any fasteners or handles must be made of brass or chrome.

▶ **Green burial sites.** Green burial advocates caution that traditional cemeteries can harm the environment in numerous ways. They deplete land needed for agriculture, a problem that will only worsen as the world's population continues to mushroom. Clearing trees and native plants to make way for gravesites can disrupt native habitat. Paving areas for parking lots and walkways can contribute to drainage problems, stormwater runoff and flooding. Mowing a cemetery's vast lawn burns fossil fuels. And the use of pesticides and herbicides to keep grounds neat and tidy can endanger local ecosystems, contaminating air, water and soil.[4]

The U.S. has a small but growing number of green cemeteries, as well as some traditional facilities beginning to offer green alternatives. An up-to-date list can be found on the website of the Green Burial Council (greenburialcouncil.com). Certified green cemeteries seek to preserve land in its natural state or, as necessary, restore the local ecosystem along with native plants and wildlife. Hardscaping is kept to a minimum, and grounds are left ungroomed or managed organically. In addition to offering a serene setting for the deceased and mourners, some green cemeteries double as nature preserves or parks, open to the public for hiking, biking and other low-impact activities. (Geologists and other experts determine the appropriate location and density of grave sites to allow for dual use of the land while preserving the integrity of burial areas.) Many green cemeteries are located on land that has been preserved in perpetuity, often by land trusts. Our purchase of burial plots may help fund the continued preservation and maintenance of the land.

▶ **Natural markers.** Green cemeteries ban traditional tombstones because their manufacture and transport can be energy intensive, contributing to green-house gas emissions.[5] Sustainable alternatives include natural markers, such as rocks already located on the grounds, which may be unmarked or adorned with engraved plaques bearing the name and life span of the deceased. Some green burial grounds forego markers altogether, planting over grave sites with native plants or trees and relying on GPS technology to locate graves.

▶ **Home-based services.** Once commonplace, home funerals are making a comeback in the many states that allow them, offering a more intimate, less institutional environment that some mourners may find comforting. Avoiding the use of a funeral parlor also can make the cost of arrangements far more affordable.

▶ **Sustainable cremation.** Some criticize cremation as interrupting the natural cycle of life and death. The practice is prohibited by certain religions, including Islam and Judaism. But about 40%[6] of Americans choose this alternative, often believing it's more sustainable than taking up space in a cemetery. It also costs substantially less than a traditional burial. Unfortunately, the cremation process typically has involved the burning of a substantial amount of fossil fuel and the emission of pollutants, including sulphur dioxide, CO_2, hydrochloric acid, hydrofluoric acid, dioxin and mercury from dental fillings.[7] Newer cremation techniques have eliminated some pollutants. The development of more effective air-filtration systems is expected to further reduce the environmental impact of cremation. Biodegradable urns also are becoming more widely available.

More information on green death care and burial is available from the Green Burial Council (greenburialcouncil.com), the Funeral Consumers Alliance (funerals.org) and the National Home Funeral Alliance (homefuneralalliance.org).

Notes

Chapter 1: Why It's Time for Holistic Sustainability

[1] Pew Research Center, pewresearch.org, "For Earth Day, here's how Americans view environmental issues," Monica Anderson, April 20, 2017

[2] Organic Trade Association, ota.com, Organic Market Analysis

[3] *Business Insider*, businessinsider.com, "The demand for 'local' food is growing—here's why investors should pay attention," Oran B. Hesterman, PhD and Daniel Horan, April 25, 2017

[4] FleetCarma, fleetcarma.com, "Electric Vehicle Sales in the United States: 2016 Final Update," Sunny Trochaniak, January 19, 2017

[5] *Time Magazine*, time.com, "Renewable Energy Continues to Beat Fossil Fuels," Justin Worland, February 8, 2017

[6] Environmental Protection Agency, "Municipal Solid Waste Generation, Recycling, and Disposal in the United States: Facts and Figures for 2012"

[7] Dodge Data & Analytics, construction.com, "New Study Suggests Strong Outlook for Green Homes," November 18, 2015

Chapter 2: Breaking It Down: Three Paths to Sustainability

[1] Some notable exceptions: The early to mid-20th century was the era of Jerome Irving Rodale, one of the earliest supporters of organic agriculture, and of Scott and Helen Nearing, whose forays into organic, self-reliant homesteading in the 1930s led to their 1970s' reputation as the "godparents" of the back-to-the-land movement. This also was the period during which President Franklin Delano Roosevelt's New Deal program initiated the Civilian Conservation Corps and the soil conservation assistance program for farmers.

[2] Earth Day Network, earthday.org, "The History of Earth Day"

[3] Atmos, ucar.edu, "How Much Has the Global Temperature Risen Since 1880?"

[4] Gallup, gallup.com, "Global Warming Concern at Three-Decade High in US," Lydia Saad, March 14, 2017

[5] Union of Concerned Scientists, ucsusa.org, "Each Country's Share of CO_2 Emissions," 2011 Total Carbon Dioxide Emissions from the Consumption of Energy (Million Metric Tons), China: 8,715.31; U.S: 5,490.63

[6] U.S. Energy Information Administration (EIA), eia.gov, "Frequently Asked Questions: How much of U.S. carbon dioxide emissions are associated with electricity generation?" 2015

[7] Natural Resources Defense Council, "Energy Facts: Simple and Inexpensive Actions Could Reduce Global Warming Emissions by One Billion Tons," March 2010

[8] *Scientific American*, scientificamerican.com, "How Much Is Too Much? Estimating Greenhouse Gas Emissions," David Biello, April 29, 2009

[9] Ratical, ratical.org, "Democracy and Renewable Energy: Why We're So Short on Both," Mike Ferner, January 19, 2002

[10] Nuclear Energy Institute, nei.org, "US Nuclear Power Plants: General U.S. Nuclear Info," 2015

[11] U.S. National Park Service, nps.gov, Theodore Roosevelt and Conservation

[12] Ibid, 11

[13] (1) USDA Forest Service, fs.fed.us, Open Space Conservation, "Loss of Open Space" (2) *The Washington Post*, washingtonpost.com, "A Treasure, Vanishing at 6,000 Acres a Day," Craig W. Culp, February 18, 2007

[14] The American Presidency Project, presidency.ucsb.edu, "Lyndon B. Johnson: Remarks Upon Signing the Air Quality Act of 1967," November 21, 1967

[15] United Nations Department of Economic and Social Affairs, "World Population Prospects: The 2017 Revision," June 21, 2017

[16] Adirondack Council, adirondackcouncil.org, Acid Rain

[17] Environmental Protection Agency, yosemite.epa.gov, News Release from Headquarters: "EPA Proposes Smog Standards to Safeguard Americans from Air Pollution," November 26, 2014

[18] *First Along the River: A Brief History of the U.S. Environmental Movement*, Benjamin Kline, PhD, page 93

[19] (1) conserve-energy-future.com, "What is Water Pollution?" (2) National Oceanic and Atmospheric Administration (NOAA), "Harmful Algal Blooms (HABs) in the Great Lakes" (3) *Scientific American*, scientificamerican.com, "How Does Mercury Get Into Fish?" (4) Environmental Protection Agency, cfpub.epa.gov, "Hydraulic Fracturing for Oil and Gas: Impacts from the Hydraulic Fracturing Water Cycle on Drinking Water Resources in the United States" (Final Report) (5) Environmental Protection Agency, epa.gov, "Basic Information about Lead in Drinking Water" (6) pollutionissues.com, Consumer Pollution (7) Harvard Health Publishing, Harvard Medical School, "Drugs in the Water," June 2011

[20] The Environmental Working Group, ewg.org, "'Erin Brockovich' Carcinogen in Tap Water of More Than 200 Million Americans," David Andrews and Bill Walker, September 20, 2016.

[21] Environmental Protection Agency, Advancing Sustainable Materials Management: 2013 Fact Sheet, June 2015

[22] (1) Energy Justice Network, energyjustice.net, "Trash Incineration More Polluting than Coal" (2) The Conversation, theconversation.com, "Garbage in, garbage out: Incinerating trash is not an effective way to protect the climate or reduce waste," Ana Baptista, February 27, 2018

[23] This term comes from the Business Alliance for Local Living Economies (BALLE), an organization committed to the idea that independently owned local businesses can help support stronger, more resilient communities while meeting people's needs, promoting social justice and protecting the environment. BALLE was co-founded by restauranteur Judy Wicks of Philadelphia's White Dog Café and Laury Hammel, a Boston business owner.

[24] "Conserving Communities," Wendell Berry, from *The Case Against the Global Economy and for a Turn Toward the Local*, edited by Jerry Mander and Edward Goldsmith

[25] "Principles of Bioregionalism," Kirkpatrick Sale, from *The Case Against the Global Economy and for a Turn Toward the Local*, edited by Jerry Mander and Edward Goldsmith

[26] *Small is Beautiful: Economics as if People Mattered*, E.F. Schumacher, Harper Perennial, 1973

[27] *Fortune*, fortune.com, "Today's Cars Are Parked 95% of the Time," David Z. Morris, March 13, 2016

Chapter 3: Food

[1] (1) foodnavigator-use.com, "Organic Trade Association: US retail sales of organics grew 11.5% to $35.1bn in 2013," Elaine Watson, May 13, 2014 (2) Ibid, "Consumer Reports: 84% of US consumers buy food with organic seal, but some are confused about its meaning," Elaine Watson, May 7, 2014

[2] Sustainable Table, sustainabletable.org, "What is local," citing "Life Cycle-Based Sustainability Indicators for Assessment of the U.S. Food System," Martin C. Heller and Gregory A. Keoleian, Ann Arbor, MI, Center for Sustainable Systems, University of Michigan, 2000:42

[3] United States Department of Agriculture, usda.gov, News Release No. 0084.16, "USDA Reports Record Growth In U.S. Organic Producers," April, 4, 2016

[4] Footnotes for entire organic benefits section: (1)*The Omnivore's Dilemma: A Natural History of Four Meals*, Michael Pollan (2) *Organic Manifesto: How Organic Farming Can Heal Our Planet, Feed the World, and Keep Us Safe*," Maria Rodale (3) *Fast Food Nation: The Dark Side of the All-American Meal*, Eric Schlosser (4) *Food Inc.*, Robert Kenner (5) *Silent Spring*, Rachel Carson, Chapter 5, Realms of the Soil, pp 53-61 (6) *The New York Review of Books*, "The Food Movement, Rising," Michael Pollan, June 10, 2010 (7) Pan North America, panna.org, "Industrial Agriculture" (8) Natural Resources Defense Council, nrdc.org, "Our Children At Risk: The Five Worst Environmental Threats to Their Health" (9) The Environmental Working Group, ewg.org, "Frequently Asked Questions About Produce and Pesticides, 2012 (10) Environmental Protection Agency, epa.gov, Data Requirements for Pesticide Registration (11) Sustainable Table, sustainabletable.org, Hormones (12) *The New York Times*, nytimes.com, "Antibiotics in Animals Need Limits, F.D.A. Says," Gardiner Harris, June 28, 2010 (13) Food Safety News, foodsafetynews.com, "Most U.S. Antibiotics Go to Animal Agriculture," Helena Bottemiller, February 24, 2011 (14) *Science Magazine*, sciencemag.org, "Are antibiotics turning livestock into superbug factories?" Giorgia Guglielmi, September 28, 2017 (15) National Public Radio, npr.org, Fresh Air, "'Big Chicken' Connects Poultry Farming to Antibiotic-Resistant Bacteria," November 2, 2017 (16) Resilient Communities, resilientcommunities.com, "After the GMO Bubble Pops..." and "The Secret to Food Independence," Paul Clarke (17) nongmoproject.org, "A Collaborative Initiative Working to Ensure the Sustained Availability of Non-GMO Options" (18) *Mother Earth News*, motherearthnews.com, "The Status of Genetically Modified Salmon," Shelley Stonebrook, April/May 2016 (19) Food Dive, fooddive.com, "USDA on GMO labeling law: 'Still on track, but a little behind,'" Megan Poinski, June 7, 2017 (20) *The New England Journal of Medicine*, "GMOs, Herbicides, and Public Health," Philip J. Landrigan, MD, and Charles Benbrook, PhD, 2015 (21) Harvard University, Graduate School of Arts and Sciences, "Challenging Evolution: How GMOs Can Influence Genetic Diversity," Heather Landry, August 10, 2015 (22) Government of the Netherlands, "Consequences of GMOs for Biodiversity" (23) Sierra Club, sierraclub.org, "Why are CAFO's bad?" (24) sustainableagriculture.net, "Conservation & Environment" (25) Ecological Society of America, "Carbon Sequestration in Soils," summer 2000 (26) Sustainable Table, sustainabletable.org, Soil Quality (27) The Week, theweek.com, "America is running out of soil," Matt Hansen, May 13, 2015 (28) The Organic & Non-GMO Report, non-gmoreport.com, "Research shows organic corn, soybean yields can exceed conventional," Bob Turnbull, Associate Editor (29) Cambridge University, Cambridge Core, cambridge.org, "Can organic agriculture feed the world?" Catherine Badgley and Ivette Perfecto, June 2007 (30) *The New York Times*, nytimes.com, "In America's Heartland, Discussing Climate Change Without Saying 'Climate Change,'" Hiroko Tabuchi, January 28, 2017 (31) National Public Radio, npr.org, "Is Organic More Nutritious? New Study Adds To

the Evidence," Allison Aubrey, February 18, 2016 (32) Columbia University, Earth Institute, blogs.ei.columbia.edu, "Can Soil Help Combat Climate Change?" Renee Cho, February 21, 2018 (33) *The Guardian*, theguardian.com, "Our best shot at cooling the planet might be right under our feet," Jason Hickel, September 10, 2016

5 (1) Rodale Institute, "Regenerative Organic Farming: A Solution to Global Warming," Tim J. LaSalle, PhD, CEO and Paul Hepperly, PhD, Director of Research and Fulbright Scholar (2) Rodale Institute, The Farming Systems Trial

6 (1) The Association of American Feed Control Officials, aafco.org, "What is in Pet Food" (2) PetMD, petmd.com, Pet Food (What You Need to Know) for Your Pet's Sake," Dr. Donna Spector

7 (1) Environmental Defense Fund, seafood.edf.org, "PCBs in fish and shellfish" (2) *Scientific American*, scientificamerican.com, "How Does Mercury Get Into Fish?" (3) Natural Resources Defense Council, nrdc.org, "Protect Yourself and Your Family: Consumer Guide to Mercury in Fish" (4) World Wildlife Fund, wwf.panda.org, "Unsustainable Fishing," citing FAO, the Food and Agriculture Organization of the United Nations, State of World Fisheries and Aquaculture (SOFIA) - SOFIA 2010, FAO Fisheries Department

8 (1) *The New York Times Magazine*, "The Lawyer Who Became DuPont's Worst Nightmare," Nathaniel Rich, January 6, 2016 (2) The Environmental Working Group, ewg.org, "'Erin Brockovich' Carcinogen in Tap Water of More Than 200 Million Americans," David Andrews and Bill Walker, September 20, 2016

9 Sustainable Business Toolkit, sustainablebusinesstoolkit.com, "What's your coffee costing the planet?—Environmental impact of the coffee trade," Victoria Moore

10 United States Department of Agriculture, Economic Research Service, ers.usda.gov, "Trends in U.S. Local and Regional Food Systems: Report to Congress," January 2015

11 United States Department of Agriculture, Economic Research Service, ers.usda.gov, "Import Share of Consumption"

12 Worldwatch Institute, worldwatch.org, "Globetrotting Food Will Travel Farther Than Ever This Thanksgiving"

13 Bureau of Labor Statistics, bls.gov, "Employment by major industry sector"

14 United States Department of Agriculture, *2012 Census of Agriculture Highlights*, ACH12-7, August 2014, "Farmers Marketing: Direct sales through markets, roadside stands, and other means up 8% since 2007"

15 (1) USDA Agricultural Marketing Service, "Local Food Demand in the U.S.: Evolution of the Marketplace and Future Potential," Debra Tropp, Deputy Director, Local Food Research and Development Marketing Services Division (2) USDA, "Emerging Market Opportunities for Small-Scale Producers, Proceedings of a Special Session at the 2008 USDA Partners Meeting," April 2009

16 Ibid, 10

17 Natural Resources Defense Council, Switchboard, switchboard.nrdc.org, "We're losing an acre of farmland every minute, according to new data," Kaid Benfield, October 4, 2010

18 (1) Think Progress, thinkprogress.org, "3 Reasons Why Foodborne Illness Outbreaks Are Getting Bigger and Deadlier Than Ever," Alex Zielinski, November 6, 2015 (2) Sustainable Table, sustainabletable.org, "Food Processing & Slaughterhouses"

19 SEED, "Sticky economy evaluation device, measuring the financial impact of a public market, 2010 Economic Survey, an economic impact report generated for Hunterdon Land Trust Farmers' Market," marketumbrella.org, March 7, 2011

[20] Ibid, 10

[21] Ibid, 10

[22] National Restaurant Association, restaurant.org, "Looking for 2016's top food trends? Yep, sustainability!" November 16, 2015

[23] Stat, statnews.com, "A study found that 92 percent of food popular with eaters dining out exceed the threshold of calories for a normal meal," Megan Thielking, January 20, 2016, citing research from the *Journal of the American Academy of Nutrition and Dietetics*

[24] The Vegetarian Resource Group blog, vrg.org, "How Often Do Americans Eat Vegetarian Meals? And How Many Adults in the U.S. Are Vegetarian? The Vegetarian Resource Group asks in a 2015 National Survey Conducted by Harris Poll," Charles Stahler, May 29, 2015

[25] Vegetarianism In America, "*Vegetarian Times* Study Shows 7.3 Million Americans Are Vegetarians. Additional 22.8 Million Follow a Vegetarian-Inclined Diet"

[26] American Cancer Society, cancer.org, "World Health Organization Says Processed Meat Causes Cancer," Stacy Simon, October 26, 2015

[27] Ibid, 18

[28] Ibid, 4

[29] *Conservation Magazine*, conservationmagazine.org, "How many people we can feed depends on how much meat we eat," Catherine Elton, July 29, 2016

[30] (1) Greenpeace, greenpeace.org, "How cattle ranches are chewing up the Amazon rainforest," Daniel Beltra, January 31, 2009 (2) *Science Magazine*, "In Brazil, cattle industry begins to help fight deforestation," Allie Wilkinson, May 15, 2015

[31] (1) United Nations Food and Agriculture Organization, fao.org, Livestock Environment and Development, "The role of livestock in climate change" (2) Ibid, "Livestock a major threat to environment; Remedies urgently needed," Christopher Matthews, November 29, 2006 (3) *Scientific American*, "How Meat Contributes to Global Warming," Nathan Fiala, February 2009

[32] Ibid, 4, 31

[33] *New Hope News,* "Why locally farmed, pastured eggs are tops," Robin Hoy, Bucks County Foodshed Alliance, March 2013

[34] (1) CNSNews.com, "Food Stamp Beneficiaries Exceed 46,000,000 for 38 Straight Months," Ali Meyer, January 13, 2015 (2) Food Research and Action Center, frac.org, "SNAP Over-the-Year Participation Dropped by Nearly 1.3 Million People in March 2016 to Its Lowest Level in Five Years" (3) USDA Food and Nutrition Service, fns.usda.gov, "Characteristics of Food Stamp Households: Fiscal Year 2007 (4) *Newsweek*, newsweek.com, "The Number of People On Food Stamps Is Falling. Here's Why," Max Kutner, July 22, 2017

[35] Ibid, 14

[36] Feeding America, feedingamerica.org, "Food Waste in America"

[37] *New Hope News,* "Focus on Food—Glorious Imperfection," Cathy Snyder, Founder/Director, Rolling Harvest Food Rescue, August 2015

Chapter 4: Home

[1] More information on sustainable building: The U.S. Green Building Council, usgbc.com and greenhomeguide.com

[2] *Small is Beautiful: Economics As If People Mattered*, E.F. Schumacher, Harper Perennial, New York, 1973

[3] (1) Earth 911, earth911.com, "EPA Estimates 170 Million Tons of Yearly Construction, Demolition Debris," Trey Granger, April 17, 2009. This article says C&D equals about 30% of total waste in the U.S., according to the U.S. Green Building Council. (2) "Construction & Demolition Waste Manual" prepared for NYC Department of Design & Construction by Gruzen Samton LLP with City Green Inc., May 2003. This article says C&D equals 25% to 40% of total waste.

[4] U.S. Energy Information Administration, eia.gov, "Analysis & Projections: Drivers of U.S. Household Energy Consumption, 1980-2009, released February 3, 2015

[5] Houzz, houzz.com, "Ecofriendly Cool: Insulate With Wool, Cork, Old Denim and More," Julia Pockett, July 18, 2013

[6] Green Home Guide, greenhomeguide.com, "Green Renovation Checklist," September 9, 2009

[7] Environmental Protection Agency, epa.gov, "Sources of Greenhouse Gas Emissions" as of 2014

[8] Environmental Defense, "Electricity Generation and Pollution," November 2002

[9] U.S. Energy Information Administration, eia.gov, "Frequently Asked Questions: What is U.S. electricity generation by energy source?" as of 2017

[10] (1) Renewable Energy Policy Network for the 21st Century, REN21, "The First Decade: 2004-2014, 10 Years of Renewable Energy Progress" (2) Wikipedia, Renewable Energy in the United States, from the U.S. Energy Information Administration, eia.gov

[11] American Council on Renewable Energy (ACORE), "Renewable Energy in Idaho," September 2014, 73% hydroelectric and 15% other renewables

[12] Yale Climate Connections, yaleclimateconnections.org, "What's Behind the Good News Declines in U.S. CO_2 Emissions?" Zeke Hausfather, May 5, 2013

[13] (1) Electric Choice, electricchoice.com, "Current State of Electricity Deregulation in the U.S. (2014)," October 27, 2014 (2) Quantum Gas & Power Services, Ltd., quantumgas.com

[14] Union of Concerned Scientists, blog.ucsusa.org, "How Many Homes Have Rooftop Solar? The Number is Growing...," Laura Wisland, September 4, 2014

[15] Union of Concerned Scientists, ucsusa.org, Clean Energy

[16] Solar Energy Industries Association, seia.org, "Solar Industry Growing at a Record Pace"

[17] Bloomberg, bloomberg.com, "What Just Happened in Solar Is a Bigger Deal Than Oil Exports—The Impact: $73 billion in new investments in the U.S.," Tom Randall, December 17, 2015

[18] Ibid, 17

[19] (1) *Mother Earth News,* motherearthnews.com, "Is a Wind Turbine Right for Me?" Dan Chiras, January 26, 2011 (2) American Wind Energy Association (AWEA), awea.org, "FAQs for small wind systems"

[20] Ibid, 19

[21] The U.S. Department of Energy, energy.gov, "Reduce Hot Water Use for Energy Savings"

[22] *Delaware Valley Living,* "The Power of Going Green: Geothermal Power Reduces Utility Bills and Conserves Natural Resources," late Spring 2011

[23] (1) *Smithsonian,* smithsonianmagcom, "Americans Are Using Less Water Than We Did in 1970," Marissa Fessenden, November 21, 2014 (2) Pacific Institute, "Water Use Trends in the United States," April 2015

[24] The U.S. Geological Survey, water.usgs.gov, "Water Questions & Answers: How much water does the average person use at home per day?"

[25] Ibid, 23

[26] Environmental Protection Agency, epa.gov/watersense, WaterSense, An EPA Partnership Program, "Water Use Today"

[27] *Mother Earth News,* motherearthnews.com, "Low-Flow Toilets: Half the Water, Twice the Flush!" Steve Maxwell, August/September 2006

[28] Environmental Protection Agency, epa.gov, WaterSense, An EPA Partnership Program, "Showerheads"

[29] Environmental Protection Agency, epa.gov, WaterSense, An EPA Partnership Program, "Bathroom Sink Faucets & Accessories"

[30] energystar.gov, "Dishwasher vs. Hand Washing Dishes"

[31] *Mother Jones,* motherjones.com, "Should You Ditch Your Chemical Mattress?" Hannah Wallace, March/April 2008

[32] (1) EcoChoices Natural Living Store, ecochoices.com, "Conventional Cotton Statistics" (2) World Wildlife Fund, panda.org, Cotton Farming: "Cotton: a water wasting crop" (3) National Wildlife Federation, wwf.nwf.org, "Cotton and Pesticides: Pick Your Cotton," Doreen Cubie, February 1, 2006 (4) Naturepedic, "Does Non-Organic Cotton Contain Pesticide Residues?"

[33] Rodale, rodale.com, "The Most Toxic Thing in Your House?" Emily Main

[34] Minnesota Department of Health, "Formaldehyde in Your Home," November 21, 2016

[35] Physicians for Social Responsibility, psr.org, "Stain-resistant…cancer-causing?" Kathy Attar, MPH (Masters in public health), January 5, 2015

[36] The Environmental Working Group, ewg.org, Guide to Healthy Cleaning

[37] (1) Rodale, rodale.com, "How to Make Green Cleaning Recipes That Really Work," Leah Zerbe (2) The Environmental Working Group, ewg.org, "PBDEs—Fire Retardants in Dust: Dust and Indoor Pollution"

[38] The Ohio State University Extension, The Invisible Environment Fact Sheet Series, CDFS-191-08, "Indoor Air Quality: Dust and Molds," Jackie LaMuth, 2008

[39] The National Institutes of Health, ncbi.nlm.nih.gov, "Pollutants in house dust as indicators of indoor contamination," W. Butte and B. Heinzow, University of Oldenburg, Faculty of Chemistry, Oldenburg, Germany, 2002

[40] greenhomeguide.com, "45 Ways to Green the Not-So-New Home," September 9, 2009, "The Washington Toxics Coalition reports that using entryway mats can reduce the amount of pesticide residue on carpets by 25% and the amount of dust on carpets by 33%. And homes where shoes are removed at the door, according to the WTC, have 10 times less dust than homes where shoes are worn."

[41] Environmental Protection Agency, epa.gov, WaterSense, An EPA Partnership Program, "Outdoor Water Use in the United States"

[42] SFGATE, homeguides.sfgate.com, "How Much Water Does One Rain Barrel Save?" David Anderson

[43] (1) *Business Insider,* businessinsider.com, "America's biggest crop is not what you think," Rebecca Harrington, February 19, 2016 (2) *Huffington Post,* huffingtonpost.com, "The American Lawn Is Now The Largest Single 'Crop' In The U.S.," Rob Wile, August 17, 2015

[44] *You Bet Your Garden,* gardensalive.com

[45] earth-heal.com, "Permaculture: A Quiet Revolution—An Interview with Bill Mollision," Scott London, March 27, 2013

[46] *Mother Earth Living*, motherearthliving.com, "Green Patio Options: Brick, Stone, Gravel, Concrete and Recycled Materials," Debra Bokur, May/June 2006

[47] U.S. Fish & Wildlife Service, January 24, 2015

[48] AARP Public Policy Institute, "Taking the Long View: Investing in Medicaid Home and Community-Based Services Is Cost-Effective," 2009

Chapter 5: Consuming

[1] (1) Frequently quoted statistic. (2) thebalance.com, "Components of GDP Explained With Its Formula and Chart," Kimberly Amadeo, March 29, 2018 (3) Tallus Capital Management, tallusadvisory.com, "Slow Evolution of Consumer Spending," Weekly Economic Commentary, August 14, 2017

[2] (1) *The New York Times*, nytimes.com, "Think Those Chemicals Have Been Tested? Ian Urbina, April 13, 2013 (2) *PBS News Hour,* pbs.org, "It could take centuries for EPA to test all the unregulated chemicals under a new landmark bill," Mark Scialla, June 22, 2016

[3] *Independent Science News,* independentsciencenews.org, "Unsafe at any Dose? Diagnosing Chemical Safety Failures, from DDT to BPA," Jonathan Latham, PhD, May 16, 2016

[4] (1) Rodale, rodalenews.com, "Is Your Shampoo Loaded with This Cancer Causer?" Leah Zerbe (2) The Environmental Working Group's Shopper's Guide to Safe Cosmetics, ewg.org (3) ewg.org, Skin Deep Cosmetics Database (4) *Green Made Easy: The Everyday Guide for Transitioning to a Green Lifestyle*, Chris Prelitz, Hay House, Inc., New York, NY, 2009

[5] (1) American Cancer Society, cancer.org, "Teflon and Perfluorooctanoic Acid (PFOA). What are these substances? Where are they found?" (2) drweil.com, "Non-Stick Cookware—Cancer Risk?" June 6, 2014 (3) The Environmental Working Group, ewg.org, "Teflon Toxicosis is deadly to pet birds. Are we at risk?" May 15, 2003 (4) *The New York Times*, nytimes.com, "Why Has the E.P.A. Shifted on Toxic Chemicals? An Industry Insider Helps Call the Shots," Eric Lipton, October 21, 2017 (5) *The New York Times Magazine*, "The Lawyer Who Became DuPont's Worst Nightmare," Nathaniel Rich, January 6, 2016 (6) The Environmental Working Group, ewg.org, "Industry calls them super plastics. What if they're also super dangerous?" Olga Naidenko, July 29, 2009 (7) National Institute of Environmental Health Sciences, niehs. nih.gov, Perfluorinated Chemicals (PFCs) (8) The Environmental Working Group, ewg.org, "EWG's Healthy Home Tips"

[6] (1) Agency for Toxic Substances and Disease Registry (ATSDR) - Centers for Disease Control, atsdr.cdc.gov, "Public Health Statement for Styrene," June 2012 (2) Future Centre Trust, businessbarbados.com, "The Dangers of Polystyrene," July 6, 2010 (3) U.S. National Library of Medicine, National Institutes of Health, ncbi.nlm.nlh.gov, "Styrene exposure and risk of cancer," James Huff and Peter F. Infante, July 1, 2011

[7] (1) Ibid, 5

[8] environmentalprofessionalsnetwork.com, "The Environmental Impacts of Using Paper," September 24, 2014

[9] *Institutional Investor,* institutionalinvestor.com, "Apple Cares About Workers But Does it Care Enough?" Imogen Rose-Smith, September 7, 2016

[10] Electronics TakeBack Coalition, "Facts and Figures on E-Waste and Recycling," citing information from the EPA

[11] (1) National Institutes of Health, ncbi.nlm.nih.gov, "Leaching of heavy metals from E-waste in simulated landfill columns," Y. Li, J.B. Richardson, Mark R. Bricka, X. Niu, H. Yang, L. Li and A. Jimenez, July 29, 2009 (2) *The Guardian*, theguardian.com, "Rare earth mining in

China: the bleak social and environmental costs," Jonathan Kaiman, March 20, 2014 (3) The Carnegie Cyber Academy, carnegiecyberacademy.com, "How Technology can Harm the Environment" (4) Yale Environment 360, e360.yale.edu, "Boom in Mining Rare Earths Poses Mounting Toxic Risks," Mike Ives, January 28, 2013

[12] American Optometric Association, "The Effects of Computer Use on Eye Health and Vision"

[13] National Institutes of Health, ncbi.nlm.nih.gov, "Occupational Overuse Syndrome (Technological Diseases): Carpal Tunnel Syndrome, a Mouse Shoulder, Cervical Pain Syndrome," Merita Tiric-Campara, Ferid Krupic, Mirza Biscevic, Emina Spahic, Kerima Maglajlija, Zlatan Masic, Lejla Zunic and Izet Masic, October 29, 2014

[14] (1) *Mother Jones*, motherjones.com, "'Game-Changing' Study Links Cellphone Radiation to Cancer," Josh Harkinson, May 27, 2016 (2) American Cancer Society, cancer.org, "Cellular Phones"

[15] (1) *PC Advisor*, pcadvisor.co.uk, "How much screen time is healthy for children? Expert tips on screen safety, education, mental development and sleep," Simon Jary, November 17, 2015 (2) *Psychology Today*, psychologytoday.com, "Gray Matters: Too Much Screen Time Damages the Brain," February 27, 2014

[16] Environmental Protection Agency: Advancing Sustainable Materials Management: Facts and Figures 2013

[17] (1) Ecology Center, ecologycenter.org, "PTF: Environmental Impacts: Pollution and hazards from manufacturing" (2) Moms Clean Air Force, momscleanairforce.org, "What's Plastic Got to Do With Clean Air?" Beth Terry

[18] State of the Planet, Earth Institute, Columbia University, blogs.ei.columbia.edu, "What Happens to All That Plastic?" Renee Cho, January 31, 2012

[19] (1) National Public Radio, npr.org, "How Plastic In the Ocean Is Contaminating Your Seafood," Eliza Barclay, December 13, 2013 (2) Greenpeace, unep.org, "Plastic Debris in the World's Oceans" (3) Sailors for the Sea, sailorsforthesea.org, "Plastic Pollution and its Solution," Maggie Ostdahl, September 2013 (4) New Jersey Environment News, njenvironmentnews.com, "Take 'plastic soup' off the menu," Michele S. Byers

[20] (1) Rodale, rodale.com, "Study: All Plastics Are Bad for Your Body," Emily Main, citing a study published in the journal *Environmental Health Perspectives* (2) breastcancer.org, "Exposure to Chemicals in Plastic"

[21] (1) The Environmental Working Group, ewg.org, "A Survey of Bisphenol A in U.S. Canned Foods," March 5, 2007 (2) Rodale, rodale.com, "Finally! FDA Considers BPA Plastic in Your Food a Health Risk," Emily Main (3) The Environmental Working Group, ewg.org, "BPA is toxic at low doses," May 23, 2007 (4) European Commission, europa. eu, "Bisphenol A: EU ban on baby bottles to enter into force tomorrow," May 31, 2011 (5) The Environmental Working Group, ewg.org, "Bisphenol A - Toxic Plastics Chemical in Canned Food," March 5, 2007 (6) National Institute of Environmental Health Science, "Bisphenol A (BPA)"

[22] (1) The Environmental Working Group, ewg.org, "Plastics: A daily dose of danger?" Mike Kernels, August 1, 2004, originally published in the *Greensboro News Record* (2) *The Guardian*, theguardian.com, "Phthalates are everywhere, and the health risks are worrying. How bad are they really?" Amy Westervelt, February 10, 2015

[23] Ibid, 20

[24] drweil.com, "Is Plastic Wrap Safe?" January 31, 2013

[25] Ibid, 20

[26] (1) nutria.co, "Choose Glass Bottles to Avoid Plastic Toxins," June 25, 2013 (2) *Huffington Post*, huffingtonpost.com, "Plastic Is Food Poisoning," Lisa Kaas Boyle, April 28, 2014 (3) Institute for Agriculture and Trade Policy, "Smart Plastics Guide: Healthier Food Uses of Plastics"

[27] Rodale, rodalenews.com, "Bottled Water: Your New Hormone Disruptor," Emily Main

[28] (1) Rodale, rodale.com, "4 Things You Must Know about Your Water," Emily Main (2) Rodale, rodalesorganiclife.com, "How Clean Is Your Drinking Water? Lori Ball, September 10, 2015

[29] (1) watoxics.org, "Vinyl Shower Curtains Dangerous for Health and Environment" (2) *Los Angeles Times*, articles.latimes.com, "That 'new shower curtain smell'? It's toxic, study says," Tami Abdollah, June 13, 2008

[30] (1) Federal Reserve of St. Louis, fred.stlouisfed.org, "E-Commerce Retail Sales as a Percent of Total Sales," as of the second fiscal quarter of 2017 (2) Ycharts, ycharts.com, "US E-Commerce Sales as Percent of Retail Sales"

[31] (1) nchannel.com, "Retail, eCommerce & Digital Marketing," Ryan Lunka, July 9, 2015 (2) RetailNext, retailnext.net, "Retail's Main Event: Brick & Mortar vs. Online," Ray Hartjen

[32] Ibid, 31

[33] Culture Change, culturechange.org, "Good News/Bad News for Consumers in an Increasingly Energy-Challenged, Shipping-Dependent World," Jan Lundberg, February 23, 2016

[34] GAS2: Green Is the New Fast, gas2.org, "One Container Ship Pollutes As Much As 50 Million Cars," Christopher DeMorro, June 3, 2009

[35] Ibid, 33

[36] Ibid, 33

[37] The Local Multiplier Effect, localmultiplier.com, "The Hidden Power of Shopping Locally… "

[38] Local First and Civic Economics, "Local Works! Examining the Impact of Local Business on the West Michigan Economy," September 2008

[39] *The True Cost*, documentary film, director Andrew Morgan, 2015

[40] *Huffington Post*, huffingtonpost.com, "Bangladesh Factory Fire: Disney, Sears Used Factory In Blaze That Killed More Than 100 Workers," Julhas Alam, November 28, 2012

[41] (1) EcoChoices Natural Living Store, ecochoices.com, "Conventional Cotton Statistics" (2) World Wildlife Fund, wwf.panda.org, "Cotton Farming: "Cotton: a water wasting crop" (3) National Wildlife Federation, nwf.org, "Cotton and Pesticides: Pick Your Cotton," Doreen Cubie, February 1, 2006

[42] National Institutes of Health, ncbi.nlm.nih.gov, "Long term respiratory health effects in textile workers," Peggy S. Lai, MD and David C. Christiani, MD, MPH, MS

[43] treehugger.com, "50 Surprising Fashion and Beauty Products Made From Oil That You Probably Use Everyday (Even if You're Green)," Meaghan O'Neill, May 7, 2010

[44] Rodale, rodalesorganiclife.com, "How to Find Organic Clothes That Are Truly Organic," Emily Main, June 28, 2011

[45] greencotton.wordpress.com, "Synthetic Dyes: A Look at Environmental & Human Risks," June 18, 2008

[46] Rodale, rodale.com, "Dry Clean Only? Nah, There Are Cheaper, Safer Ways," Leah Zerbe

[47] Environmental Protection Agency, epa.gov, "Municipal Solid Waste Generation, Recycling, and Disposal in the United States: Facts and Figures for 2012"

[48] *National Geographic*, news.nationalgeographic.com, "Eight Million Tons of Plastic Dumped in Ocean Every Year," Laura Parker, February 13, 2015

[49] Ibid, 19

[50] Ibid, 19

[51] Ibid, 19

[52] Ibid, 8

[53] Environmental Protection Agency, Advancing Sustainable Materials Management: Facts and Figures

[54] Stanford University, Buildings & Grounds Maintenance, Land, Buildings & Real Estate, bgm. standford.edu, "Frequently Asked Questions: Benefits of Recycling"

[55] Resource Recycling, resource-recycling.com, "Study finds half of U.S. is automatically enrolled in curbside recycling," Lacey Evans, August 10, 2016

[56] Ibid, 10

[57] Ibid, 11

[58] (1) Rainforest Connection, rfcx.org, "Our Work" (2) *National Geographic*, news. nationalgeographic.com, "Your Old Cell Phone Can Help Save the Rain Forest," Christina Nunez

[59] Environmental Protection Agency, "Materials and Waste Management in the United States Key Facts and Figures," from Advancing Sustainable Materials Management: Facts and Figures, June 2015, with 2013 data

[60] Pew Research Center, pewresearch.org, "For Earth Day, here's how Americans view environmental issues," Monica Anderson, April 20, 2017

[61] Ibid, 59

[62] Ibid, 59

Chapter 6: Transportation

[1] Environmental Protection Agency, epa.gov, "Sources of Greenhouse Gas Emissions," 2015

[2] U.S. Energy Information Administration, eia.gov, "Frequently Asked Questions: How many alternative fuel and hybrid vehicles are there in the U.S.?" May 16, 2013

[3] (1) Natural Resources Defense Council, "Energy Facts: Simple and Inexpensive Actions Could Reduce Global Warming Emissions by One Billion Tons," Sasha Lyutse, March 2010 (2) Environmental Protection Agency, epa.gov, "Emissions by Country," 2011

[4] Yale Climate Connections, yaleclimateconnections.org, "What's Behind the Good News Declines in U.S. CO_2 Emissions," Zeke Hausfather, May 5, 2013

[5] Union of Concerned Scientists, ucsusa.org, "Fuel Efficiency"

[6] Environment Protection Agency, "Greenhouse Gas Emissions from a Typical Passenger Vehicle," EPA-420-F-11-041, December 2011

[7] Union of Concerned Scientists, ucsusa.org, "Advanced Vehicle Technologies"

[8] HybridCars, hybridcars.com, "Norway Is Fourth Country to Register 100,000 Plug-in Cars," Jeff Cobb, May 9, 2016

[9] *Who Killed the Electric Car: A Lack of Consumer Confidence…Or Conspiracy?* a documentary written and directed by Chris Paine, 2006

[10] Ibid, 7

[11] (1) EVObsession, evobsession.com, "Electric Car Charging 101—Types of Charging, Charging Networks, Apps, & More!" Zachary Shahan, September 10, 2015 (2) Plug In America, pluginamerica.org, "Understanding Electric Vehicle Charging," January 31, 2011 (3) plugincars.com, "Buying Your First Home EV Charger," Brad Berman, May 26, 2016

[12] *Wired,* wired.com, "How GM Beat Tesla to the First True Mass-Market Electric Car," Alex Davies, January 2016. The earliest entrants are the Chevy Bolt and Tesla Model 3.

[13] Ibid, 12

[14] WHYY, *Radio Times,* Marty Moss-Coane, February 2015, Interview with Timothy Searchinger, Princeton University research scholar at the Woodrow Wilson School, Senior Fellow at the World Resources Institute and lead author of a report on biofuels and global food supplies

[15] Union of Concerned Scientists, blog.ucsusa.org, "8 Ways Science Can Save Gas On Your Summer Road Trip," Dave Cooke, June 22, 2015

[16] Ibid, 15

[17] (1) Medscape, medscape.com, "Long-term Effects of Repealing the National Maximum Speed Limit in the United States," Lee S. Friedman, PhD, Donald Hedeker, PhD and Elihu D. Richter, MD, MPH (2) "Relationship of Traffic Fatality Rates to Maximum State Speed Limits," Charles M. Farmer, April 2016, based on a report from the Insurance Institute for Highway Safety. According to the report, a five-mph increase in the maximum speed limit results in a 4% overall increase in fatalities and an 8% increase on interstates and freeways. (3) Edmunds, edmunds.com, "Speed Limit Increases Equal More Deaths, Study Finds," Anita Lienert, April 18, 2016 (4) *Wired*, wired.com, "Raising Speed Limits Is Irresponsible, But States Keep Doing It Anyway," Aarian Marshall, May 4, 2016

[18] triplepundit.com, "Remotely Green: Why Working from Home is the Ultimate Green Move," Phil Green, May 27, 2011

[19] *The Atlantic*, theatlanticcities.com, "The Rise of the Sharing Economy," Emily Badger, December, 20, 2011

[20] The Atlantic CityLab, citylab.com, "America's Ongoing Love Affair With the Car," Richard Florida, August 17, 2015

[21] American Public Transportation Association, apta.com, fact sheet

[22] *Fortune,* fortune.com, "Today's Cars Are Parked 95% of the Time," David Z. Morris, March 13, 2016

[23] conservationmagazine.org, "How much carbon dioxide can car-sharing slash?" Elliot Martin and Susan Shaheen, August 11, 2016

[24] *The Sharing Solution: How to Save Money, Simplify Your Life & Build Community,* Janelle Orsi and Emily Doskow, NOLO, Berkeley, CA, 2009

[25] Shareable, shareable.net, "The History of Carpooling, from Jitney's to Ridesharing," Jef Cozza, February 7, 2012

Chapter 7: Work, Play and Retirement

[1] *Forbes,* forbes.com, "Find Happiness At Work," Jenna Goudreau, March 4, 2010, reporting on the book *Happiness At Work* by Jessica Pryce-Jones, Wiley-Blackwell

[2] AARP, aarp.org, "Nonprofit Organization Job Tips: Jobs in the nonprofit sector offer many encore career opportunities for workers over 50," Kerry Hannon, November 18, 2011

[3] Examples from Resilient Communities, resilience.org

[4] U.S. Federation of Worker Cooperatives, usworker.coop, "Frequently Asked Questions About Worker Cooperatives"

[5] (1) Wikipedia, Mondragon Corporation (2) toomuchonline.org, "Alternate Approaches: A Manufacturer of Equality," Sam Pizzigati, June 1, 2015

[6] Pew Research Center, pewsocialtrends.org, "Three-in-Ten U.S. Jobs Are Held by the Self-Employed and the Workers They Hire," October 22, 2015

[7] (1) Upwork, upwork.com, "Freelancers Union and Upwork release new study revealing insights into the almost 54 million people freelancing in America" (2) usnews.com, "1 in 3 Workers Employed in Gig Economy, But Not All By Choice," Andrew Soergel, October 11, 2016 (3) smallbiztrends.com, "20 Surprising Stats About the Gig Economy," Paul Chaney, July 25, 2016 (4) Shareable, shareable.net, "How Freelancers Are Reinventing Work Through New Collective Enterprises," Christopher D. Cook, October 11, 2016

[8] *Radical Homemakers: Reclaiming Domesticity From a Consumer Culture*, Shannon Hayes, Left to Write Press, Richmondville, New York, 2010

[9] *Stanford Social Innovation Review*, ssir.org, "The Time Bank Solution," Edgar S. Cahn and Christine Gray, Summer 2015

[10] yesmagazine.org, "Time Banking: An Idea Whose Time Has Come?" Edgar Cahn, November 17, 2011

[11] (1) "Agora Gallery, agora-gallery.com, "Going Green: Environmentally Friendly Practices for Artists," April 22, 2015 (2) observer.com, "Toxic Art: Is Anyone Sure What's In A tube of Paint?" Daniel Grant, October 19, 2016

[12] National Recreation and Park Association, "NRPA's Park and Recreation Month OUT is IN Survey National Findings," July 2014

[13] National Wildlife Federation, nwf.org, "Whole Child: Developing Mind, Body and Spirit through Outdoor Play"

[14] (1) Career Builder, careerbuilder.com, "Number of Senior Workers Delaying Retirement Reaches New Post-Recession Low," February 19, 2015, citing a retirement survey (2) money.usnews.com, "Why More Americans Are Working Past Age 65," Emily Brandon, February 11, 2013

Chapter 8: Money

[1] *Local Dollars, Local Sense: How to Shift Your Money from Wall Street to Main Street and Achieve Real Prosperity*, Michael H. Shuman, Chelsea Green Publishing, White River Junction, Vermont, 2012, Investing in Ourselves, pp 208-230

[2] Federal Deposit Insurance Corporation (FDIC), FDIC Community Banking Study, "Chapter 1: Defining the Community Bank," December 2012. Community banks typically have less than $1 billion and no more than $10 billion in bank assets.

[3] FDIC Quarterly, 2014, Volume 8, No. 2, "Community Banks Remain Resilient Amid Industry Consolidation"

[4] Institute for Local Self-Reliance, ilsr.org, "One in Four Local Banks Has Vanished Since 2008. Here's What's Causing the Decline and Why We Should Treat It as a National Crisis." Stacy Mitchell, May 5, 2015

[5] Federal Reserve Bank of Richmond, Economic Brief, EB15-03, "Explaining the Decline in the Number of Banks since the Great Recession," Roisin McCord, Edward Simpson Prescott and Tim Sablik, March 2015. The Riegle-Neal Interstate Banking and Branching Efficiency Act of 1994 removed most remaining restrictions on interstate branching. The number of small banks declined as a result.

[6] Ibid, 5

[7] Ibid, 5, Figure 1: "Number of Independent Banks in the United States." Sources cite different numbers depending on how they define "community banks."

[8] (1)Times Free Press, timesfreepress.com, "Credit unions grow in size and services, shrink in number," Dave Flessner, June 15, 2015 (2) Shareable, shareable.net, "The Trickle Down Economics of Credit Unions," Kelly McCartney, March 10, 2015

[9] Ibid, 3

[10] Ibid, 4. Counties with more than the average number of community banks have experienced fewer foreclosures.

[11] Ibid, 4, referencing a Federal Reserve Study

[12] Ibid, 4

[13] kresge.org, "Credit unions and human services agencies combine forces to serve the unbanked, underbanked," August 25, 2014

[14] Securities and Exchange Commission, sec.gov, "SEC Adopts Rules to Permit Crowdfunding," October 30, 2015

[15] Shareable, shareable.net, "It Takes An Ecosystem: The Rise of Worker Cooperatives in the US," Nina Misuraca Ignaczak, July 16, 2014, citing a University of Wisconsin study

[16] Ibid, 1, The Hidden Power of Cooperatives, pp 56-61

[17] Ibid, 1, Investing in Ourselves, pp 208-230

[18] YouTube, "Amplify the money you give," Katherina M. Rosqueta, Founder/Director, Center for Impact Philanthropy at the University of Pennsylvania, TEDx talk, March 28, 2014

Epilogue: A Green Afterlife

[1] The Green Burial Council, greenburialcouncil.org, "What Is Green Burial?"

[2] *Business Insider*, businessinsider.com, "Traditional burials are ruining the planet—here's what we should do instead," Max Plenke, April 7, 2016

[3] Ibid, 1, 2

[4] (1)*The Star Ledger*, blog.nj.com, "Eco-funerals are increasing in popularity in New Jersey," Jeff Diamant, February 14, 2010 (2) *Huffington Post*, huffingtonpost.com, "How Your Death Affects Climate Change," Katrina Spade, December 3, 2014

[5] Ibid, 4

[6] *The Capital Times*, "Proposed green cemetery near Verona sparks controversy," Steven Elbow, August 28, 2010

Bibliography

The ideas expressed in this book were inspired by these and other sources, including those listed in Notes.

Books

Addison, John. *Save Gas, Save the Planet: Ride Clean. Ride Together. Ride Less.* U.S.A.: Optimark, Inc., 2009.

Byrd, Rosaly and Lauren DeMates. *Sustainability Made Simple: Small Changes for Big Impact.* New York: Rowman & Littlefield, 2017.

Caradonna, Jeremy L. *Sustainability: A History.* Oxford, U.K.: Oxford University Press, 2014.

Carson, Rachel. *Silent Spring.* New York: Houghton Mifflin Company, 1962.

Christianson, Gale E. *Greenhouse: The 200-Year Story of Global Warming.* New York: Walker and Company, 1999.

De Young, Raymond and Thomas Princen, ed. *The Localization Reader: Adapting to the Coming Downshift.* Cambridge, Massachusetts: The MIT Press, 2012.

McDilda, Diane Gow. *365 Ways to Live Green: Your Everyday Guide to Saving the Environment.* Avon, Massachusetts: Adams Media, 2008.

Hayes, Shannon. *Radical Homemakers: Reclaiming Domesticity From a Consumer Culture.* Richmondville, New York: Left to Write Press, 2010.

Hopkins, Rob. *The Transition Companion: Making your community more resilient in uncertain times.* White River Junction, VT: Chelsea Green Publishing, 2011.

Horn, Greg. *Living Green: A Practical Guide to Simple Sustainability.* Topanga, CA: Freedom Press, 2006.

Jacobs, Jane. *The Death And Life Of Great American Cities.* New York: The Modern Library, 1993. (Originally published in 1961 by Random House, Inc.)

Kline, Ph.D., Benjamin. *First Along the River: A Brief History of the U.S. Environmental Movement*, third edition. New York: Rowman & Littlefield Publishers, Inc., 2007.

Mander, Jerry and Edward Goldsmith, ed. *The Case Against the Global Economy and for a Turn Toward the Local.* San Francisco, CA: Sierra Club Books, 1996.

Nearing, Scott and Helen Nearing. *The Good Life: Helen and Scott Nearing's Sixty Years of Self-Sufficient Living.* New York: Schocken Books, 1990. (Originally published as *Living the Good Life* in 1954)

North, Peter. *Local Money: How to Make it Happen in Your Community.* Totnes, Devon, England: Transition Books, 2010.

Orsi, Janelle and Emily Doskow. *The Sharing Solution: How to Save Money, Simplify Your Life & Build Community.* Berkeley, CA: Nolo, 2009.

Pahl, Greg. *Power From the People: How to Organize, Finance, and Launch Local Energy Projects.* White River Junction, VT: Chelsea Green Publishing, 2012.

Perry, Stewart E. and Mike Lewis. *Reinventing the Local Economy: What 10 Canadian Initiatives Can Teach Us About Building Creative, Inclusive, & Sustainable Communities.* Vernon, British Columbia, Canada: Centre for Community Enterprise, 1994.

Pollan, Michael. *The Omnivore's Dilemma: A Natural History of Four Meals.* New York: Penguin Books, 2006.

Prelitz, Chris. *Green Made Easy: The Everyday Guide for Transitioning to a Green Lifestyle.* Carlsbad, CA: Hay House, Inc., 2009.

Rodale, Maria. *Organic Manifesto: How Organic Farming Can Heal Our Planet, Feed the World, and Keep Us Safe.* New York: Rodale, 2010.

Schlosser, Eric. *Fast Food Nation: The Dark Side of the All-American Meal.* New York: Perennial, 2002.

Schumacher, E.F. *Small Is Beautiful: Economics as if People Mattered.* New York: Harper Perennial, 1973. (Originally published in London by Blond & Briggs Ltd in 1973.)

Shuman, Michael H. *Going Local: Creating Self-Reliant Communities in a Global Age.* New York: Routledge, 2000.

Shuman, Michael H. *Local Dollars, Local Sense: How to Shift Your Money from Wall Street to Main Street and Achieve Real Prosperity.* White River Junction, VT: Chelsea Green Publishing, 2012.

Articles

Diamant, Jeff. "Eco-funerals are increasing in popularity in New Jersey." *The Star Ledger*, February, 14, 2010.

Elbow, Steven. "Proposed green cemetery near Verona sparks controversy." *The Capital Times*, August 28, 2010.

Meoli, Daria. "Call it a final act for the environment: Natural burials, around since the start of time, are seeing a resurgence of popularity in the state." njbiz.com, April 18, 2016.

Miller, Ruth. "Landscapes of the Dead: An Argument for Conservation Burial." *The Urban Fringe*, September 19, 2012.

Plenke, Max. "Traditional burials are ruining the planet—here's what we should do instead." *Business Insider*, April 7, 2016.

Spade, Katrina. "How Your Death Affects Climate Change." *Huffington Post*, December 3, 2014.

Togneri, Chris. "Simple green burials create serene final resting spots." *TribTotal Media*, April 16, 2016.

Index

About the Author

Mindy Mutterperl is a communications consultant and writer with a passion for living sustainably and helping others find their own sustainable paths. She publishes sustainablechoices.net (formerly Fresh in the Delaware River Valley), which offers ideas, insights, resources and inspiring stories to help readers continue their journey toward a more sustainable way of life. Since creating Bankhouse Communications more than two decades ago, Mindy has developed influential marketing content and educational materials for business and nonprofit clients, earning accolades and awards. In addition to writing about sustainable living, she has written extensively about such topics as health, disability issues, financial literacy, retirement planning, charitable giving, education and the arts. Mindy's informative articles have appeared online and in newspapers and magazines. She earned a B.A. in English Literature from Rutgers, the State University of New Jersey.

You can find additional ideas, inspiration and resources to help you live more sustainably at **sustainablechoices.net.**

Made in the USA
Middletown, DE
14 August 2019